GOSPEL *mysteries*

Typological Coding as Evidence of the Bible's Inspiration

By Darek Barefoot

Grandling Valley Press
Grand Junction, CO

Unless otherwise noted, Scripture quotations are from the HOLY BIBLE, NEW INTERNATIONAL VERSION®. Copyright © 1973, 1978, 1984 by International Bible Society. Used by permission of Zondervan Publishing House. All rights reserved. The "NIV" and "New International Version" trademarks are registered in the United States Patent and Trademark Office by International Bible Society. Use of either trademark requires the permission of International Bible Society.

Where noted as from NASB, scripture quotations are taken from the NEW AMERICAN STANDARD BIBLE®, Copyright © 1960, 1962, 1963, 1968, 1971, 1972, 1973, 1975, 1977, 1995 by the Lockman Foundation. Used by permission.

ISBN   0-615-23419-9
          978-0-615-23419-9

Cover design by QuigsPlace Graphics
Cover photo by Emlyn Addison; source: Morguefile

Grandling Valley Press
PO Box 2332
Grand Junction, Colorado 81502

For Ryan, Ian, Josiah & Ezekiel

Acknowledgments

Since typological study has long been a part of Christian tradition, it is to that tradition that I am most heavily indebted for the material in this book. Credit is due also to individuals from whom I have learned of interpretations that are not common currency in Christian literature. I thank Andrew Hopkins of Alexandria, Virginia for several points concerning the typology of Jonah. My brother, Ross Barefoot, drew my attention to the typology of the Good Samaritan story from Luke's Gospel. My wife, May, supplied the seed that grew into chapters concerning the four-way pattern of the canonical Gospels.

Some of the ideas in this book may have precedents unknown to me. The volume of Biblical commentary is so large that even someone who believes he has a fresh observation to make must be cautious with claims of originality. I feel safe in saying that the material here presented has never been organized the same way in order to construct an apologetic argument.

All the members of my family, including my parents Clark and Ruthie Barefoot, offered valuable encouragement. My son Ian assisted with manuscript preparation as did my wife, whose help in other ways too numerous to mention and whose personal sacrifices over a period of years made it possible for me to write this book.

Contents

Contents

(continued)

Introduction

In the early 1990s, Israeli mathematician Eliyahu Rips and two colleagues, Doron Witzum and Yoav Rosenberg, announced that they had found a secret code in the Hebrew Bible. Using a computer, they selected Hebrew letters occurring at regular intervals in the text of Genesis, such as every fourth letter, then every fifth letter, and so on. Searching through the long character strings they had compiled they found the names of nearly three dozen prominent rabbis from past centuries.[1]

The findings of the three Israeli scientists touched off an avalanche of books and articles by others who likewise claimed that acrostic codes in the Hebrew text of the Old Testament either confirm the divine inspiration of the Bible or foretell the future or both. The public appetite for Bible code speculation has been damped only slightly by the fact that generating myriads of random letters stands a good chance of producing words and phrases related to whatever subject the "code breakers" are interested in. While it would be unfair to dismiss the original work of Rips offhandedly, anyone who investigates the "skip sequence" method he uses will find reason to remain skeptical.

The attention lavished on the "Bible codes" is disconcerting not just because Bible's actual language fails to hint at the existence of such codes or even because sensational theories tend to reinforce skepticism toward religion in general and the Bible in particular. It is frustrating as well because the Scriptures do contain a kind of code, explicit in some passages and latent in others, that is more profound in its implications

---

1   Eliyahu Rips *et al.*, "Equidistant Letter Sequences in the Book of Genesis," *Statistical Science* 9, no. 3 (August, 1994).

than anything churned out by letter-counting computers. I am referring to typological prophecy, a method of foreshadowing that uses characters and circumstances early in a narrative to portray what will occur later.

Typology at first looks unpromising as an area of study because it can be—and too often has been—whimsically subjective. Representation of one thing by another can be read into almost any literary work or set of circumstances. Jacob shepherding his flock in the Old Testament might represent Jesus shepherding the church in the New, but equally St. George battling the dragon might represent Winston Churchill confronting the Nazi threat, not to mention a number of other historical situations.

By treating the Bible's language as figurative, early church fathers were able to make it say nearly anything they wanted it to. Third century bishop Origen of Alexandria was so imaginative in his symbolic reconstructions that, as one scholar put it, the Bible in Origen's hands became a "divine crossword puzzle" that no one but Origen could decipher.[2]

Typology need not be arbitrary, however. An example of controlled use of types is Jesus' parable of the "wheat and the tares" from the thirteenth chapter of Matthew's Gospel. Jesus tells his audience about a farmer who planted and cultivated a field of wheat, explaining later that he has the church in mind. Between the tale of the farmer in verses 24-30 and the historical fulfillment in verses 40-43, he identifies his symbols: "The one who sows the good seed is the Son of Man, the field is the world, and the good seed are the children of the kingdom" (vv. 37-39). Here we have the ingredients of an informal code including a key that allows us to align the encrypted and decrypted forms of the message based on something other than vague resemblance.

Might coded and decoded messages occur more widely separated, in Biblical books as far apart in time of composition and content as Genesis is from Matthew? And might the "key," or list of symbol identifiers, consist not of a single passage but of verses scattered throughout the Bible text? In this book I argue that the Bible does indeed contain the three elements of a literary code: encrypted narratives from the Hebrew Scriptures, decrypted messages in the New Testament and symbol identifiers that relate the first class of material to the second.

2   R. P. C. Hanson, *Allegory and Event: A Study of the Sources and Significance of Origen's Interpretation of Scripture* (Richmond: John Knox Press, 1959), 248.

To distance the discussion from subjective interpretation, I will identify features of Biblical typology that can be sought in non-Biblical literature and must be found there if type coding is to be explained other than by divine inspiration. Mathematical precision may not be possible and judgments are involved, but they are judgments that can be recommended on reasonable grounds to whoever is willing to examine the evidence, no matter what opinion they hold otherwise about the Bible or Christianity.

To say that coded alignment between sections of the Bible can be evaluated objectively is not to deny that it has spiritual implications. As a Christian I see prophetic foreshadowing as a confirmation of the New Testament gospel about Jesus. Faith may not be a cold decision comparable to solving an equation, but neither is it raw emotional heat detached from facts.

Each of us charts his or her spiritual course by consulting the constellation of our personal experience, taking into account our knowledge of the world, the testimony of conscience, our appreciation of the beautiful and sense of wonder at the awe-inspiring. A single class of evidence, such as typological coding, is rarely decisive when it comes to religious belief. But we will make a wiser decision for having explored a part of the spiritual landscape neglected even by most scholars.

The question of the Bible's status is especially important given the challenge to belief posed by the social and intellectual climate of our time. Whatever magnetism the gospel may exert on our spiritual compasses is opposed by powerful forces. In addition to being politically incorrect the Bible is likely to be seen by educated people as scientifically uninformed and historically questionable. If those liabilities were not enough to savage its credibility, the Bible comes across as overbearing, particularly on the subject of sexual morals, to a society in pursuit of guilt-free gratification.

"You say, 'The way of the LORD is not right,' " God tells the people of Israel, acknowledging their distaste for his standard of virtue, and then counters, "Is My way not right? Is it not your ways that are not right?"[3] If the message of the Scriptures about the relationship between God and man, about the toxic effects of sin and a divine rescue operation through Jesus—if that message is true in spite of being wrapped in

---

3   Ezek 18:25, NASB.

what strikes our modern sensibilities as unattractive packaging, we must
come to terms with it. The study of Biblical type coding is worth the effort for that reason alone, but it pays dividends as well by enlivening
passages of Scripture that seldom get a second look.

In the New Testament the apostle Paul says that he and other
Christian ministers are "stewards of God's mysteries," the Greek *muste-
rion* here referring neither to an incomprehensible paradox nor to a
secret intended only for the few but to a divine truth so surprising that
it requires specific disclosure.[4] That kind of mystery might originally be
hidden in what the Hebrew Bible calls a "riddle," *chiydah*, that is, a saying
that alludes to something beyond the concrete sense of the words.[5] In
that case the revelation of the mystery would also be the solution to the
riddle; though the riddle was too difficult for us to solve without the answer in hand, we could see afterward that the answer was present in the
riddle just as meaning was present in Egyptian hieroglyphics before the
discovery of the Rosetta Stone.

With these thoughts in mind concerning mysteries, riddles and unex-
pected solutions, we are ready to begin an investigation of prophetic
types.

---

4   1 Cor 4:1.
5   Prov 1:6.

1

Jacob's Bargain

During the reign of Tiberius Caesar, when John the Baptist began to "clear a way for the LORD in the desert" by calling Jews to repentance,[1] paths of a different kind were being cleared on the other side of the world, in the coastal desert of what is now Peru. The Nazca people were moving dark volcanic rocks aside to form what at first appear to be walkways across the light-colored sand. Viewed from an airplane the pathways form immense figures called "geogliphs," which include simple geometric shapes as well as drawings of animals hundreds of feet in length.

Author Erik von Daniken once claimed that the geogliphs marked off landing areas for extraterrestrial spacecraft.[2] A more credible theory is that they were drawn as a devotion to various Nazca gods who were thought to be looking down from the sky. While it is not clear just how these lines were created, no one attributes them to accident. The random appearance of the lines to a grounded observer only makes their large-scale orderliness more impressive.

Typological coding poses a mystery that in certain ways resembles the Nazca Lines. The Bible consists of scores of separate documents, varying widely in style and purpose, composed in three languages over the course of at least six centuries. The words, phrases and narratives of these documents form connected patterns that can only be seen clearly from above, that is, by comparing the texts in a way only possible after the last of them had been written.

---

1   Isa 40:3; Matt 3:3.
2   Erik von Daniken, *Chariots of the Gods?* (New York: Putnam, 1970), 32-33.

Are these patterns and their common theme having to do with the Jewish Messiah proof of divine inspiration or instead the product of co-incidence magnified by wishful thinking? Could common cultural themes or myths have influenced the writers, perhaps subconsciously, to concoct stories that seem to portray future events? Were later Bible writers, in particular the "evangelists" who wrote the Gospels, prepared to falsify history to create the appearance of inspired harmony between what they wrote and what had been recorded centuries earlier?

The last explanation is favored by commentators such as Randel Helms, who popularized historical criticism of the Bible in the books *Gospel Fictions* and *Who Wrote the Gospels?*[3] Modern critics generally see Jesus as a wandering rabbi, exorcist and faith healer who somehow ran afoul of Roman authorities and was crucified. We have no way of knowing the details of his life beyond those bare facts and neither did the early Christians who elevated him to the status of Messiah. Having little to draw upon, the Gospel writers combed through the Scriptures—specifically, the Septuagint Greek translation of the Hebrew Bible—lifting out words, phrases and even whole stories and then stitching them together to create a fictional account of Jesus' life.

A common example of how this might occur has to do with King David of Israel, who is identified in the Hebrew Scriptures as both a forefather and forerunner of the promised Messiah. Hypothetically, in order to reinforce the resemblance of Jesus to David the writers of the Gospels of Matthew and Luke imagined circumstances that led to the birth of Jesus in David's home town of Bethlehem. The writers created their stories about Jesus' birth independently of one another, so the two nativity accounts differ in their details.

I will leave the question of Jesus' birth to one side until a later chapter, but it serves to illustrate the approach of an entire generation of scholars influenced by the late German theologian Rudolf Bultmann. Another member of that contingent was Robert Funk, organizer of the scholar's forum known as the Jesus Seminar, who claimed that the Gospel writers used their stock of Jewish tradition and material from

---

3   Randel Helms, *Gospel Fictions* (Amherst, NY: Prometheus Books, 1988); *Who Wrote the Gospels?* (Altadena, CA: Millennium Press, 1997).

the Septuagint Greek Bible to flesh out a portrait of Jesus as the Messiah.[4]

Perhaps, since the Hebrew Bible has Moses miraculously feeding Israel in the desert, the evangelists needed to invent a story about Jesus supernaturally feeding the crowds; since Elijah and Elisha were believed to have performed resurrections, yarns had to be spun about Jesus raising the dead; and so on.

What "demythologizers" have proposed looks plausible on its face. They argue that the Gospel writers were not being deliberately dishonest but simply using their ingenuity to reconstruct events that their faith told them must have taken place. What these scholars failed to notice is that the Hebrew Scriptures encode the coming of Jesus as Messiah and Savior in ways that would have been difficult or impossible for the evangelists to have exploited. To demonstrate this, I first have to make some observations about Jesus as the Gospels present him.

The Shepherd's Mottled Flock

One of the intriguing characteristics of Jesus from a historical perspective is his association with sinners. Jesus ministered even to the least regarded members of Jewish society, including tax collectors (notorious for their corruption) and prostitutes. His ministry to the disreputable did not mesh well with Jewish expectations about the coming Deliverer. In various places the Hebrew Scriptures confirm that all human beings are sinners before God, and one passage in Isaiah does say that God's "servant" would atone for the sins of Israel. But neither Scripture nor Jewish tradition predicts that the Messiah would gather to himself a crowd of persons shunned by respectable society.

Before Jesus no Jew would have considered it appropriate to describe the Messiah as "a friend of tax collectors and sinners."[5] And it was not only Jews who found such an association scandalous. The pagan critic Celsus chided Christians because their leader had surrounded himself with "sailors and tax-gatherers of the most worthless character" and because rather than targeting the most virtuous citizens for recruitment, as

---

4   Robert Funk, Roy Hoover and the Jesus Seminar, *The Five Gospels* (New York: Macmillan, 1993), 4.

5   Matt 11:19.

did other religions, Christianity appealed instead to "everyone . . . who is a sinner, who is devoid of understanding, who is a child, and, to speak generally, whoever is unfortunate."[6]

From Jesus' unusual career we turn to a Biblical oddity of a different sort, an event from the life of the patriarch Jacob, whose alternate name "Israel" later became the national designation for his descendants. A story from the Old Testament book of Genesis tells how the rivalry between the young man Jacob and his twin brother Esau becomes so heated that Jacob is forced to leave his father's household and seek refuge with his uncle Laban in Syria. Like the rest of Jacob's family, Laban is a herder of sheep and goats. Jacob ends up marrying Laban's two daughters and working for Laban as a herdsman for twenty years. The odd episode is the negotiation of Jacob's pay, in which Jacob asks Laban for certain animals in order to form his own small flock, namely, "every speckled or spotted sheep, every dark colored lamb and every spotted or speckled goat."[7]

Genesis goes on to devote a surprising amount of space to Jacob's acquisition of spotted livestock. Why? One of the features not only of Genesis but of the historical Scriptures in general is their brevity. Several years can be passed over between sentences. A few lines might summarize decades or more. Certain events such as the journey of Abraham to Canaan or God's covenant declarations have such significance that their inclusion seems natural, while innumerable minor happenings necessarily are omitted. In one or two sentences the writer of Genesis could have conveyed the information that Jacob, while working for Laban, acquired "flocks and herds" through the blessing of God.[8] Instead, something made him lavish the equivalent of several paragraphs on it.

Does the story in Genesis 30 contain coded symbolism, and if so what meaning could it have? A correspondence might be suspected between Jacob as a peaceful herder of sheep and the promised Messiah, future King of Israel, who is likened to a shepherd of God's people. Genesis says that in contrast to his aggressive brother Esau, "Jacob was

---

6 Origen, *Against Celsus* 1:62; 2:46; 3:59, from *Ante-Nicene Fathers,* Vol. 4 (Peabody, MA: Hendrickson, 1994), 423, 449, 487.

7 Gen 30:31-32.

8 Cf. Gen 26:12-14.

a quiet man, staying among the tents." Decades after their rift Jacob encounters Esau, who true to character has acquired an entourage of armed men. Jacob reconciles with his brother but begs off from accompanying him. "My lord knows that the children are tender and that I must care for the ewes and cows that are nursing their young," he says. "So let my lord go on ahead of his servant, while I move along slowly at the pace of the droves before me and that of the children."[9]

Jacob's tender care of his flock and family anticipates God's promise that eventually he will place over his people "one shepherd, my servant David, and he will tend them."[10] "I will put my Spirit on him," God says of the messianic shepherd, "and he will bring justice to the nations. He will not shout or cry out, or raise his voice in the streets. A bruised reed [the sick] he will not break, and a smoldering wick [the weak] he will not snuff out."[11]

"He tends the flock like a shepherd: He gathers the lambs in his arms and carries them close to his heart; he gently leads those that have young."[12] The last verse is a description of Israel's God Yahweh (Jehovah) himself, yet the prophetic context leaves little doubt that Yahweh carries out the shepherding of his people through his "arm," that is, his Messiah.[13] To these references may be added one in which God's special servant is in fact called by the name "Israel," the other personal name of the man Jacob:

> "[God] said to me, 'You are my servant, Israel, in whom I will show my splendor . . . It is too small a thing for you to be my servant to restore the tribes of Jacob . . . I will also make you a light to the Gentiles, that you may bring my salvation to the ends of the earth.'"
> —Isaiah 49:3-6.

The one here described cannot be simply a personification of the Jewish nation, since he is said to gather back the various tribes of that nation. Yet another passage from Isaiah confirms that the one given as

---

9   Gen 33:13-14.
10 Ezek 34:23.
11 Isa 42:1-4.
12 Isa 40:11.
13 Cf. Isa 40:9-10; Mic 5:4.

"leader" of the Gentile nations is the greater David, the promised Shepherd King.[14] In the New Testament, Jesus assumes this role, saying, "I am the good shepherd."[15]

Deciphering the Narrative

If typological coding is present in the tale of Jacob and his sheep, it must concern the Messiah and the people who constitute his flock. What then is the significance of Jacob's asking for streaked and spotted animals? We find the key in the New Testament book of 1 Peter. Besides casting Jesus as a shepherd at 5:4, 1 Peter pictures him as a sheep when it reminds first-century believers that they "were not redeemed with corruptible things, like silver or gold . . . but with the precious blood of Christ as of a lamb without blemish and without spot [Gr., *aspilos*, 'unstained' or 'unsoiled']."[16] Jesus' state of sinlessness, in contrast with that of humankind as a whole, is represented here as a lack of "blemishes" or "stains." The passage necessarily implies that a spot on a sheep can stand for sin in a human being.

Jacob's request was for those goats, ordinarily solid black, that had white markings and for sheep that were either spotted or uniformly dark in contrast to their usual color of light gray. This dappled or charcoal coloring did not in Jewish tradition constitute a defect barring such animals from sacrificial use, as was the case with injury, sickness or deformity. However, when we study carefully the images of purity contained in both Old and New Testaments, the possibility that any kind of spot on a sheep's coat could stand for sin begins to emerge:

> " 'Come now, let us reason together,' says the LORD. 'Though your sins are like scarlet, they shall be as white as snow; though they are as red as crimson, they shall be like wool.' " —Isaiah 1:18.

> "The Ancient of Days [God] took his seat. His clothing was as white as snow; the hair of his head was white like wool." —Daniel 7:9.

---

14 Isa 55:3-4.
15 John 10:14.
16 1 Pet 1:18-19, *New King James Bible* (Nashville: Thomas Nelson, 1983).

Christ also loved the church and gave himself for it that he might sanctify and cleanse it . . . that he might present it to himself a glorious church, not having spot or wrinkle or any such thing.
—Ephesians 5:25-27, KJV.

"His [Christ's] head and hair were white like wool, as white as snow."
—Revelation 1:14.

If white sheep's wool is ideal for portraying sinlessness, then in a symbolic context even a natural mark on such wool could stand for sin. Spots or stains are equated with sins in the Old and New Testaments.[17] In the story of Genesis 30, this symbolism would mean that the messianic shepherd claimed sinful mankind—the spotted and speckled animals—as his own. This is precisely what the New Testament says about Jesus. "I have not come to call the righteous, but sinners," he says in answer to the derisive comments of his opponents that "this man welcomes sinners and eats with them."[18] We find it written in 1 Timothy that it is "a trustworthy saying" that "Christ Jesus came into the world to save sinners."[19]

Jesus' association with the "dregs" of Jewish society is not an example of tolerance of sinful behavior, but a reminder that all men and women need cleansing of their sins through Jesus and none are so stained as to be past reclaiming. Jesus said that the virtue of tax collectors and prostitutes was that large numbers of them were painfully aware of their flawed natures and were ready to accept spiritual assistance, while those suffering from more subtle kinds of sin were not.[20]

The story of Jacob and the spotted sheep appears to be a coded prophecy that the Messiah would reach out to sinful humanity, but it is not the only one in the Hebrew Bible. The other concerns an even more prominent messianic type, David. Before ascending the throne of Israel, David spent years on the run from his predecessor, King Saul. During that time David's fugitive status served to attract the lowly and rejected class of Israelite society. "All those who were in distress or in debt or discontented gathered around [David], and he became their leader."[21]

---

17 Jer 2:22; Jas 3:6.
18 Mark 2:17; Luke 15:2.
19 1 Tim 1:15.
20 Matt 21:31-32.
21 1 Sam 22:2.

In the New Testament, sin is likened to indebtedness. The words *hamartolos*, sinner, and *opheiletes*, debtor, are used interchangeably by Jesus at Luke 13:2-4. Elsewhere he teaches the disciples to ask God for forgiveness of their "debts," meaning their sins.[22] The symbolic equivalence of "debt" and "sin" allows us to see Jesus' ministry as a fulfillment of debt-ridden men being gathered to David. The other terms from 1 Samuel describe men who are "in difficulty" and "embittered" (literally, "bitter of soul"), the latter capable of meaning either "resentful" or "distraught." Again, the correspondence with Jesus' appeal to troubled humanity is easy to see. "Come to me, all you who are weary and burdened," Jesus tells the crowds, "and I will give you rest. Take my yoke upon you and learn from me, for I am gentle and humble in heart, and you will find rest for your souls."[23]

Whether or not Jacob's sheep and David's army of outcasts are prophetic of the Messiah's people, I cannot be accused of forcing a comparison by arbitrarily making one thing stand for another. The symbolism of a spot on sheep's wool representing sin in a human being is not one I proposed for convenience' sake, and is established by verses that cannot have been written to rig the significance of the Genesis story. The same may be said for equating "debtors" joining themselves to David with "sinners" coming to Jesus for salvation.

These examples demonstrate an important principle of typological coding—that key symbols must be confirmed objectively from the Scriptures. The second-century apologist Justin Martyr, in his *Dialogue with Trypho*, correctly observes that Jacob represents Christ and the animals stand for mankind.[24] Justin then weakens his interpretation by speculating that the spotted appearance of the sheep typifies humanity's mixture of different races and nationalities, rather than the universality of human sin.

Justin and other believers from the first few centuries of Christianity may be forgiven a degree of laxness, since they made do without the modern concordances, lexicons and computer programs that allow for word studies. They lacked what we would consider basic conveniences, as well. Bible books at first circulated as independent documents or

---

22 Matt 6:12; cf. 18:21-35; Luke 7:41-47.
23 Matt 11:28-29.
24 Justin Martyr, *Dialogue with Trypho* 134.

small compilations, and few believers would have had the means to acquire a single book let alone all those that comprise the Bible as we know it. For those who did have ready access to the sacred writings, finding a particular text in a scroll of the Hebrew Scriptures meant tedious spooling past one page at a time. Even when the scroll gave way to the codex, or leaved book, modern chapter and verse divisions did not exist to aid in the location of passages. Analysis of Biblical types today is easier than ever not only due to the abundance of Biblical study tools but even, as we will see later, because of archaeological discoveries.

If our interpretation of the story of Jacob's sheep avoids the wholesale subjectivity sometimes evident in the writings of the church fathers, it can be explained in only one of two ways. The first of these is that God, having planned in the remote past to send his Son to lay claim to the fallen human family, moved Jacob to make his strange proposal to Laban. God then saw to it that the story was preserved, first through oral tradition and afterward in the writing of Genesis. Finally, he inspired later writers to record those clues necessary to unlock the episode's meaning.

The second explanation is coincidence. Coincidences occur in literature and history as in everyday life. Some of us may be tempted to meet cost of disbelief in the present case by writing a check against the Long Odds account at the Bank of Statistical Probability. I must caution them that we have just begun our survey of prophetic episodes. Does coincidence have reserves enough to cover them all? Chance will have to be tapped more heavily even before we leave the subject of Jacob's sheep, since the story contains further symbolic meaning.

Bringing Sins to Light

As the account in Genesis continues, Laban agrees to Jacob's seemingly modest request for the spotted animals of the flock. To deny Jacob any breeding stock and thereby reduce his financial exposure, Laban violates the agreed-upon terms by removing all existing sheep and goats with unusual coloration. He and his sons herd these animals, which rightfully belong to Jacob, to a distant location. "And he put a distance of three days' journey between himself and Jacob, and Jacob fed the rest of Laban's flocks." Jacob responds by attempting a crude form of genetic engineering. "Then Jacob took fresh rods [Hebrew, *maqqel*] of poplar and almond and plane trees, and peeled white stripes in them, exposing the white that was in the rods." Jacob places the rods in the watering troughs where the livestock drink, " . . . and they mated when they came to drink. So the flocks mated by the rods, and the flocks brought forth striped, speckled, and spotted."[25]

Jacob incises the bark of tree branches in the mistaken belief that if the sheep and goats are forced to stare at a streaked pattern, similar marks will be generated sympathetically in their offspring. The trick seems to work, but Jacob himself later admits that it is really the hand of God that has caused his flocks to increase.[26] If the rods are introduced as part of the allegory, they should not be difficult to decode. In Bible times the rod as a symbol most often represented legal authority. Proverbs 22:15, for example, refers to parents wielding the "rod of discipline" within the family. In turn, "discipline," from the Hebrew *musar*, denotes not simply correction but direction in a broad sense. At Deuteronomy 11:1-2, the Israelite nation is reminded that they have received God's laws and experienced his *musar*, his discipline.

Down through the centuries, the rod in the form of the king's scepter continued to stand for the rule of law.[27] Several Biblical Hebrew words with overlapping meanings can be translated as "rod," "staff," "scepter" or the equivalent, all having an association with governmental and legal power, as the following passages illustrate:

The scepter [*shebet*] will not depart from Judah nor the ruler's staff [*chaqaq*] from between his feet. —Genesis 49:10.

Mourn for [the kingdom of Moab], all who live around her, all who know her fame; 'How broken is the mighty scepter [*matteh*], how broken the glorious staff [*maqqel*]! —Jeremiah 48:17.

---

25 Gen 30:34-39, NASB.
26 Gen 31:7-9.
27 The rod as a symbol of law also can be seen in, for example, the bundled rods of the Roman *fasces*.

Fire spread from one of [Judah's] main branches and consumed its fruit. No strong branch [*matteh*] is left on it for a scepter [*shebet*].
—Ezekiel 19:14.

As I judged your fathers in the desert of the land of Egypt, so I will judge you, declares the Sovereign LORD. I will take note of you as you pass under my rod [*shebet*], and I will bring you into the bond of the covenant. —Ezekiel 20:36-37

Among these roughly synonymous terms is the same one, *maqqel*, used of the rods made by Jacob. Another of them, *chaqaq*, though clearly referring to a rod or staff at Genesis 49:10, is from a root word meaning "to engrave," specifically to engrave laws or statutes on tablets; the King James Version translates *chaqaq* as "lawgiver." The equivalence of the various terms for "rod" is clear from the ancient Greek Old Testament, the Septuagint, which uses the same Greek word, *rabdos*, to describe Jacob's rods at Genesis 30:37 and the rod associated with the Mosaic Law Covenant at Ezekiel 20:37.

Jacob set his rods in the water troughs for the livestock, and it turns out one of water's metaphorical meanings also has to do with law. At Amos 5:24 God advises his people, "Let justice [*mishpat*, legal verdict, ruling] roll on like a river, righteousness like a never-failing stream!"[28]

God caused the rods placed in the water troughs to have the effect of multiplying animals with spots and streaks. If the rods stand for law, then the meaning, paradoxically, must be that law placed before people causes sins to multiply. Anyone familiar with what the New Testament says about law and sin will immediately be reminded of a statement made by Paul in his letter to the Romans: "The law was added so that the trespass [or, sin] might increase."[29] Paul is speaking about the law God gave Israel through Moses in the "desert of Egypt," a law that included the Ten Commandments.

---

28 Amos not only commands that justice is to pour forth like a river but also that it must be "maintained" or "established" in Israel (5:15), employing the seldom used verb *yatsag* that also describes the placing of the rods in front of the flocks at Genesis 30:38.

29 Rom 5:20.

How could the law, an instrument for promoting honest behavior, instead cause transgressions to multiply? Paul explains in the seventh chapter of Romans that the Mosaic Law set a high standard intended to make the Israelites aware of sins they were committing in ignorance. Paul uses the example of the tenth commandment, which condemns coveting the possessions of someone else. "Coveting" or envying is not committed externally, but in the mind. The tenth commandment revealed that while a person might be adhering to a strict code of conduct outwardly, he could yet be sinning in the confines of his private thoughts. The law therefore caused sins to multiply in the sense of exposing them. "I would not have known what sin was," Paul says, "except through the law."[30]

Paul had made the same point when writing to Christians in Galatia, asking rhetorically, "Why, then, the law?," and answering, "It was added for transgressions, until the descendant [Jesus] came to whom the promise had been made."[31] Admittedly, the Greek phrasing at Galatians 3:19 is vague. It may mean that the law was introduced "because of" transgressions. On the other hand, it may mean that the law "caused" or promoted transgressions.

Some Bible translators understandably hesitate to make God's law a source of sin. As we have seen from Romans, however, Paul believed that the law caused sin to spread in that it caused guilt, the recognition of sin, to spread. Various translators have seen this as the most likely meaning in Galatians 3:19 as well:

> Then what of the law? It was added to make wrongdoing a legal offense.[32]

> What was the purpose of the law, then? It was added in order to show what wrongdoing is.[33]

> Why then was the Law necessary at all? It was introduced to show what transgressions are.[34]

---

30 Rom 7:7.
31 Gal 3:19, *The New American Bible.*
32 *The New English Bible* (New York: Oxford Univ. Press, 1971).
33 *Today's English Version* (New York: American Bible Society, 1971).
34 *Translator's New Testament* (London: British and Foreign Bible Society, 1973).

Then what about the Law? Well, it was interpolated for the purpose of producing transgressions.[35]

Then what about the Law? It was a later addition, designed to produce transgressions.[36]

What is the point of the law then? It was an extra dispensation, introduced in order that transgressions might be brought to light.[37]

The *New American Bible,* noteworthy for its scholarship, comments that in light of Paul's other arguments concerning the law, Galatians 3:19 implies "that the law in effect served to produce transgressions."[38] The exposing of sin is preparatory to faith, part of a process of claiming sinners that began long before Jesus' earthly ministry.

The spots on sheep in the Genesis story are merely symbols of sin. Real sins also were connected with the animals—the sins of Laban, who tried to defraud Jacob of his wages. Laban compounded his original transgression by repeatedly amending his agreement with Jacob, hoping to restrict the size of Jacob's flock. Jacob complains to his wives about Laban's shameless double dealing but admits that he has prospered in spite of it. "If [Laban] said, 'The speckled ones will be your wages,' then all the flocks gave birth to speckled young; and if he said, 'The streaked ones will be your wages,' then all the flocks bore streaked young. So God has taken away your father's livestock and given them to me."[39]

As the symbolic marks of sin multiplied, the sins of Laban increased as he attempted to keep as many animals as possible in his possession. Yet God's blessing upon Jacob more than compensated for Laban's maneuvering. Uncannily, the outcome corresponds again with a statement of Paul's respecting sin, law and the purpose of God. Just after observing that the law caused sins to multiply, Paul continues, "But where sin

---

35 James D. Moffatt, *A New Translation of the Bible* (NY: Harper, 1935).

36 Edgar Goodspeed, *The Complete Bible: An American Translation* (Chicago: Univ. of Chicago Press, 1939).

37 F. F. Bruce, *An Expanded Paraphrase of the Epistles of Paul* (Exeter, NJ: Paternoster, 1965).

38 *The New American Bible* (NY: Catholic Book Pub. Co., 1986).

39 Gen 31:6-9.

increased, grace increased all the more, so that, just as sin reigned in death, so also grace might reign through righteousness to bring eternal life through Jesus Christ our Lord."[40] "Grace" simply refers to favor or kindly treatment. Divine grace pushed aside everything in Jacob's way, and through God's grace Jesus' redemptive work overcame every obstacle raised against it.

Another detail concerns Laban's first effort to keep Jacob from collecting the animals that were due him. Laban gathers the animals with markings, put his sons in charge of them and then herds them to a place three days removed from Jacob. A fairly obvious parallel is evident in what happened to Jesus. Even in the context of his arrest and impending death Jesus' disciples are described as sheep of his flock. "This very night you will all fall away on account of me," Jesus tells the apostles, "for it is written: 'I will strike the shepherd, and the sheep of the flock will be scattered.' "[41] The gulf between life and death is infinite, but because Jesus rose again it also is true that he was separated from his flock by an exile in the grave of approximately three days' duration. (Although this part of the story occurs out of chronological order of fulfillment, we will see later such disjunctions are common in illustrations.)

Further Parallels in Jacob's Story

So far, we have established objectively from the Bible itself that the "sheep" story of Jacob and Laban makes sense as a coded portrayal of sin, law and guilt, and further, of the redemptive role of Jesus, the "greater Jacob." In this prophetic drama, Laban acts as antagonist, standing in for all the individuals, both Jewish and gentile, who would later oppose Jesus. One of those turned out to be Pontius Pilate, the Roman governor who appeased the demands of Jewish priests and other leaders by ordering Jesus' execution. We should not be surprised, then, to find that what Laban says to Jacob at their parting reflects what happens as Pilate is deciding Jesus' fate.

When Jacob furtively departs for Canaan his father-in-law gives chase, but God comes to Laban "in a dream" to warn him, according to Genesis 31:24. "It is in my power to do you harm," the offended Laban

---

40 Rom 5:20-21.
41 Matt 26:31.

tells Jacob upon overtaking him, "but the God of your father spoke to me last night, saying, 'Be careful not to speak either good or bad to Jacob.' "[42] Compare these words with passages from Matthew and John about Pilate:

> While Pilate was sitting on the judge's seat [with Jesus before him], his wife sent to him this message: "Don't have anything to do with that innocent man, for I have suffered a great deal today in a dream because of him." —Matthew 27:19.

> "Do you refuse to speak to me?" Pilate said. "Don't you realize I have power either to free you or to crucify you?" Jesus answered, "You would have no power over me if it were not granted from above . . . " From then on, Pilate tried to set Jesus free, but the Jews kept shouting, "If you let this man go, you are no friend of Caesar."
> —John 19:10-12.

The caution given to Laban not to "speak either good or bad" had to do not only with speaking but with taking any action against Jacob. It is the equivalent of what Pilate is told about Jesus: "Have nothing to do with that man." In both cases the warning is associated with a dream, in Pilate's case coming through his wife as intermediary. Both Laban and Pilate insist that they have power over God's chosen one even as it becomes obvious that each is able only to allow him to proceed along on his ordained course.

The typological meaning we have so far discovered in one small portion of the book of Genesis is more remarkable for defying the limited value placed on the books of the Bible by critics. Genesis is widely supposed to be a collection of legends calculated to engender a sense of ethnic superiority in the ancient Hebrews. The Law of Moses is an artifact preserving the practical ethics and customs of the Israelite people, while the writings of the prophets are an archaic form of social commentary. The Gospels reflect the beliefs of early Christian sects projected back onto the man Jesus, about whose life relatively little can be said with confidence. The New Testament letters document the sometimes conflicting schools of opinion that typically develop within a new religion.

---

42 Gen 31:29, NASB.

Put differently, modern scholarship lays the Bible before us dissected like a laboratory specimen. Moreover, dissection, including dissection of a human body, may be performed for various reasons. Autopsy is dissection for the purpose of gathering information. The coroner may sense a residual sacredness still attached to the object before him, but for the most part his work is a cold disembowelment of something no longer alive. A surgeon, by contrast, cuts into the body in order to keep it alive, to determine the cause of the patient's illness and to separate diseased and healthy tissues. Even in surgery, however, the body lies prostrate while the surgeon wields power over it.

Some Biblical scholars are cast in the mold of coroners, others in that of surgeons. Graham Stanton belongs in the second category. In his book *Gospel Truth?*, Stanton affirms his own Christian faith and makes the case for a core of historical fact at the heart of the Gospels. At the same time, he argues that the tools of literary analysis expose certain Gospel passages as being in all probability "legendary expansions," giving as one example the report in Matthew of the dream of Pilate's wife.[43]

It is fascinating that Stanton should identify as fiction the warning given to Pilate. We saw above that this very text, when set alongside a statement of Pilate to Jesus from John's Gospel, forms a parallel to Laban's confrontation with Jacob. Since the prophetic fulfillment may be seen only by combining passages from different Gospels, no possibility exists that it was noticed, let alone fabricated, by the evangelists themselves. The resemblance might be passed off as an intriguing coincidence if it were not for many other texts that forge a solid link between Jacob and Jesus, and between Jacob's actions and the New Testament themes of law, sin and the need for redemption.

Typological Coding Outside the Bible?

As will become more evident, in the light of typological study the sacred canon lying corpse-like under the scalpel of the specialist undergoes a transformation. The parted bones and severed tendons mend themselves. The body opens its eyes and leaps off the examining table. Unexpectedly but undeniably, the word of God is again "living and active." Once alive, the inspired word itself becomes the examiner

---

43 Graham Stanton, *Gospel Truth?* (Valley Forge, PA: Trinity Press, 1995), 54.

who wields a razor's edge to divide between "soul and spirit, joints and marrow" and expose "thoughts and attitudes of the heart."[44]

In the next chapter I will examine the characteristics of literary symbolism that ordinarily lead us to conclude that it is planned rather than accidental. Even if Biblical typology exhibits those same characteristics, readers who are sufficiently motivated will find reasons to reject its implications. By definition, so the argument goes, a Scriptural passage has no meaning outside its historical context nor may it have a meaning that points toward supernatural inspiration. It might be conceded that a divine influence acted upon the minds of the writers from a cosmic distance like a breeze wafting ocean waves imperceptibly toward the shore. The idea that God would actively direct the writing of the Scriptures, however, is for many critics unthinkable. Evidence of divine authorship is ruled inadmissible before the trial can proceed, so the verdict is never in doubt.

Coded prophecy is likely to be classed along with other conjunctions that inevitably occur between sacred stories from one historical era and those of another or between folk tales and real events. Who is to say that our imaginations are not more ingenious than we realize at exaggerating such conjunctions out of all proportion to their true significance? In the eyes of skeptics typology is best likened to stage magic, combining illusion with an audience's desire to be dazzled.

If typological coding is a trick, it should be easy enough to expose. The raw material of such prophecy ought to be available outside the Bible. The Jews are not the only ethnic group with a written tradition that includes history, legend, poetry and proverbial wisdom. Among others the cultures of Greece, Persia (modern Iran), Arabia, North Africa, China and Japan are obvious candidates. The thousands of stories, proverbs and historical memories contained in these traditions should yield patterns just as apparently mysterious as those we may find in the Bible.

Exactly what would typological coding from extra-Biblical traditions have to portray in order to duplicate the Scriptural evidence? It would prove nothing to find types from non-Jewish sources that seem to reflect what the Bible says about Jesus. Jesus, according to the New

---

44 Heb 4:12.

Testament, is the Savior of the world of mankind and the focal point of all history before and since. In preparing the way for Jesus' coming, God revealed himself primarily but not exclusively to Israel. No one can say that amid the distortions of other religious traditions some seeds of prophetic truth were not sprinkled as well.

Instead of seeming to focus on Jesus, the literary heritage of another culture would have to give the appearance of predicting the life and contributions of a prominent person who later arose within that same culture. After all, Jesus is not the only man revered either as a source of divine wisdom or as the savior-hero of a particular people. A list beginning with Buddha, Plato, Confucius, Mohammad and other spiritual/philosophical figures could extend to Solon, Alexander the Great, Charlemagne, Queen Elizabeth I of England, Napoleon, Simon de Bolivar, Peter the Great, Abraham Lincoln, Charles de Gaulle, Gamal Nasser and dozens of others.

Embedded in Arthurian legends and Chaucer's *Canterbury Tales* could be a symbolic portrayal of the career of Winston Churchill. Or we might examine the mythology in the Hindu Vedas for depictions of Mohandas "Mahatma" Gandhi. Someone could even attempt to show that the Hebrew Scriptures can be made to appear just as predictive of the medieval Jewish rabbi Maimonides as of Jesus of Nazareth. If they could do so we would have to conclude that prophetic "codes," no matter how compelling, fall short as objective evidence of inspiration.

For counterexamples to be of value they must exhibit the same economy of distribution and interrelatedness as those from the Bible. This has to do with how many type sketches are identified relative to the length of the body of literature in which they are found, and whether they are interconnected by shared symbols and concepts. If the Hebrew Bible contained scores of personal histories and incidents to choose from, then the appearance of coded alignment in a few instances could more easily be explained as accidental. In fact, we are talking about documents with the combined length of a bulky novel. If we can relate many of its narratives to Jesus in surprising yet specific ways, as with the example of Jacob, then the phenomenon we face will be that much more difficult to duplicate elsewhere or to account for except as divine revelation.

We have glimpsed the case for typological coding in the Bible, but it remains a hazy outline because we have looked at no more than a fraction of the relevant material. Before considering other examples, I will make some general observations about typology and metaphor in the Scriptures.

2

"All Things Occur as Parables"

As we saw in our study of Jacob and his sheep, a "type" is a person or object that is used to stand for someone or something else. Types are often used outside the Bible in novels, plays or movies as part of the technique of foreshadowing. The 1999 film *The English Patient* offers an example. In the movie an archaeologist named Katherine Clifton reads a story to a group of her colleagues who are on an expedition in North Africa. The story anticipates what will happen to Katherine, her husband and one of the other men in the group.

Since the author of a work of fiction is free to plan the storyline from beginning to end, it is easy for him or her to use foreshadowing to tie it together. The Bible, however, is not the product of a single human author but was written by dozens of men over the course of many centuries. How could these men have coordinated their efforts to create what I have referred to as "typological coding"?

Literary critic Frank Kermode says that if typological foreshadowing was not fabricated by the Bible writers, then perhaps Christ actually was prophesying about himself in the Old Testament. Kermode implies that we can never know for sure because imagination is our only guide.[1] Is Kermode right? Does imagination alone tell us when a human author is using the technique of foreshadowing? Does the Bible leave us no signposts about coded types?

---

1   Frank Kermode, *The Genesis of Secrecy: On the Interpretation of Narrative* (Cambridge, MA: Harvard University Press, 1979), 106-7.

Consider how we might determine whether a screenwriter has consciously employed foreshadowing. Our example is another movie, *On the Waterfront*, from the 1950s. The main character is a New York City dockworker, Terry Malloy, whose brother is an accountant for the longshoremen's union. The union leadership is made up of mobsters who care only about extracting money from union members and who resort to bribery, extortion and even murder to hold on to their power.

When one of Terry's friends, another dockworker, agrees to testify against corrupt union officials, the friend is killed by union thugs. Later, when Terry is walking in the park with the friend's sister, he begins talking about his hobby of keeping racing pigeons. He tells her about the prevalence of hawks who "sit up on the tops of the big hotels" and look for pigeons to swoop down on. On the surface the comment has nothing to do with corruption in the longshoremen's union.

We have good reason to suspect that what Terry Malloy says about birds really has to do with union gangsters and the workers they prey on. Later in the film, the camera looks steeply upward at the union bosses smoking cigars as they peer down at workers in the hold of a cargo ship. In the same scene, a local Catholic priest accuses the bosses of wearing expensive suits and diamond rings paid for by dues and extortion money.

The wealth of the bosses also seems to be reflected in Terry's remark about where the "hawks" like to perch—"on the tops of the big hotels"—since that is also where penthouses and luxury suites are located. The close resemblance between the hawks and pigeons Terry refers to and the union bosses and workers is enough to make it more than likely that the writer is using the birds as types.

There is also another clue that confirms our suspicion. A couple of scenes after Terry's comments the corrupt union president and his henchmen find Terry and tell him that another worker has agreed to testify for government prosecutors. "The little pigeon," says the union chief with contempt, "he ought to have his neck wrung." By actually calling one of the workers a pigeon the scriptwriter has provided a marker or identifier. The odds that both a close resemblance of one thing to another plus a supporting identifier would occur by chance in the same work are small.

This combination of circumstantial resemblance and symbol identifiers was also what helped us decode the meaning of Jacob and his sheep. Circumstantial resemblance refers to features of one character or event that remind us of another. Resemblance is strengthened by the occurrence of identical words, or words that can be shown to be synonyms, in the descriptions of the objects being compared. Symbol identifiers are passages that equate one thing with another.

We would not demand that every feature of a type sketch in a novel or movie be confirmed by an identifier before we would accept that it was intentionally created, so we cannot make that demand in the case of the Bible either. Still, the presence of at least some identifiers is necessary because resemblance alone can occur too easily by chance. It is even possible that resemblance plus an identifier or two could occur by chance, but the odds of this happening are so small that if we found the combination over and over again in the same work, the odds approach zero. And, as was noted in the previous chapter, typological coding in the Bible has the additional characteristics of economy of distribution and interconnectedness. This four-way combination of factors will become apparent as we explore the subject further.

Typology in a Parable

Typology exists in the Bible alongside ordinary metaphors and parables. The relationship between God and his ancient people, the Israelites, is compared to a king and his subjects, a shepherd and his sheep, a father and his children, a mother and her baby, and a husband and wife in various passages. In Isaiah 5, God is a farmer and Israel is a vineyard he creates by turning over the earth, clearing away stones and planting vines. The farmer also builds a tower in the vineyard, digs a well and sets up a wine press. He waits patiently for a good crop, but the grapes turn out to be of poor quality.

"Now you dwellers in Jerusalem and men of Judah," God says to his people, "judge between me and my vineyard." What will the farmer do? "I will take away its hedge," God warns, "and it will be destroyed . . . The vineyard of the LORD Almighty is the house of Israel. And he looked for justice, but saw bloodshed; for righteousness, but heard cries of distress."[2]

---

2 Isa 5:1-7.

Illustrations such as the vineyard parable depend on approximate rather than precise resemblance. God's provision for his people and his expectations of an obedient response bore comparison in certain respects to a landowner owner tending his vines in hopes of a successful grape harvest. When Jesus later repeated the parable he wanted to emphasize the responsibility borne by Israel's leadership. He also wanted to point beyond destructive judgment on the fleshly nation to the emergence of a new kind of people defined not by ancestry but by an obedient response to God's grace.

To get these points across Jesus introduced hired cultivators to represent judges and priests, and servants to represent the prophets sent by God to correct Israel. He also introduced a son of the vineyard owner to represent himself. In the expanded story, the owner sends his servants to receive the harvest only to see them mistreated and his son murdered by the hired men.[3]

Both the original vineyard parable and Jesus' retelling of it contain important prophetic details. The version from Isaiah leaves no doubt that God's disappointment with Israel is deep and that his patience is not inexhaustible. Catastrophe is predicted if the nation does not alter its course: "I will break down its wall and it will be trampled. I will make it a wasteland."[4] A generation or so after Isaiah, the prophet Jeremiah alludes to the parable and indicates that its terrible conclusion is imminent.[5] Such a destruction, including a literal demolition of Jerusalem's wall and razing of Yahweh's temple, did take place in the sixth century BC by the Babylonians.

By reviving Isaiah's story Jesus implied that the nation was due for a repeat of the cataclysm experienced centuries before. The parable did prove durable when, forty years after Jesus' death, Roman armies suppressed the First Jewish Revolt and, like the Babylonians, breached Jerusalem's walls and tore down its temple. However, Jesus' modifications to the story include a new ending. Instead of describing the destruction of the vineyard's wall, Jesus says that the evil caretakers will be swept away while the vineyard itself will survive in order to be leased out to faithful tenants.

---

3   Matt 21:33-41 and parallels.
4   Isa 5:6.
5   Jer 12:10.

To the Jewish establishment of Jesus' day the horrific message had been clear: the blessing of God that had rested on the nation for more than a millennium was going to be transferred to another people. Once replaced by something new, the system of national worship centered on the holy city of Jerusalem and its temple would become obsolete.[6] The point was not anti-Jewish in any racial sense, since like Jesus the Christian apostles and early disciples were themselves Jews. Nevertheless, the suggestion was so abhorrent to Jewish sensibilities that it galvanized opposition to Jesus into a conspiracy seeking his execution.

The vineyard parable effectively focuses attention on certain facts— the spiritual history of the nation, the antagonism of the Jewish establishment to Jesus' ministry, the rift between Judaism and the first century church, the eventual devastation of Judea by Roman armies— and organizing them into a coherent picture of the divine purpose at work. This would remain true of the parable even if, as some scholars presume, it was not actually told by Jesus but was attributed to him fifty years later.

For now, simply note that the story works well despite its mechanical imperfections. Take the chronology of its conclusion, for example: "What then will the owner of the vineyard do? He will come and kill those tenants and give the vineyard to others."[7] Punishment comes before the property changes hands because if murderous men were to occupy a real vineyard it would hardly be possible to usher in new tenants before overpowering the criminals. In the fulfillment contemplated by the evangelists, the spiritual leasehold is transferred to the apostolic church shortly after Jesus' death, decades before Roman troops lay siege to Jerusalem. In spite of the small misalignment, the parable resembles the reality closely enough to showcase critical information.

In another parable, Jesus tells about a farmer sowing seed. Some of the seed either fails to germinate or withers before maturity because of having fallen on rocks, among weeds or beside the road. Other seed falls on fine soil and produces grain. After Jesus relates the parable to the crowd, he explains to his disciples that what the farmer sows is "the word," meaning the gospel message. Some people hear the message but the devil snatches it out of their hearts the way birds eat seed that falls

---

6　John 4:21; Heb 8:13.
7　Mark 12:9.

on the hard-packed roadside. Others hear the word and respond at first but in the end bear no fruit. Finally, there are those who, "like seed sown on good soil, hear the word, accept it, and produce a crop."[8]

By the end of the parable, the "seed" seems to represent hearers of the word and not just the word itself. This slight shift violates a rigid equation of typical and antitypical objects, but not illogically. The story effectively shows that the process of spreading the gospel or "good news" is much like scattering seed to produce a crop. Likewise, typological coding of New Testament salvation history in the Old Testament might lack precision in every detail and still be recognizable for what it is—and be impossible to explain other than as the result of inspiration.

Snakes, Poles and the Logic of Metaphor

When evaluating the symbolic value of historical episodes in the Old Testament, we must remember the characteristics of typological stories that we know were deliberately created. Like the parables of the vineyard and of the sower, effective typology must be brief and pointed, not encumbered by excess detail. We can expect minor incongruities. By its very nature it cannot be pressed beyond the limits of illustration, yet it will reveal connections between seemingly isolated facts.

Our example above, the vineyard narrative, is openly presented as a parable both in its original Old Testament context and in its retelling by Jesus. From it we turn to a historical incident with no obvious prophetic meaning that nevertheless is claimed by Jesus to be messianic. As recorded in John's Gospel, Jesus says, "Just as Moses lifted up the snake in the desert, so the Son of man must be lifted up, that everyone who believes in him may have eternal life."[9]

Jesus is referring to an event from Israel's long years of wilderness wandering as recorded in the Old Testament book of Numbers. The people complain bitterly against God and Moses, calling the miraculous bread that sustains them "miserable food." As a punishment God sends poisonous snakes into the Israelite camp. When the people cry out in anguish, God tells Moses to take a sculpture of a snake and mount it

---

8   Mark 4:13.
9   John 3:14-15.

high on a pole. Anyone who is bitten merely has to look at the figure of the snake in order to survive.[10]

The way Jesus applies the story defies expectation. Jesus compares his own crucifixion, during which he will be nailed high on an executional stake, to the raising of the bronze serpent on a pole. A couple of elements in the odd comparison do make sense. In John, where the application is found, Jesus accuses the devil of being a murderer, implying that death is the result of the devil's having lured the human family into sin.[11] Since elsewhere in the Scriptures the devil is compared to a serpent or snake, death could be likened to a poisonous snake bite.[12] Further, John equates "looking to" Jesus with believing in him as God's Son and the Savior of mankind, the only one who can reverse the process of death and decay.

In these respects the picture of Israelites dying of snakebite and looking upward at God's provision for healing is an understandable portrayal of dying humanity looking toward Jesus, the crucified one, for everlasting life. What does not seem appropriate is the equivalence between Jesus hanging on the cross and the figure of a snake, a symbol more appropriate to Satan than to God's Son.

The solution to the riddle of the snake on the pole is found in two passages from the writings of Paul. "God made him [Jesus] who had no sin to be sin for us," Paul says, "so that in him we might become the righteousness of God."[13] He writes elsewhere that "Christ redeemed us from the curse of the law by becoming a curse for us, for it is written: 'Cursed is everyone who is hung on a tree.' "[14] In the second passage Paul quotes from Deuteronomy, which says that a criminal whose body is "hung on a tree" should not be left out after dark. "Be sure to bury him that day," the law commands, "because anyone who is hung on a tree is under God's curse."[15]

Paul's argument has come under fire from critics who complain that the Mosaic Law never contemplates vicarious punishment, in which one

---

10 Num 21:4-9.
11 John 8:44.
12 Rev 12:9.
13 2 Cor 5:21.
14 Gal 3:13.
15 Deut 21:22-23.

person can take upon himself the sins of others. Further, they say, the command from Deuteronomy has more to do with the vileness of exposing a corpse than with divine justice. We will not take time here to deal with these objections in detail. Although substitutionary atonement, like other profound realities, can be understood only upon reflection, it is easy to grasp the general truth that to help someone in the grip of evil is to accept a measure of suffering oneself.

As for the passage in Deuteronomy, undeniably it assumes public execution of heinous criminals to be just as well as horrific. Rather than setting aside the procedure for punishing wickedness, the Mosaic Law insists that it be concluded swiftly and sin's grisly debris not left long before the eyes of God and man. Paul is on firm ground when he argues that Jesus' death on an executional tree is a repugnant one under the law.

The statement about someone hanging on a tree or timber being under a curse acts as an identifier to unlock the allegory of the serpent on the pole. In the Hebrew Bible the serpent is the only animal specifically placed under God's curse. The familiar narrative of the temptation of Adam and Eve includes God's sentence against the serpent, "Because you have done this, cursed are you above all the livestock and all the wild animals!" He continues, "You will crawl on your belly and you will eat dust all the days of your life. And I will put enmity between you and the woman, and between your offspring and hers; he will crush your head, and you will strike his heel."[16]

Some people are repulsed by snakes, but as part of God's creation snakes are no better or worse than other animals. As noted earlier, the serpent in Genesis chapter three serves as a visible cipher for God's invisible adversary, calling attention to the low moral level on which Satan chooses to exist. When "offspring of snakes" occurs later in the Bible it describes, not legless reptiles, but lying, murderous human beings who show themselves to be "children of the devil" in a metaphorical sense.[17] In English usage "snake in the grass" continues to denote a malicious schemer.

God's instructions to Moses about putting a bronze serpent on a pole therefore had been a puzzle from the beginning. Why would God

16 Gen 3:14-15.
17 Isa 59:4-5; Matt 12:34; cf. John 8:44.

use the image of a cursed animal, symbolic of evil, to provide life and healing to his people? According to Paul, it is because Jesus had to assume the full weight of God's condemnation of sin in order to lift it off of mankind. He had to be seen as the human version of a serpent, namely a liar, rebel and blasphemer who deserved to die nailed to a rough wooden frame in public view. For an agonizing moment the moral order of the universe had to turn upside-down.

We will see later how many other allegories reveal themselves in light of the paradox that Jesus, the most innocent man who ever lived, suffered a punishment appropriate to the worst of criminals. In the case of the serpent on the pole the significance is veiled to a degree by language.

The original Hebrew for the curse pronounced on the serpent is *arar*, whereas the word used in Deuteronomy to describe the curse upon an executed criminal is *qelala*. The two words are close in meaning, however, as can be seen from passages where they are exchanged for one another in parallel phrases.[18] The Septuagint Greek Old Testament translates both *arar* and *qelala* by the Greek word *epikataratos*. By a happy coincidence the verses leading up to Paul's statement about Jesus becoming "a curse" demonstrate the equivalence of the two original Hebrew terms:

> All who rely on observing the law are under a curse, for it is written: 'Cursed [*epikataratos*, from Heb. *arar*] is everyone who does not continue to do everything written in the Book of the Law' . . . Christ redeemed us from the curse of the law by becoming a curse for us, for it is written: 'Cursed [*epikataratos*, from Heb. *qelala*] is everyone who is hung on a tree.'
> —Galatians 3:10-13.

Just as in the account of Jacob's sheep, in the serpent-on-the-pole story we are confronted with an Old Testament narrative that corresponds typologically to one of Paul's teachings about the redemptive role of Jesus. Uncovering the mystery is easier because the identifier at John 3:14-15 is a flashing neon sign pointing us in the right direction. From this example alone we would suspect that typology is not limited to fictional illustrations like the vineyard parable of Isaiah, but that

---

18 Gen 27:12-13, 29; Deut 27:13-15.

prophetic meaning underlies a number of other Old Testament narratives as well.

A different line of reasoning leads to the same conclusion. The Gospels claim that in teaching the crowds Jesus "did not say anything to them without a parable," but that "when he was alone with his own disciples, he explained everything."[19] With Jesus' fondness for parables in mind, consider his claim that he did nothing on his own initiative, but only what he observed his Father to do.[20] If Jesus depended so heavily on parables or allegories that he virtually never taught without them, and if his teaching methods reflect those of God the Father, then the implication is that the Father himself has never spoken apart from illustrations of one kind or another.

The history of the Old Testament period was sculpted by God into representations that lie open only to those who, like the disciples, turn toward Jesus for their explanation. Furthermore, we have already begun to see that these episodes, which I referred to earlier as type sketches, do not stand apart from each other but are cross-linked like the strands of a finely woven net.

Water in the Desert

Nowhere is the linkage between typological episodes more apparent that in another historical event, the provision of water during the Exodus wandering. Like the serpent on the pole, this story too is claimed in the New Testament to have a prophetic dimension. Paul says that "our forefathers," the ancient Israelites, "were all baptized into Moses in the cloud and in the sea" at the time of the exodus from Egypt. "They all ate the same spiritual food and drank the same spiritual drink," he says, "for they drank from the spiritual rock that accompanied them, and that rock was Christ."[21]

"Rock" or "stone" is a symbol of solidity and strength in both Old and New Testaments, used of God, of the Messiah and of prominent servants of God such as Abraham and Jesus' apostles. Paul sees Jesus prefigured in the rock outcrops that God caused to split open and pour

---

19 Mark 4:33-34.
20 John 5:19.
21 1 Cor 10:1-4.

forth water for the Israelites. The miracle was performed once shortly after the departure from Egypt and again decades later after the Israelite people refused to enter the Promised Land and were condemned to sojourn in the desert for forty years.

In both instances the people react to lack of water not by entreating but instead by angrily denouncing Moses, at which Moses in fear for his life beseeches Yahweh: "What am I to do with these people? They are almost ready to stone me." God instructs Moses to take in his hand the staff he had used to strike the Nile River during the Egyptian plagues and to summon the elders of the people to a large rock face at or near Mt. Horeb (probably another name for Mt. Sinai). "I will stand there before you by the rock at Horeb," God tells him. "'Strike the rock, and water will come out of it for the people to drink." Moses performs this act "in the sight of the elders of Israel" and water erupts from the crag.[22]

In the second occurrence, Moses and Aaron his brother, who has since been installed as High Priest, are again besieged by the people over the issue of water. At the entrance to the makeshift temple, the tabernacle, Moses is told once again to take his staff in hand and, along with Aaron, to gather the assembly in front of a large rock. Moses is to speak to the rock so that water will begin to flow from it.

"So Moses took the staff from the LORD's presence, just as he commanded him." Moses angrily asks the crowd if he and Aaron must bring water out of the rock for them. "Then Moses raised his arm and struck the rock twice with his staff. Water gushed out, and the community and their livestock drank."[23] If viewed prophetically, the double occurrence of the water miracle serves to give it emphasis.[24]

Foremost among several symbolic meanings of water in the Scriptures is as a representation of the miraculous power of God's Spirit. "I will pour out water on the thirsty land, and streams on the dry ground," God declares in Isaiah. "I will pour out my Spirit on your offspring, and my blessing on your descendants."[25] Since divine knowledge is communicated through the Spirit—giving rise to the term "inspiration"—such knowledge or teaching is also likened to water. "As the rain and the

---

22 Exod 17:4-6.
23 Num 20:6-11.
24 Gen 41:32.
25 Isa 44:3.

snow come down from heaven, and do not return to it without watering the earth . . . so is my word that goes out from my mouth."[26] Proverbs adds, "The words of a man's mouth are deep waters; the fountain of wisdom is a bubbling brook."[27]

The image of water coming out of the rock suggests various manifestations of God's Spirit coming from the Messiah, the "stone laid in Zion" by Yahweh.[28] In agreement, the Gospels present Jesus as the source from which miraculous power, including healing and divine knowledge, pours forth. The correspondence continues to hold when we examine the details of the Exodus stories.

Moses was commanded to procure the water both by striking the rock and by speaking to it. The second instruction is significant in that the healing power of Jesus was generally available to those who asked for it either by their words or actions. In a story from the Gospels, a blind beggar is told that Jesus is passing by and begins calling out loudly for Jesus to show him mercy. Bystanders rebuke the blind man and try to silence him, but he cries out the more. Jesus stops to speak with him and in the end he is cured of his blindness.[29]

The meaning of Jesus' parables, too, was given to those who took the trouble to ask. Before providing an interpretation of the parable of the sower, for example, Jesus is approached by the twelve and certain others who want an explanation. "He told them, 'The secret of the kingdom of God has been given to you. But to those on the outside, everything occurs in parables so that "they may be ever seeing but never perceiving." ' "[30] Instructions on prayer also come after a disciple says, "Lord, teach us to pray, just as John taught his disciples."[31]

If these and other examples leave any doubt that spiritual water was available to anyone who spoke receptively to the Messiah, a familiar story from John's Gospel settles the question. Jesus is resting next to a well and a Samaritan woman comes to draw water. When Jesus asks her for a drink, she wonders aloud why he is willing to engage in conversa-

---

26 Isa 55:10-11.
27 Prov 18:4, NASB.
28 Isa 28:16.
29 Luke 18:35-43.
30 Mark 4:10-11.
31 Luke 11:1-2.

tion a member of a race despised by Jews. "Jesus answered her, 'If you knew the gift of God and who it is that asks you for a drink, you would have asked him and he would have given you living water.'"

The word used by Jesus to say that he would "give" living water, *didomi*, is the same word used in the Septuagint Greek Old Testament at Numbers 20:8 to say that the rock would give its water when Moses spoke to it. When the Samaritan woman speaks further to Jesus and asks for the water he describes, he responds with miraculous knowledge of her past followed by a disclosure that he is the long-awaited Messiah.[32] The realization that Jesus is the Messiah or Christ, the unique Son of Yahweh and Lord of heaven and earth, is an insight representing deep spiritual waters.[33]

The significance of Jesus' bold self-identification to the Samaritan woman can be appreciated by remembering that most of the time Jesus took pains to avoid it, much to the frustration of his adversaries.[34] He finally offered the information to his opponents at his trial when they angrily bound him to do so under judicial oath. "Again the high priest asked him, 'Are you the Christ, the Son of the Blessed One?' 'I am,' said Jesus. 'And you will see the Son of Man sitting at the right hand of the Mighty One and coming on the clouds of heaven.'"[35]

The audience for this proclamation, the Sanhedrin, is described by Luke as "the council of the elders of the people, both the chief priests and teachers of the law," the counterpart of the assembly consisting of the elders of Israel who were present when Moses caused water to come forth from the rock.[36]

A Double Blow Against the Messianic Stone

It is now apparent how God's instruction, "Speak to that rock and it will pour out its water," was fulfilled in Jesus. Even more prominent in the Hebrew Scriptures, however, is God's first command concerning the provision of water: "Strike the rock with your staff." On the second

---

32 John 4:6-26.
33 Matt 16:16-17.
34 Mark 8:29-30; John 10:24.
35 Mark 14:60-62.
36 Luke 22:66-67.

occasion, in fact, Moses strikes the rock twice to get water, even though he has been commanded only to speak to it. We have a head start on what the striking of the rock means because of what we understood from the story of Jacob's sheep, that "rod" or "staff" as a symbol is most often representative of legal authority. The implication is that the Jesus would be attacked by means of law.

The Hebrew word for "struck" in the passages about water from the rock is *naka*, a word that is found in at least three passages that may concern the Messiah. Isaiah says of God's "servant" that "we considered him stricken by God, smitten [*naka*] by him, and afflicted."[37] Micah foretells, "They will strike [*naka*] Israel's ruler on the cheek with a rod" and Zechariah says to "strike [*naka*] the shepherd, and the sheep will be scattered."[38]

The fifty-third chapter of Isaiah was widely seen as descriptive of Jesus by the early church, as for example at Acts 8:32-35, but not because of a connection with what Exodus and Numbers say about the striking of the rock. The same is true of the Zechariah passage, applied by Jesus to his own impending execution at Matthew 26:31 and Mark 14:27. Although the water-from-the-rock narratives had nothing to do with the original application of these verses to Jesus by Christians, under scrutiny the coded meaning reveals itself.

Micah 5:1 is not applied to Jesus in the New Testament. However, the very next verse of chapter five, which says that the ruler of Israel will be born in the town of Bethlehem, was considered to be messianic by both Jews and early Christians.[39] The "rod" that Micah says would strike the Messiah is translated from the Hebrew *shebet*. We saw in the previous chapter that this is one of several Hebrew words that can be translated "rod" or "staff." The word for "staff" in the water-from-the-rock stories is *matteh*. Isaiah furnishes us with a verse to confirm the equivalence of the terms when it declares, "Woe to the Assyrian, the rod [*shebet*] of my anger, in whose hand is the club [*matteh*] of my wrath!"[40]

This text from Isaiah equating *matteh* and *shebet* further illustrates that "rod" as a symbol of legal power entails the ability to inflict punishment

---

37 Isa 53:4.
38 Micah 5:1; Zech 13:7.
39 Matt 2:6.
40 Isa 10:5-6.

on lawbreakers, as God used the Assyrian empire to punish the faithless northern ten-tribe kingdom of Israel. The southern kingdom of Judah with its capital at Jerusalem escaped destruction by Assyria, but eventually came under Babylonian, then Persian, Greek and finally Roman domination.

Rome allowed the Jews a vassal dynasty in the house of Herod the Great (who probably was not even ethnically Jewish), and permitted local institutions such as the Sanhedrin to exercise certain law-enforcement functions. But in the early years of the first century, unrest among the Jews led Rome to tighten its grip on the Jewish capital, removing Jerusalem from the jurisdiction of Herod's son Archelaus and installing a Roman "procurator" or governor instead. The key events are recorded by the Jewish historian Josephus:

> And now Archelaus's part of Judea [including Jerusalem] was reduced into a province, and Coponius, one of the equestrian order among the Romans, was sent as a procurator, having the power of life and death put into his hands by Caesar.
> —Wars of the Jews, 2.8.1.

One of Coponius's successors was Pontius Pilate, whose administration of Jerusalem posed an obstacle to Jewish leaders when they sought to execute Jesus. According to John, when Pilate demands to know the charges against Jesus, the elders say that if he were not a criminal they would not be handing him over. Pilate tries to dismiss them, telling them to deal with Jesus according to Jewish law. " 'But we have no right to execute anyone,' the Jews objected."[41]

In practice the Sanhedrin could get away with extralegal execution of someone of low social status such as the disciple Stephen.[42] Jesus, by contrast, was popular enough that the Jewish leadership earlier had feared an outbreak of rioting if he were arrested near the temple during daylight hours. Execution of a public figure in defiance of Roman authority was too risky, so instead the elders had to induce the Roman governor to do the killing.

---

41 John 18:28-31.
42 Acts 7:57-58.

The elders might well have expected that Pilate, who had a reputation for responding savagely to the least infraction, would be easily persuaded to dispose of one more troublesome Jew. It is the fashionable albeit naive opinion even of many contemporary historians that Pilate would automatically have conferred a death sentence on any Jew who was brought to him. As the Gospels tell it, Pilate was suspicious of the Sanhedrin's motives and resistant to being manipulated. What other than jealousy had led the Jewish leadership to accuse this itinerant rabbi, who was not known to him as a rebel? And what kind of disturbance might his execution provoke?

Pilate must have known that when Jesus had entered Jerusalem the welcome he received from his followers was enthusiastic but not riotous. If Pilate knew that Jesus had created a disturbance at the temple, he is just as likely to have heard from the Roman-sympathizing party followers of Herod that Jesus had supported—with careful qualification—the paying of taxes to Caesar. Finally, the charge that Jesus claimed to be God's Son seems to have aroused Pilate's superstitious fear.

Pilate decided to fob the problem off on the brother of Archelaus, Herod Antipas, who was in Jerusalem for the Passover festival. His rationale was that Jesus came from Galilee, which was under Herod's jurisdiction. Herod might take Jesus into custody and then remove him to Galilee for execution, imprisonment or even release. Like Pilate, the Jewish ruler felt no particular threat from Jesus and was hoping to be entertained by one of the Nazarene's famous miracles. Yet, as a politician he scarcely would have been anxious to make enemies in the Sanhedrin. Herod sent Jesus back to Pilate, thereby casting doubt on the charge of sedition but in practical terms upholding the high council's decision.

Unable to dodge the issue, Pilate finally understood that there was greater danger in letting Jesus live than in ordering his crucifixion.

The maneuvering to have Jesus killed resulted in his being tried and convicted on two different charges under two different authorities, one Jewish and the other Roman. The charge against Jesus under Jewish law was blasphemy, for his having claimed to be the messianic Son of Man destined to judge the world. The charge under Roman law was sedition, for making himself a rival to Caesar by claiming to be a king. The final arbiter of Jewish law, in this case Herod Antipas, silently upheld the charge against Jesus, as did the administrator of Roman law, Pontius Pilate.

The apostles' prayer from book of Acts draws attention to this double condemnation. "Indeed Herod and Pontius Pilate met together with the Gentiles and the people of Israel in this city," it says, "to conspire against your holy servant Jesus, whom you anointed."[43] Herod and Pilate are paired together, as are the two classes of people they represent, namely, Jews (Israel) and Gentiles in the form of the Romans. In fact, on the night of his arrest Jesus was held alternately in the custody of Jewish temple police and Roman soldiers and endured beatings at the hands of both.[44] The "double blow" fulfills the detail from the Numbers narrative that says Moses struck the rock twice with his staff.

If we take another look at Matthew's account of Jesus' beating by Roman soldiers we find further confirmation of the symbolism of Jesus, the "rock," being struck by the "staff" of the law. The soldiers ridicule the idea of Jesus as king by draping him in a royal cloak (possibly the one put on him earlier by Herod[45]), setting a crown of thorns on his head and finally placing in his hand a mock scepter—the symbol of legal sovereignty—with which they then hit him repeatedly.

The Greek word for the object put in Jesus' hand is *kalamos*, which often describes a fine reed used as a pen. In Greek literature, however, *kalamos* also is used of a fishing pole and of the shaft of an arrow, which shows that it can denote a stick heavy enough to raise welts if used to strike someone on the face and head. The Bible book of Revelation, in the first verse of chapter eleven, refers to a measuring stick as "a reed [*kalamos*] like a rod [*rabdos*]." In turn, "rod," *rabdos*, is the word used in the Septuagint Greek Bible in both Exodus and Numbers to describe the staff with which Moses strikes the rock.

Streams from the Rock

At the conclusion of the water-from-the-rock stories, water gushes forth and the people drink. We saw that even before Jesus' death, spiri-

---

43 Acts 4:27-28.
44 Mark 14:64-65; Matt 27:27-30.
45 Luke 23:11.

tual refreshment poured forth from him for those who requested it. These early manifestations of God's Spirit were limited in comparison with the "water" that would become available after his death.

As reported in John, Jesus announces at the Feast of Booths in Jerusalem that anyone who is "thirsty" can come to him and "drink." "Whoever believes in me," he says, will have "streams of living water" flowing within him. John then adds, "By this he meant the Spirit, whom those who believed in him were later to receive. Up to that time the Spirit had not been given, since Jesus had not yet been glorified."[46] Showing that the glorification of Jesus and therefore the sending of the Spirit depended upon his sacrificial death, Jesus later tells the disciples that "unless I go away [in death], the Counselor [the Spirit] will not come to you; but if I go, I will send him to you."[47]

The infusion of "power from on high" into the tiny Christian congregation of Jerusalem took place at the Jewish festival of Pentecost a few weeks after the crucifixion.[48] Believers received the miraculous ability to speak in foreign languages, allowing them to witness to Jews who had traveled to Jerusalem from the far corners of the Roman empire.[49] The apostle Peter explained the manifestation by citing an Old Testament verse that, like Isaiah, uses language about the "pouring out" of the holy Spirit as if it were water:

> Then Peter stood up with the Eleven, raised his voice and addressed the crowd: 'Fellow Jews and all of you who live in Jerusalem, let me explain this to you; listen carefully to what I say. These men are not drunk, as you suppose. It's only nine in the morning! No, this is what was spoken by the prophet Joel: 'In the last days, God says, "I will pour out my Spirit on all people.' "
>
> —Acts 2:14-17.

Peter links this "pouring out" to the death and resurrection of Jesus, saying that he was put to death according to God's purpose and foreknowledge but afterward raised to life. "Exalted to the right hand of

46 John 7:37-39.
47 John 16:7.
48 Luke 24:49.
49 Acts 2:7-11.

God," Peter continues, "he has received from the Father the promised Holy Spirit and has poured out what you now see and hear."[50] John and Acts therefore leave no doubt about how water for the spiritually thirsty resulted from the striking of the rock.

An important note to this typological episode is what John reports about Jesus' final moments on the cross. When at the end of the day Roman soldiers find that the two crucified robbers are still alive, they break their legs, a procedure that caused a victim's own weight to compress his rib cage and bring about death by suffocation. Jesus appears lifeless, but to make sure he is dead one of the soldiers jabs his side with a spear, "bringing a sudden flow of blood and water."[51]

The water that came from Jesus was probably in the form of clear fluid that had gathered in the chest or abdominal cavity. Some commentators have tried to determine the precise physiological condition involved while others have questioned its plausibility. The truth is that we have too few details to make a firm medical judgment about the source of the fluid. Our present interest lies in the event as the equivalent of the soldiers beating Jesus with a mock scepter, that is, as a dramatization of a larger fulfillment underway. Significantly, one text in the Hebrew Bible, Habakkuk 3:14, demonstrates that in rare instances the Hebrew word for Moses' staff, *matteh*, can refer to a shaft with a point for piercing—in other words, a spear.

The story of water pouring from the rock intersects that of Jacob's sheep by using the same symbol, the rod, to stand for law. The two prophecies are therefore mutually reinforcing. In a later chapter I will present a more detailed typological sketch that also shares symbolism with the water-from-the-rock episode. Moreover, certain texts we have already looked at will be revisited in the course of deciphering yet other prophecies, since these passages serve as anchor points from which lines of meaning radiate outward.

By now we should have put behind us any objection that the typological method, carefully applied, is alien to the Bible text. In the examples from this chapter, the plain language of the Bible itself at John 3:14 and 1 Corinthians 10:4 put us on the trail of typological meaning.

---

50 Acts 2:23-24, 32-33.
51 John 19:34.

The consistency between story and fulfillment in the cases we have examined justifies the expectation that even where coding is unheralded, clues in the text may show it to be present. Clues are nowhere more sought after than in the matter of whether Jesus of Nazareth was who his disciples claimed he was. A traveling rabbi, no matter how gifted, would hardly seem to qualify as the warrior-king expected by the Jewish people. Can typology settle the question of messianic credentials? That is the question I will address next.

3

Credentials of the Liberator

In view of the prominence of miracles in the Gospels, it seems strange at first that Jesus rebuked those who asked him to show them one. In the Gospel of Mark, with a bluntness characteristic of that book Jesus says that his generation will be given "no sign."[1] Versions of this saying found in Matthew and Luke deny that any sign will be given except for some kind of resemblance between Jesus and the prophet Jonah. John's Gospel records Jesus' complaint that the people will not believe unless they see "signs and wonders."[2]

Some scholars infer from these sayings that Jesus never intended his works to be viewed as miracles and that he did not see himself as the divine figure his adherents later claimed him to be. Even rabbinic tradition did not necessarily associate miracle-working with the expected Messiah. The *International Jewish Encyclopedia* says that the messianic deliverer was not expected to be "superhuman" nor did the rabbis consider performance of miracles to be a qualification of the Messiah.[3] But it is hard to imagine that the author of Mark, whose Gospel contains the starkest version of the "no sign" remark, would have failed to see the contradiction between such an understanding and the rest of his narrative.

---

1   Mark 8:12.
2   John 4:48.
3   *The International Jewish Encyclopedia*, ed. Ben Isaacson (Englewood Cliffs, NJ: Prentice-Hall, 1973), 208.

Early in Mark Jesus calls attention to his ability to heal a paralytic as proof that he also has the power to forgive sins.[4] Jesus' authority to teach the meaning of divine law is in the very next chapter authenticated by his healing of a man with a withered hand on the Sabbath.[5] Also in the third chapter of Mark, Jesus cites his ability to exorcise demons as proof that he can overcome Satan.[6]

Although John and Luke are the only evangelists to use the word *semeion*, "sign," to describe Jesus' powerful works, all four Gospels effectively present those works as proof of Jesus' identity as the Messiah, God's beloved Son.[7] If Jesus in fact performed signs, how then do we explain his insistence that "no sign" would be given? Part of the answer lies in Jesus' disinclination to perform feats on demand as if he were a paid entertainer. In all the Gospels the challenge to produce a sign comes from Jesus' enemies.[8]

There is also the question of what kind of sign would have been most popular with Jesus' audience. Jewish society in the first century was a volatile mixture of nationalism and religious fervor born of the Jews' unique history. Widespread poverty kept this brew simmering near the flash point, as did the frequently harsh and sometimes barbarous tactics of the Roman occupying force. The plight of first century Jews is graphically demonstrated by what archaeologists found when they excavated four tombs north of Jerusalem in 1968. Most sensational was the recovery of the bones of a crucifixion victim whose ossuary is inscribed with the name "Jehohanan" (in English, "John"). Like Jesus, he was executed sometime in the first century.[9]

The case of Jehohanan proves that the Romans did occasionally release the bodies of crucifixion victims for interment. It also testifies to the horror of the times. Of the thirty-five individuals whose remains were found with those of Jehohanan, at least five had died violently, including a teenage boy who had been burned on an iron grill, an elderly

---

4   Mark 2:3-12.
5   Mark 3:1-5.
6   Mark 3:22-27.
7   John 3:2; 4:54; 12:18; Acts 2:22.
8   Matt 12:38; Mark 8:11; Luke 11:16; John 2:18.
9   See Nicu Haas, "Anthropological Observations on the Skeletal Remains from Giv'at ha-Mivtar," *Israel Exploration Journal* 20, 1-2 (1970): 38-59.

woman who had been clubbed to death and a four-year-old who had been shot through the head with an arrow—all presumed victims of a Roman crackdown. Other remains bear witness to less dramatic but no less agonized deaths, like that of a young woman who had died in child-birth and three children who had simply starved.[10]

Jehohanan's face bore the stamp of harrowing circumstances. His crooked skull and cleft palate likely resulted from his mother's poor diet, prenatal stress and injuries he sustained in childbirth.[11] He and those buried with him leave little doubt as to why the torture of crucifixion was for the Romans an indispensable tool of social control. The threat of quick death under a Roman sword may have been less than intimidating for people so deeply immersed in misery.

With the historical setting of Jesus' ministry in mind, it is easy to understand what kind of miracle many Jews of the first century were looking for and why the works of Jesus fell short in their eyes. The Hebrew Scriptures promised that the Messiah would gloriously triumph over Israel's enemies and inaugurate an era of prosperity. Never had the realization of the messianic prophecies been more desperately longed for than under Roman rule. Compromise with the Roman occupiers was the order of the day for all but the most brazen of zealots, but only an oligarchy at the top of Jewish society actually relished it.

The vast majority of Jews, rich and poor, would have applauded a Messiah who could with a display of heavenly power rid them of the Roman presence. The caustic demand of one of the criminals crucified alongside Jesus, "Are you not the Christ? Save yourself and us!," was in a way that of the greater part of the nation.[12] The taunt of Jesus' enemies, "He is the king of Israel; let him now come down from the cross, and we will believe in him," is in the same spirit as the demand for a sign. "If your power is not greater than the enemy's legions," they seemed to say, "then as Messiah you are a fraud."

Such sentiments were not unanimous, of course. To those who put faith in Jesus the force of his words along with his mighty works testified that he was the Anointed, who in God's time would rule the world.

---

10 Ibid., 40-49.
11 Ibid., 54.
12 Luke 23:39.

It was not that they lacked experience with teachers and healers. Sages, healers, mystics and self-proclaimed prophets were commonplace throughout the ancient world. From these Jesus stood out. He taught as no one else taught and healed as no one else healed, or at any rate that is what the Gospel writers would have us believe.[13] It did not matter to the disciples, as it does to critics, that the Hebrew Scriptures nowhere say that the Messiah would begin his career as an itinerant preacher.

Apart from the question of whether miracles identify Jesus as the Messiah, the number of scholars who are prepared to treat Jesus' exorcisms and healings as pure fantasy is smaller than might be expected. Consider the book *Putting Away Childish Things*, which in a jacket blurb promises to debunk such Biblical narratives as those about the virgin birth and the empty tomb. The author, Uta Ranke-Heinemann, claims that enlightened Christianity can dispense with such beliefs.[14]

It would be hard to find within the field of Biblical studies anyone with less respect for the Bible than Ranke-Heinemann. Her comments on the New Testament are sprinkled with such pejorative descriptions as "fables," "fairy tales," "manipulation," "nonsense" and "propaganda."[15] Yet even as partisan a voice as hers is forced to acknowledge that when it comes to the cures and exorcisms attributed to Jesus we cannot simply dismiss the Gospel narratives as unhistorical.[16]

In *Gospel Fictions* Randel Helms cites with approval the opinion of German higher critic Ernst Kasemann. Kasemann proclaimed in the early 1960s that scientific scrutiny reveals the bulk of Gospel reports of Jesus' miracles to be legendary. Only healings such as that of Peter's mother-in-law from a fever and the cure of "so-called possessed persons," in other words exorcisms, ought still to be regarded as historical, according to him. Kasemann called these accounts "harmless" in that they are easy to explain in naturalistic terms.[17]

---

13 Matt 7:28-29; Mark 2:12; John 7:46; 9:25, 32.

14 Uta Ranke-Heinemann, *Putting Away Childish Things*, trans. Peter Heinegg (New York: HarperCollins, 1994).

15 *Ibid.*, 95, 96, 98, 106, 116, 116, 287.

16 *Ibid.*, 88.

17 Ernst Kasemann, *Essays on New Testament Themes*, trans. W. J. Montague (London: SCM Press, 1964), 48, 50-51.

A common view among scholars and historians is that Jesus had a gift for making people feel better psychosomatically, which was misinterpreted at the time as exorcism of demons and supernatural healing of the sick.

Jesus and Moses

To understand what typology can contribute to our understanding of Jesus' powerful works we must first turn to the Old Testament figure to whom Jesus is most frequently and most closely compared, Moses. So prominent is Moses as liberator and lawgiver that he is distinguished from the prophets who followed, as in the common New Testament phrase, "Moses and the prophets."

All four Gospels parallel Jesus and Moses in various ways, and at least one strand of Jewish tradition holds that the Messiah will resemble Moses. The key Hebrew text in this regard, from Deuteronomy, quotes Moses as saying that in order to set Israel apart from the nations that "practice sorcery or divination" God "will raise up for you a prophet like me from among your own brothers. You must listen to him."[18]

The verse of Deuteronomy about the coming prophet anticipated the prophetic office filled by Joshua, Samuel, Elijah, Elisha and others. But an ultimate fulfillment in terms of the general line of prophets is ruled out by another passage in Deuteronomy that states that "since then [the days of the wilderness wandering], no prophet has risen in Israel like Moses, whom the LORD knew face to face, who did all those miraculous signs and wonders the LORD sent him to do." "No one," it continues, "has ever shown the mighty power or performed the awesome deeds that Moses did in the sight of all Israel."[19]

When the epilogue to the story of Moses was written, long after the prediction had been made about a prophet "like Moses," no such man had yet appeared. According to the Scripture only a deliverer who communed with God "face to face" and performed signs like those of Moses would qualify. If we carry the comparison with Moses to its logi-

18 Deut 18:14-15.
19 Deut 34:10-12.

cal end, we must envision a prophet who functions as emancipator, lawgiver and covenant mediator as well.

What concerns us here are those miraculous powers that Moses was
endowed with specifically to corroborate the claim that he had been sent
by God. Three signs were to serve that purpose according to the story
of the burning bush. God speaks to Moses out of the bush and gives
him the mission to liberate the Israelites enslaved in Egypt. When Moses
asks how he will prove to his people that he has been sent by God, he is
told to throw his shepherd's staff to the ground. The staff instantly becomes a snake. "Reach out your hand," God tells him, "and take it by
the tail." When Moses does so, the snake changes back into a staff.
"This," says God, "is so that they may believe that the LORD, the God
of their fathers—the God of Abraham, the God of Isaac and the God
of Jacob—has appeared to you."

Yahweh further instructs Moses to put his hand inside his cloak.
When Moses withdraws it again, the hand is white with leprosy. When
Moses puts the hand inside his cloak a second time, the leprosy vanishes
and the hand is restored. "If they do not believe you or pay attention to
the first miraculous sign," God says, "they may believe the second. But
if they do not believe these two signs or listen to you, take some water
from the Nile and pour it on the dry ground. The water you take from
the river will become blood on the ground."[20]

The revered Jewish rabbi Maimonides denied that Moses appealed to
miracles. "Israel did not believe in Moses, our teacher, because of the
miracles he worked," he claimed in one of his treatises. "Whenever anyone's belief is based on seeing miracles, he has doubts that remain,
because it is possible the miracles were performed through magic or
witchcraft."[21] Maimonides was probably attempting to counter Christian
claims based on Gospel accounts of Jesus' miracles.

Maimonides' learned opinion notwithstanding, Exodus says that
Moses was given miraculous abilities expressly to prove to Israel that
God had sent him. And the signs described in Exodus chapter four had
their intended effect, for when Moses and his brother Aaron performed
them, the narrative says, "the people believed."[22]

---

20 Exod 4:1-9.
21 Maimonides, *Foundations of Torah*, ch. 8.
22 Exod 4:30-31.

Decoding the Signs

The first two powers are demonstrated and paired together as "these two signs," and then a third is given if necessary to settle the issue. At a glance the signs resemble magician's tricks. Once the possibility of a connection to Jesus is raised, a symbolic interpretation suggests itself. Moses' rod in this episode has a meaning derived less from its association with law than from its long serpent-like shape. The rod becomes a serpent when thrown to the ground and can be controlled by Moses. In the New Testament the devil is portrayed as a great serpent who is cast down to the earth along with the demonic angels who serve him.[23]

The first sign may be described as "power over the serpent," meaning ability to overcome Satan and his forces, and could correspond to Jesus' power to subdue evil spirits and free people from demonic oppression.

The second sign, by which Moses causes his hand to become leprous and then instantly heals it, might be described as "power over disease." In the Bible leprosy refers to skin ailments generally and is considered the most loathsome of diseases. The Mosaic Law contains more instructions about leprosy than about all other sicknesses put together.

Some characters in the Bible, including Moses' sister Miriam and one of Israel's kings, Uzziah, were stricken with leprosy as a punishment for their sins. Leprosy therefore makes a fitting symbol for disease in general, which springs from the spiritually unclean condition of mankind. Jesus' authority to forgive sins is associated in the Gospels with his power to cure diseases of all kinds, including leprosy.[24]

On occasion Jesus miraculously fed crowds, raised the dead and controlled the physical elements, but exorcism and healing were the "wonders" he was known to do nearly everywhere he went. Passing through Perea east of the Jordan on his way to Jerusalem Jesus summarizes his activities by saying, "I will drive out demons and heal people today and tomorrow, and on the third day I will reach my goal."[25] When Jesus sends out the apostles as his representatives, he gives them "authority to drive out evil spirits and to heal every disease and sickness."[26]

---

23 Rev 12:9.
24 Mark 1:40-42; 2:9-12.
25 Luke 13:32.
26 Matt 10:1; cf. Mark 6:13.

There appears to be a good fit between the first two signs of Moses and the two types of miracles Jesus most commonly performed. We might discern a connection as well between the third sign—water turning to blood as it is poured out—and the pouring out of Jesus' blood. The question now is whether a closer examiination will support these impressions.

Subduing the Snake

We begin with the figure of Satan. As difficult as it is for the modern secular mind to take the devil and demons seriously, in the Bible evil spirits are presented not only as real but as superior to humans in capabilities and intelligence. The Scriptures imply that Satan, the most powerful of the demons, was once an angel whose pride led him into rebellion and the desire to incite others against God. Satan "fell" in the sense that he lapsed into sin. Falling or being thrown down is also a metaphor for being hindered, humiliated or even destroyed. In English usage, "downfall" describes not a physical fall but a defeat.

Satan has fallen more than one time in more than one way. During Jesus' ministry the devil was overcome both morally by Jesus' integrity and physically by Jesus' power of exorcism. An intriguing passage on the subject is found in Luke, when Jesus welcomes back his disciples at the end of a preaching mission. The disciples excitedly report to him that "even the demons submit to us in your name." Jesus replies, "I saw Satan fall like lightning from heaven." He goes on to tell them, "I have given you authority to trample on snakes and scorpions and to overcome all the power of the enemy; nothing will harm you. However, do not rejoice that the spirits submit to you, but rejoice that your names are written in heaven."[27]

Jesus' comment on the success of the disciples resonates with the first sign of Moses. Just as Moses can grasp the serpent by the tail to render it harmless again, Jesus and his representatives have authority to neutralize "all the power of the enemy." Jesus leaves an identifier by referring to the devil's forces as "snakes and scorpions." He also says that the de-

---

27 Luke 10:19-20.

feat of occult power amounts to Satan taking a fall, much as the rod of Moses is thrown to the ground in the course of being transformed into a serpent.

Jesus' reference to "trampling" likewise calls to mind "casting down" because the terms are associated with each other in the Bible. In Daniel chapter eight, for example, the two terms are alternated in such a way as to demonstrate their equivalence as metaphors for domination.[28] The words for "casting down" in that passage are the same as those used of Moses' rod in the Hebrew Masoretic and Greek Septuagint texts of Exodus, while the Greek term for "trample" in the Septuagint text of Daniel is a form of the same word used by Jesus in Luke 10. A comparison of other Scriptures confirms that the meaning of the two expressions is the same when used metaphorically.[29]

Luke's narrative concerning the fall of Satan and the trampling of demonic spirits is a key identifier in its own right. It also leads on to still other identifiers by pointing back to a passage from the book of Isaiah:

> How you have fallen from heaven,
> O morning star, son of the dawn!
> You have been cast down to the earth,
> you who once laid low the nations!
> You said in your heart,
> "I will ascend to heaven . . . "
> But you are brought down to the grave,
> to the depths of the pit. —Isaiah 14:12-15

A previous verse says that this passage is about the "king of Babylon," yet Jesus echoes its language when he says that Satan has "fallen like lightning from heaven." The Greek word *astrape* usually means lightning but can refer to any bright light. Similarly, the Hebrew for "morning star" in Isaiah 14:12 literally means "shining one" and is rendered "Lucifer" or "light bearer" in Latin. Scholars who reject an application of the Lucifer passage to Satan overlook what is apparent from our investigation so far, namely, that more than one layer of meaning may be present in a Biblical passage.

---

28 Dan 8:10-13.
29 Cf. Luke 21:6, 24; Rev 11:2.

Isaiah chapter fourteen relies on a type of descriptive allusion that is still used today. When a dictator is referred to as a "little Hitler" we understand the expression to say something about the egomania of the individual so described as well as that of Hitler himself. The city-state of Babylon, in what is now the nation of Iraq, became dominant in the seventh century BC under rulers who enthroned themselves "in heaven" by subjugating a large part of the ancient world. As an imperial power in the ancient Near East, Babylon was preceded by by Egypt and Assyria and succeeded by Media-Persia, Greece and Rome. The rulers of these nations with few exceptions were prideful and ruthless, and therefore bore comparison with the devil, whom Jesus calls the "ruler of the world."[30]

Evil as Assyria was, in the eighth century BC it unknowingly acted as God's agent—the "rod of his anger"—by punishing the northern state of Israel for its corruption. God saved Jerusalem, capital of the southern kingdom of Judah, from the Assyrian army to give the remainder of his people time to repent. When Judah's moral condition instead deteriorated it was delivered the following century into the hands of Assyria's successor, Babylon, which likewise is called a "rod."[31] During several centuries and by means of various prophets God foretold doom upon the Israelites, upon Israel's neighboring enemies such as Philistia, Moab and Edom, and on the great powers Egypt, Assyria and Babylon. The idolatry, sexual license, injustice and violence of the time would generate rushing tides of war in which strong and weak nations alike eventually would founder.

The fourteenth chapter of Isaiah contains three prophetic condemnations arranged poetically in order of significance rather than chronologically. The first of these says, as we read above, that Babylon will rise like a star in the pre-dawn sky only to fall back to earth. The second, in verses twenty-four through twenty-seven, foretells that Assyria, after spreading devastation through much of the ancient world, will itself be crushed.

The third prophecy, in verses twenty-eight through thirty-two, is about Philistia on the coast of Palestine, a warlike nation and traditional

---

30 John 14:30.
31 Isa 14:5-6.

enemy of Israel. "Do not rejoice," the Philistines are warned, "that the rod that struck you is broken; from the root of that snake will spring up a viper, its fruit will be a darting, venomous serpent." Here is something peculiar: the "rod" that punished Philistia becomes a serpent in mid-verse, a shift of metaphor that calls to mind the transformation of Moses' rod into a snake. The rod in this case refers to Assyria. When the Philistines resisted Assyria's control of their territory, the empire-builder Sargon II responded by razing Ashdod, one of Philistia's three great coastal cities.[32]

Sargon was later ambushed and killed while on a campaign in Persia. Sargon's heir, Sennacherib, who called himself "king of the world," was assassinated by two of his own sons.[33] With the passing decades political intrigue and civil war loosened Assyria's grip on its western vassals and ultimately led to the empire's collapse.

A century after Sargon's campaign against Ashdod, the Philistines may have thought that at last they were free to pursue their national ambitions. But in southern Mesopotamia, the land from which the earliest Assyrians had migrated, Babylon was rising like a star through the military brilliance of Nebuchadnezzar II. Nebuchadnezzar swiftly subdued the western reaches of what had been Assyria's empire. He dealt with the Philistines in much the same way Sargon had, by destroying the jewel of Philistia, the wealthy port of Ashkelon.[34] In vindication of Isaiah's warning the Mesopotamian stock from which the Assyrian "rod" or "serpent" sprang had produced in its place an even more deadly enemy, Babylon.

The Babylonian power that by implication is called a "darting" or "flying" snake in verse 29 of Isaiah fourteen is just a few verses earlier referred to as the "shining one," "Lucifer," fallen from heaven to earth. As noted above, the image of a great serpent thrown forcefully down is repeated in the New Testament book of Revelation: "The great dragon was hurled down—that ancient serpent called the devil, or Satan, who leads the whole world astray."[35]

The defeat of the king of Babylon mirrors what is said about Satan, for whom the venomous tyrants of Assyria and Babylonia are ideal rep-

---

32 Isa 20:1.
33 Isa 37:38.
34 Jer 25:9, 20.
35 Rev 12:9.

resentatives. God used the dynasties of both of those nations as retributive "rods" by allowing them to bring other corrupt nations to ruin before they themselves came to an end. In the New Testament, wrongdoers are "handed over to Satan" for punishment in that they are at their own insistence deprived of divine protection and abandoned to the corrosive vices and random cruelties of the devil's world.[36]

The Casting Down of the Serpent in Ezekiel

The passages we have analyzed from Isaiah, Luke and Revelation confirm what we suspected about the meaning of Moses' first sign. The identifiers, once spotted, are as easy to follow as footprints in wet sand. They lead us to yet another Old Testament prophecy, this one concerning the king of the island city of Tyre:

> You were anointed as a guardian cherub [angel],
>> for so I ordained you.
> You were on the holy mount of God;
>> you walked among the fiery stones.
> You were blameless in your ways
>> from the day you were created
>> till wickedness was found in you.
> Through your widespread trade
>> you were filled with violence,
>> and you sinned.
> So I drove you in disgrace from the mount of God,
>> and I expelled you, O guardian cherub,
>> from among the fiery stones.
> Your heart became proud
>> on account of your beauty,
>> and you corrupted your wisdom
> So I threw you to the earth;
>> I made a spectacle of you before kings.
>
> —Ezekiel 28:14-17

Tyre lay off the coast of the verdant, garden-like territory of Lebanon. Prosperous and nearly invulnerable to attack, during its heyday Tyre felt

---

36 1 Cor 5:5; 1 Tim 1:20.

free to intimidate neighboring peoples.[37] Nebuchadnezzar partly carried out God's judgment on the city by demolishing its mainland quarter and subjecting the island stronghold to a punishing siege. Several generations later Tyre was captured and destroyed by the armies of Alexander the Great.

The translators of ancient Greek and Syriac versions of the Hebrew Bible modified portions of Ezekiel chapter twenty-eight to avoid describing the king of Tyre as a "cherub," apparently finding it hard to understand how a human king could be called an angel even as poetic hyperbole. We saw in Isaiah fourteen, though, that the proud kings of the pagan world may serve as representatives of the devil, and that Satan may be prophetically addressed through them. A dual application to the Tyrian king and to the devil—who was worshiped by Tyre's inhabitants as a form of the god Baal—is the only way that Ezekiel's prophecy makes sense.

That identification in turn draws our attention to the phrase "I threw you to the earth" in verse seventeen. The verb there for "throw" and the noun for "earth" are the same as those used of Moses "throwing" his rod to the "ground" to transform it into a serpent. Both the Hebrew Masoretic Text and the Greek Septuagint (abbreviated "LXX") manifest this correspondence of terms:

Moses threw [*salak*] it on the ground [*erets*]. —Exodus 4:4, MT.

I threw [*salak*] you to the earth [*erets*]. —Ezekiel 28:17, MT.

He [Moses] cast [*rhipto*] it on the ground [*ge*].
                                        —Exodus 4:3, LXX.

I have cast [*rhipto*] you to the ground [*ge*].
                                        —Ezekiel 28:17, LXX.

In Revelation twelve where Satan the "old serpent" is similarly "hurled down to the earth," we find not the Greek verb *rhipto* but the slightly more forceful word *ballo*. Nevertheless, we can demonstrate that in Biblical usage these words are synonyms by comparing two Gospel versions of a saying of Jesus.

---

37 Ezek 26:17.

In Mark Jesus says that anyone who tempts a young believer into sin would be better off having a millstone hung around his neck and then be thrown, *ballo*, into the sea; in Luke the same saying is reproduced almost verbatim but with the verb *rhipto* in place of *ballo*.[38] The interchangeability of these terms proves that the throwing down of the rod/serpent is the rhetorical equivalent of the casting down of the devil. It also provides a linguistic link to Jesus' expulsion of demons, since the word most often used in the Gospels to describe that action is *ekballo*, an expanded form of *ballo* meaning literally "to out-cast."

The coding of the first sign of Moses to Jesus' power over demonic forces will be corroborated further if we can make a case for the coding of the other two signs as well. In the next chapter, therefore, I will look closely at the miracles of the leprous hand and water turning to blood.

---

38 Mark 9:42; Luke 17:2.

4

Healing and Bloodshed

In the previous chapter we saw that God gave Moses three signs to serve as credentials and that the first of these, in which Moses' rod was transformed into a serpent, functions well as a symbol of Jesus' power of exorcism. We now come to Moses' second sign, in which he causes his hand suddenly to become leprous and then just as quickly heals himself. The order of this sign, in second place after the casting down of the rod/serpent, is significant because in all three Synoptic Gospels Jesus must overcome Satan before he can begin to heal disease.

After Jesus' baptism but before he can begin his ministry, he treks alone into the Judean desert (or "wilderness") where Satan engages him in a psychological battle. Jesus is tempted to misuse his God-given authority in various ways but refuses to do so. In Matthew the contest ends when Jesus dismisses Satan with the command, *Hupage*, "Go!"[1] This is the same command Jesus later issues to evil spirits when driving them out of a Gadarene man and his companion.[2]

---

1 Matt 4:10.
2 Matt 8:32.

The defeat of Satan by Jesus in their desert encounter is not itself an exorcism, but it is the first manifestation of the power by which Jesus goes on to free people from demonic possession. Satan is forced to retreat without finding a foothold in Jesus' personality.[3]

After his initial victory over the devil, Jesus commences preaching about the kingdom of God and curing his listeners of various maladies. In Matthew the first healing that is recounted in detail occurs after the Sermon on the Mount. A man with leprosy kneels before Jesus and entreats him, "Lord, if you are willing, you can make me clean." Jesus holds out his hand and touches the man, saying, "I am willing," and then, "Be clean!" The man is immediately cured. Jesus tells him to go show himself to the priest and to "offer the gift Moses commanded, as a testimony to them."[4]

I will return to the healing of the leper in Matthew after comparing the way the other evangelists treat the duel with Satan and the order of Jesus' miracles. John does not help us with this question because it skips over the temptation and early Galilean healings and alludes only in the most general way to Jesus' power of exorcism.[5] Mark and Luke cover more of the key events, but in their own distinct ways.

Mark mentions Jesus' desert ordeal only briefly and Luke reverses the order of the last two temptations as compared with Matthew. Mark and Luke leave no doubt that Jesus withstands Satan's testing, but they omit the emphatic rebuke that in Matthew's narrative prompts Satan to withdraw. Instead, they demonstrate Jesus' defeat of the devil by giving a dramatic account of an exorcism just before their first episode of healing.

The exorcism occurs as Jesus begins teaching in the synagogue at Capernaum. A man in the audience who is possessed by a spirit shouts, "What do you want with us, Jesus of Nazareth? Have you come to destroy us? I know who you are—the Holy One of God!" Jesus orders the spirit to be silent and then commands it, "Come out of him!" The demon shakes the man violently and departs from him "with a shriek."[6]

---

3   John 14:30.
4   Matt 8:1-4.
5   John 12:31.
6   Mark 1:23-25; Luke 4:33-35.

Jesus' first healing, as related by Mark and Luke, occurs immediately after the exorcism in the synagogue. When worship is finished, Jesus goes with James and John to the home of Simon Peter and finds Peter's mother-in-law in bed with a fever. Jesus approaches the sick woman and takes her hand. "The fever left her and she began to wait on them."[7]

Mark and Luke therefore maintain the order of the signs, with the sign of power over the serpent preceding that of power over disease, although they reflect this order slightly differently than does Matthew. Something else about Mark's narrative that bears comparison with Matthew's is the importance of Jesus' hand. In order to heal Simon Peter's mother-in-law, Jesus "takes her hand," meaning that he holds her hand in his; in Matthew, Jesus cures the man with leprosy by "reaching out his hand" and touching him. Throughout the Synoptics we find that the touch of Jesus' hand, while not necessary to every healing, is the principal means by which healing takes place.[8]

The use of Jesus' hand or hands to accomplish healings is another point of resemblance to the second sign of Moses, which involves Moses' hand. The subject of Moses is raised by Jesus himself after the cure of the man with leprosy, quoted above from Matthew 8:1-4. Jesus instructs the man to present himself to the priest and offer the appropriate sacrifice as "Moses commanded" in the law.

To do as he was ordered the man would have to give the priest a testimony about Jesus' ability to heal what was at the time an intractable condition. The priest, who would be versed in the events of Moses' life, might be led to reflect on Moses' power over leprosy as a proof of his claim to represent God. He might also remember that Moses' sister Miriam was stricken with leprosy as punishment for the sin of rebellion and afterward was healed through the intervention of Moses. These stories, found in the second and fourth Bible books (Exodus and Numbers), would have had even more significance to priests than to other Jews of the day, since the priestly class was made up largely of Sadducees who held that the Pentateuch (first five books) was the only part of the Scriptures to have been divinely inspired.

Finally, the priest may have sensed the importance of Jesus having healed a leper given the harsh quarantine measures the Mosaic Law en-

---

7 Mark 1:29-31; Luke 4:38-39.
8 Cf. Matt 9:29; Mark 5:22-23; 6:2, 5; 7:32; 8:25; Luke 13:12-13.

joins upon such people. The law portrays skin disease, a corruption of the flesh, very much as it does sin, a corruption of the heart and spirit. Like Adam and Eve, who were expelled from the garden of God for their sin, lepers were forbidden to live within the cities and villages of Israel. The leper was required to advertise his loathsome condition by wearing torn clothes, letting his hair become unkempt, covering the lower part of his face and crying out "Unclean!" to any healthy person who might be tempted to approach him. Lepers were commanded to live in their own ghettos separate from other Israelites.[9]

In Biblical Hebrew, the word for "unclean" used to to describe leprosy is also the word used of uncleanness due to sin. The same is true in Biblical Greek. And in either language, the "cleansing" of leprosy may be described using the same word as that for the "cleansing" of sins. The leper healed in Matthew asks to be made "clean," *katharizo*, and Jesus uses the same word in healing him, saying, "Be clean!" The book of 1 John, a letter to early Christian congregations, says that "if we walk in the light, as he is in the light, we have fellowship with one another, and the blood of Jesus, his Son, purifies [*katharizo*] us from all sin."[10]

The connection between sin and leprosy is of special interest given the symbolism of the second sign of Moses, where leprosy must represent all forms of disease. Evidence for that interpretation is found in a story from Mark's Gospel, where sins come up in connection, not with leprosy, but with paralysis. Jesus says to a paralytic man, "Son, your sins are forgiven." Certain scribes who are present consider this blasphemous, since only God can forgive sins. Their learning would have told them that insofar as forgiveness was possible it could be obtained only through priestly services at the temple. Jesus was claiming to wield God's own authority, supreme over even the Law of Moses and the House of Yahweh in Jerusalem.

Jesus senses the scribes' disapproval "in his spirit" and asks them, "Which is easier: to say to the paralytic, 'Your sins are forgiven,' or to say, 'Get up, take your mat and walk'?" Jesus then shows his authority over human infirmity by healing the man. "He got up, took his mat and walked out in full view of them all."[11]

---

9 Lev 13:45-46.
10 1 John 1:7.
11 Mark 2:8-11.

The passage does not claim that an ailment such as paralysis is a punishment for a specific sin; when the disciples try to make such a connection in the case of a blind man, Jesus dismisses it.[12] It does, however, imply a general relationship between sin and disease. In the book of Romans Paul says that ultimately death results from sin, and when death comes, disease is most often the door by which it enters.[13]

The relationship between sin and disease in the New Testament flows naturally out of the Old. I have already noted the case of Moses' sister Miriam. A more detailed and dramatic story is found in the fifth chapter of 2 Kings, in which a Syrian army officer with leprosy comes to the prophet Elisha seeking a cure. The officer, Naaman, is told to bathe in the Jordan river and is "cleansed" of his leprosy when he does so.

The cure prompts Naaman to forsake the idol gods of Syria and vow to worship only Yahweh, the God of Israel. As Naaman is on his way back to Syria, Elisha's personal attendant Gehazi approaches him and, falsely claiming to speak for Elisha, asks Naaman for a gift. Elisha later unmasks Gehazi's fraud and as punishment strikes him with leprosy, declaring that "Naaman's leprosy will cling to you and to your descendants forever."[14] The story ends leaving Naaman cleansed, through baptism, not only of the disease of leprosy but of the sin of idolatry, while Gehazi has become guilty of the sins of greed and deceit and physically stricken as well.

Healing and Forgiveness in the Story of Hezekiah

A relationship between sin and disease can also be detected in the final story of healing in the Old Testament. The incident takes place in the southern kingdom of Judah near the end of a long period of moral and political decline likened by the prophet Isaiah to physical deterioration. "From the sole of your foot to the top of your head," he writes to the kingdom of Judah, "there is no soundness—only wounds and welts and open sores, not cleansed or bandaged or soothed with oil."[15]

---

12 John 9:1-3.
13 Rom 5:12.
14 2 Kgs 5:27.
15 Isa 1:6; cf. Jer 6:7.

This troubled state of affairs confronts the young man Hezekiah when he ascends the throne of Judah late in the eighth century BC. King Hezekiah institutes reforms aimed at ending idolatry and reinstilling respect for the Mosaic Law. His program has only temporary success but his personal integrity is rewarded by two instances of divine deliverance. In one of them the formidable army of Assyria is forced to retreat from Judah when a large number of Assyrian troops suddenly and mysteriously die, slain by God's angel according to the Scriptural account. In the other Hezekiah falls gravely ill but is miraculously healed, and is told through the prophet Isaiah that an additional fifteen years have been added to his life.

Hezekiah sees his recovery as evidence of God mercifully having overlooked his sins. "In your love you kept me from the pit of destruction," he says in a prayer of thanksgiving. "You have put all my sins behind your back."[16] Besides confirming the connection between sin and disease on one hand and forgiveness and healing on the other, what happens to Hezekiah is noteworthy because one man, in this case the ruler of the southern Israelite kingdom, is afflicted in a way that mirrors the nation as a whole.

God likens the waywardness of his people to cuts, bruises and running sores. When Hezekiah falls ill the sickness is due to a boil, a skin sore, which is either malignant or infected so seriously that it threatens his life. It is as if Hezekiah is made to bear in his own flesh the morally ulcerous condition that has threatened the national existence first of Israel and then of Judah.

God has said that the sores in the nation's body have not been treated and bandaged. When Hezekiah pleads for relief, God tells Isaiah that healing will take place when a poultice is applied to the boil. Hezekiah becomes a representative of Israel, experiencing its fatal disease and receiving the life-restoring treatment God longs to provide for the nation: "The LORD binds up the bruises of his people and heals the wounds he inflicted."[17]

Hezekiah suffered from one boil, a single physical manifestation of the nation's illness. The full picture painted in Isaiah the first chapter is

---

16 Isa 38:17.
17 Isa 30:26.

more grievous, consisting of multiple injuries as would result from a vicious attack:

> Why should you be beaten anymore?
>   Why do you persist in rebellion?
> Your whole head is injured,
>   your whole heart afflicted.
> From the sole of your foot to the top of your head
>   there is no soundness—
> only wounds and welts
>   and open sores.
>
> —Isaiah 1:5-6.

Overshadowing the limited application of this passage to Hezekiah is its ultimate fulfillment upon Jesus. As we saw in Chapter 2, Jesus endured separate beatings from Jewish and Roman soldiers. He then was "scourged," *phragelloo*, meaning beaten on the back or abdomen with a many-stranded, studded whip designed to tear the skin of the victim. Jesus did not die during scourging, as prisoners occasionally did, so he was suspended from rough timbers by means of square-edged iron nails driven through his hands and heels. From his scalp, pierced by a crown of thorns to his feet, skewered by nails, he became the horrifying embodiment of Isaiah 1:5-6.

The agony of Jesus' death was, according to the Scriptures, a necessary part of the healing work begun during his ministry. In order to put an end to sin, disease and suffering, Jesus had to take them upon himself. "Surely he took up our infirmities and carried our sorrows," says the famous "suffering servant" passage of Isaiah. "He was crushed for our iniquities; the punishment that brought us peace was upon him, and by his wounds we are healed."[18]

"He himself bore our sins in his body on the tree," says the New Testament book of 1 Peter, "so that we might die to sins and live for righteousness; by his wounds you have been healed."[19] In 1 Peter as in Isaiah, expiation of sin and healing of disease blend inseparably. In these we have an identifier that reveals the full significance of the second of

---

18 Isa 53:4-5.
19 1 Pet 2:24.

Moses' signs, requiring Moses to take upon himself the plague of leprosy for one terrifying moment only to rid himself of it the next.

During his brief time on earth God's Son looked like anyone else and became subject to the physical sufferings common to fallen humanity. "God," Paul writes, "sent his Son in the likeness of sinful [spiritually 'leprous'] flesh."[20] Jesus faced the hardships that were part of growing up in the household of a Jewish laborer in first century Galilee. Foregoing the joys of marriage and family he undertook an exhausting ministry that yielded no material rewards to speak of and generated insults and threats in as great a measure as acclaim and appreciation. He burdened himself further by "stretching out his hand" to perform healings, since healing apparently taxed Jesus' physical stamina.[21] Finally, during his execution Jesus endured torture that approximated the effects of an ulcerous, wasting sickness.

According to 1 Peter 2:24, Jesus' assumption of the penalty of sin had the goal of bringing sin, and with it disease, to an end. Just as Moses rids himself of the leprosy he takes upon his hand, Jesus through his triumph on the cross leaves behind the effects of sin and gains the power eventually to end it throughout the universe. Paul in his discussion of sin and death in Romans says that Jesus "died to sin once for all" and that "death no longer has mastery over him."[22] The same thought is repeated in Hebrews, which says that Jesus "did away with sin by the sacrifice of himself."[23]

The Sign of Water and Blood

By drawing our attention to the circumstances of Jesus' death, the second of Moses' signs leads naturally into the third, the pouring out of water that becomes blood on the ground. In Chapter 2 we saw in detail that "water" gushing out of a "rock" is an illustration of the infusion of God's Spirit into the early Christian congregation and, even before that, of the flow of inspired teachings and miraculous deeds from Jesus during his ministry. For that reason Jesus can offer "living water" to the

---

20 Rom 8:3, NASB.
21 Cf. Luke 6:19; 8:46.
22 Rom 6:9-10.
23 Heb 9:26.

woman at the well of Sychar and can tell his disciples that "the words I have spoken to you are spirit and they are life."[24] A change occurs at the crucifixion, when it is no longer simply the water of divine wisdom that pours out of Jesus, but drops of real blood.

Jesus implies the two-fold provision of water and blood in Mark when he says that "even the Son of Man did not come to be served, but to serve, and to give his life as a ransom for many."[25] Jesus came to serve mankind, to be a "water carrier." When guests arrived at a house in the Middle East of Jesus' day, the first duty of the servant was to bring water to wash their feet.[26] Jesus performed this act for the apostles at the Last Supper, perhaps with the water they earlier saw being taken to the house where the supper was held.[27] The washing was understood later as representative of the spiritual cleansing Jesus accomplished by the "water" of the "word."[28]

If "to serve" means to provide water, then "to give life" means to offer blood. The word for "life" at Mark 10:45 is the Greek word for "soul," *psuche*. According to the Septuagint rendering of Leviticus 17:11, the "life [*psuche*, soul] of flesh is its blood." Jesus later confirms that his service to the world will culminate in the shedding of his own blood when he gives wine to the apostles and tells them, "This is my blood of the covenant, which is poured out for many."[29] The verb he uses for "poured out," *ekcheo*, is a form of the same verb found in the Septuagint at Exodus 4:9 to describe the "pouring out" of water/blood by Moses.

From these identifiers we can infer the symbolism of water from Jesus changing to blood even if we limit ourselves to the Synoptic Gospels. But there is a reason why this water motif only comes to the fore in John, having to do with the special place held by that book. John was in all likelihood the last of the canonical Gospels to be written. It contains only an abbreviated version of Jesus' teachings, as can be seen by comparing its contents with the detailed ethics from Matthew's "Sermon on the Mount." The author takes for granted his readers' ac-

---

24 John 4:10; 6:63.
25 Mark 10:45.
26 Cf. Luke 7:44.
27 Mark 14:13.
28 John 13:5-7; Eph 5:26.
29 Mark 14:24.

quaintance with Jesus' themes of the nearness of God's kingdom, the need for moral purity free from self-righteousness, and principled compassion toward others. He also assumes his readers' access to information about the Lord's Supper, which he alludes to but fails to narrate.[30]

John's Gospel effectively is the "last word" in terms of purported eye-witness testimony to Jesus of Nazareth, and as such it leaves no doubt as to the issue raised by his life, ministry and death. John emphasizes that acceptance of Jesus as God's unique Son is crucial to salvation and that Jesus' identity arose as a point of controversy early and repeatedly during his ministry. Since it wraps up the testimony about Jesus first presented in the Synoptics, we would expect John's Gospel to reflect most clearly the final, deciding sign of Moses, the sign of water and blood.

John not only contains straightforward statements about spiritual water coming from Jesus, it has more occurrences of the Greek word for water, *hudor*, than do the three Synoptic Gospels combined. John also contains information not found in Matthew, Mark or Luke about the shedding of Jesus' blood. By saying that Jesus was beaten, scourged and finally crucified the Synoptics necessarily indicate that Jesus bled, but only John makes the pouring out of blood explicit, saying that "one of the soldiers pierced Jesus' side with a spear, bringing a sudden flow of blood and water."[31]

The flow of blood and water described in John is much ridiculed for the simple reason that it is said to occur after Jesus' death, and corpses do not bleed. The narrative in these verses is not so easily discounted, however. The breaking of the legs of the men crucified with Jesus is another gruesome event recorded only in John. Breaking a victim's legs forced him to hang heavily from his outstretched arms, constricting the chest cavity and causing suffocation after several minutes. Only someone familiar with Roman crucifixion would be likely to supply this detail.

Physiologically, what John describes is improbable, not impossible. Most importantly in the present context, it underscores the fulfillment of the third sign of Moses. It is as if John shows us the actual transfor-

30 John 6:53-57.
31 John 19:32-34.

mation of water to blood as it spills onto the ground. The narrative of John 19:34 is a graphic token that the expenditure of Jesus' energy during his ministry has turned into the expenditure of his life at a spot called "The Place of the Skull."[32]

As we will see shortly, John's Gospel is not alone in reporting a visible event that illuminates the invisible reality of Jesus pouring out his life. But in John that reality jumps off the page as if printed in boldface type. It does so as well in the letter of 1 John, which says that Jesus "did not come by water only" like John the Baptist, who delivered an inspired call for repentance accompanied by water baptism, "but by water and blood"—blood that was poured out on the ground as sacrificial blood routinely was under the Mosaic Law.[33]

In John the sign of water and blood is foreshadowed at the very outset of Jesus' ministry, when he turns water into wine at a wedding feast in the Galilean city of Cana. John calls this event, which is recorded in none of the Synoptics, "the first of Jesus' miraculous signs."[34] The Old Testament sometimes compares wine to blood.[35] Therefore, to turn water into wine is to turn it into a kind of blood, which lawfully can be consumed because it is illustrative rather than literal.

The setting of the miracle at Cana also is revealing inasmuch as wine at a wedding has to do with joy. The joyous relationship between Jesus and the church is compared to that of a bridegroom and a bride, and the gathering of believers to Christ at his return is likened to a wedding feast.[36] The pouring out of Jesus' blood therefore involves the paradox that ultimate happiness has been purchased at the cost of ultimate suffering. In Mark Jesus mingles the symbolism of wine as sacrificial blood with that of wine as a drink to accompany celebration. "I tell you the truth, I will not drink again of the fruit of the vine until that day when I drink it anew in the kingdom of God."[37]

A popular assumption among skeptics is that legends of the Greek god Dionysius turning water into wine lie behind the miracle Jesus per-

---

32 Mark 15:22.
33 1 John 5:6; Exod 29:12; Lev 4:7.
34 John 2:11.
35 Gen 49:11; Deut 32:14; Isa 63:3.
36 Matt 22:2; 25:1; Mark 2:19; Luke 12:36; John 3:29.
37 Mark 14:24-25.

formed at the wedding in Cana. Greek mythological influence was per-
vasive in the Jewish homeland as it was in the rest of the Roman
Empire, and especially so in the region of Galilee. However, such a theory fails to take into account the correlation between the first two signs
of Moses and Jesus' works of exorcism and healing. Ignorant of that
correspondence, critics stumble blindly past clues about meaning of the
crucial third sign as well. The reason is that they contemplate only those
fulfillments that can be dismissed as the evangelists' inventions.

Any attempt to explain away John's theme of water from Jesus turning into wine or blood must account for the way that theme mirrors the
third sign of Moses. It must do the same for miniature fulfillments in
the Synoptic Gospels. One of these is an act performed by Pilate and
recorded only in Matthew. When Pilate realizes that the riotous crowd
calling for Jesus' crucifixion will not be quelled by any milder measure,
he takes water and washes his hands in front of the mob, saying, "I am
innocent of this man's blood."[38]

Washing the hands as a declaration of innocence has a long tradition
behind it, as can be seen from a reference to it in the Mosaic Law at
Deuteronomy 21:6. In Pilate's case it is less than convincing, not least
because he himself insists that he has the power to spare Jesus if he decides to do so.[39] Instead, the gesture evokes a picture of Jesus' blood
already covering Pilate's hands. Washing blood off the hands of a
Roman governor would entail clear water becoming bloody upon being
poured out, since a man of status ordinarily washed his hands by having
a servant pour water over them from a vessel.[40] In any case, washing
blood-drenched hands would require that clear water become reddened
in the process.

The other portrayal is in Luke, and occurs as Jesus is praying in the
Garden of Gethsemane just before his arrest. "He prayed more
earnestly," with the approach of his arrest, "and his sweat was like drops
of blood falling to the ground."[41] The absence of verses 43 and 44 from
some of the oldest manuscripts of Luke's Gospel raises the possibility
that they were inserted into the book. From the fact that they were

---

38 Matt 27:24.
39 John 19:10.
40 Cf. 2 Kgs 3:11.
41 Luke 22:41-44.

being quoted as early as the second century we know they were added not long after the original writing and may represent an independent but not necessarily fictional tradition. As likely as not, the source of these verses is an anecdote reflecting what one or more of the disciples saw during the hours spent in Gethsemane.

The Greek wording does not say that Jesus' sweat actually became bloody or even red in color. Apparently, the heavy perspiration formed large, dense drops that in the shadowy light looked dark, "as if drops of blood"—*hosei thromboi aimatos*. Besides conveying the great stress Jesus was under as he contemplated the ordeal ahead of him, the image of water from his body turning to blood as it falls to the ground forms a vivid reprise of Moses' third sign.

The Continuing Testimony of the Signs

How do we explain the typological correspondence between the signs given to Moses and the signs performed by Jesus, the "greater Moses"? Can coincidence, already creaking like an overloaded wheelbarrow, stand to have more weight thrown upon it? Manipulation by the Gospel writers is the only other naturalistic explanation available, but it hardly is more satisfactory than pure chance. Since internal evidence from the Gospels indicates that they were written at different places and times, the evangelists would not have been in a position to conspire with one another even if they had wanted to do so. If we assume in the teeth of the evidence that they did conspire, we would still be left with nothing better than coincidence to explain the identifiers from the Old Testament, such as the passages from Isaiah and Ezekiel, that help to align the signs of Moses and the signs of Jesus.

Those signs have yet one more point of correspondence to take note of. At the burning bush God tells Moses that if Israel fails to believe because of the first two signs, the third will convince them. Ordinarily this kind of detail is included in a story with a view toward what will occur later on. Strangely, however, nothing is said about Moses displaying the first two signs, encountering skepticism, and then winning his people over with the third. The account says simply that he performed the signs and the people believed, leaving us in the dark about whether all three of them proved necessary. It has been suggested that the third

sign was lacking in the original narrative.[42] But we know from its presence in the Dead Sea Scrolls and in the Septuagint that the third sign
was part of the story long before Jesus was born.

The enigma of the third sign is resolved when we look not to its original enactment but to the fulfillment in Jesus. Crowds flocked to Jesus
to see him perform exorcisms and healings, but the number of people
who became steadfast disciples was small. The book of Acts says that in
the weeks after the crucifixion only a few dozen believers were meeting
together for worship.[43]

Then, at the Jewish festival of Pentecost, the disciples were imbued
with the Spirit of God and began preaching to Jews and proselytes who
had come to Jerusalem from the far corners of the Roman empire. The
Pentecost sermon of Peter reviews briefly Jesus' career and then says
that Jesus had been delivered up to death "by the plan and foreknowledge of God" only to be resurrected three days later.[44] Three thousand
or so Jews were so struck by the message that they were baptized as disciples.

The large-scale conversions necessary to establish the Christian
church became possible only after the pouring out of Jesus' blood at
the crucifixion. The third sign did indeed engender faith—committed
faith—in a way that the first two signs did not.

In the view of many historical critics, the only hard facts we can take
from the Gospels are that Jesus of Nazareth was a wandering teacher or
rabbi, that to some extent he relieved sick people and those thought to
be in the grip of the demons, and that he was executed by the Romans.
The collective opinion of the Jesus seminar is little better.[45] The secular
historians who arrive at such a conclusion have no inkling that they are
pinpointing the qualifications foreshadowed by the signs of Moses.

---

42 Dewey M. Beegle, *Moses the Servant of Jahweh* (Grand Rapids, MI: Eerdmans,
    1972), 79.
43 Acts 1:15.
44 Acts 2:22-23.
45 Along with exorcism, healing, teaching and execution by Romans the Jesus
    Seminar includes Jesus' association with outcasts and sinners as being
    historically probable. See Robert Funk and the Jesus Seminar, *The Acts of
    Jesus: The Search for the Authentic Deeds of Jesus* (New York: HarperCollins,
    1998), 527.

I noted at the beginning of the previous chapter that Jesus himself mentioned yet another sign, "the sign of Jonah," as confirmation of his identity. To it we turn next.

5

The Sign of Jonah

"Search, and see that no prophet arises out of Galilee" was the response of members of the Sanhedrin to messianic claims about Jesus, according to John 7:52. They were almost correct. Prophets whose places of origin are mentioned in the Hebrew Bible came from outside Galilee with a single exception: Jonah the son of Amittai of Gath Hepher.[1] Even if Jonah and Jesus were raised in the same region they seem to have little else in common. Jonah, who ran away from one of his assignments and was swallowed by a large fish, appears to be among the least messianic of the prophets. Defying the apparent dissimilarity, Jesus said that "the sign of Jonah" was the only grand miracle he would offer to his opposers.

In Luke, Jesus compares his preaching to that of Jonah.[2] In Matthew, Jesus additionally says that the three days he will spend "in the heart of the earth" are like the three days spent by Jonah in the fish.[3] The reason for the allusion in Matthew would seem to be the coincidence of three-day periods and that fact that a huge fish would become the grave of whomever it swallowed. By now, however, we ought to suspect that Jesus was hinting at a typological connection.

---

1   2 Kgs 14:25; see note to John 7:52, *NIV Study Bible* (Grand Rapids: Zondervan, 1995), 1533.

2   Luke 11:29-30, 32.

3   Matt 12:39-40.

In the Old Testament book of Jonah, the prophet of the same name boards a ship to run away from the Lord. The vessel encounters rough weather as Jonah naps below deck. The ship's captain finds it incredible that Jonah can sleep as disaster overtakes them, and he urges Jonah to pray for deliverance. The sailors cast lots to find out who may have brought ill fortune upon them. When the lot falls on Jonah and they confront him, he tells them that the only way to save the ship is to throw him into the sea. The crew battles heroically to make landfall with the prophet still aboard, but the storm increases in violence until the sailors are forced to throw Jonah over the side. The sea becomes calm, leaving the sailors so awe-stricken that they make vows to Jonah's God.

The events that befall Jonah resemble those leading up to Jesus' crucifixion. To start with, both Jonah and Jesus appear to be indifferent to their peril. "How can you sleep?," the captain asks Jonah. "Get up and call on your god! Maybe he will take notice of us, and we will not perish."[4] Compare the words of Pilate to Jesus: "Don't you hear the testimony they are bringing against you?" Matthew adds that "Jesus made no reply, not even to a single charge—to the great amazement of the governor."[5] John has Pilate saying, "Do you refuse to speak to me? Don't you realize I have power either to free you or to crucify you?"[6]

The resemblance extends further, to the interrogation of Jonah concerning his identity and origin. "Tell us, who is responsible for making all this trouble for us?," the ship's crew demands of the prophet. "What do you do? Where do you come from? What is your country? From what people are you?"[7] Pilate similarly asks Jesus, "Are you the king of the Jews?," and, "Where do you come from?"[8] Once the special status of the man of God is discovered it arouses fear. When Jonah declares, "I am a Hebrew and I worship the LORD, the God of heaven, who made the sea and the land," the ship's crew is "terrified."[9] When Pilate is told by Jesus' accusers that the Galilean "claimed to be the Son of God," Pilate likewise becomes fearful.[10]

---

4   Jonah 1:6.
5   Matt 27:14; cf. Mark 15:4-5.
6   John 19:10.
7   Jonah 1:8.
8   Mark 15:2; John 19:9; cf. Luke 23:3.
9   Jonah 1:9-10.
10 John 19:7-8.

In both instances, the parties responsible for the fate of the man of God battle hostile forces in an effort to spare his life and then declare themselves innocent of his blood.[11] In each narrative the man of God ultimately must be consigned to oblivion.[12] Onlookers in both accounts are moved to recognize God's hand at work.[13] Note how vivid the correspondence becomes when the climactic moments are read together:

> The men rowed desperately to return to land but they could not, for the sea was becoming even stormier against them. —Jonah 1:13.

> Pilate said to them, "Then what shall I do with him whom you call the King of the Jews?" They shouted back, "Crucify him!" But Pilate said to them, "Why, what evil has he done?" But they shouted all the more, "Crucify him!" —Mark 15:12-14.

> Pilate, wanting to release Jesus, addressed them again, but they kept on calling out, saying, "Crucify, crucify him!" And he said to them the third time, "Why, what evil has this man done? I have found in him no guilt demanding death; therefore I will punish him and release him." But they were insistent, with loud voices asking that he be crucified. And their voices began to prevail.—Luke 23:20-23.

The question the sailors put to Jonah, "What should we do to you that the sea may become calm for us?," is paralleled by Pilate's question to the mob, "Then what shall I do with Jesus who is called Christ?"[14] Jonah's answer as related in the Septuagint Greek Bible is, "Take me up [*airo*] and cast me into the sea." The narrative continues, "So they took [*lambano*] Jonas, and cast him out into the sea." The mob's answer to Pilate on the subject of what should be done with Jesus is, "Take him away [*airo*]! Take him away [*airo*]! Crucify him!" In compliance with the answer of the crowd, "the soldiers took charge [*paralambano*] of Jesus" to prepare him for execution.[15]

---

11 Jonah 1:13-14; Matt 27:21-24.
12 Jonah 1:15; Matt 27:26 and parallels.
13 Jonah 1:16; Matt 27:54; Mark 15:39; Luke 23:47.
14 Jonah 1:11; Matt 27:22.
15 John 19:15-16.

Not only does one set of events mirror the other, the narratives have the same urgent, fatalistic momentum. They also share the notion of ransom or redemptive death, since Jonah's life becomes the price of the lives of the other men aboard the ship.

We need not rely on resemblance alone, because the major symbols of the story are confirmed by identifiers elsewhere in the Scriptures. The Psalmist shows us that sleep may connote seeming indifference by likening God's apparent unconcern over Israel's plight to his being asleep.[16]

A stormy sea as a metaphor for a violent mob occurs in two passages in Isaiah. One of these, at 17:12, says, "Alas, the uproar of many peoples who roar like the roaring of the seas," and another, at 57:20, says that "the wicked are like the tossing sea, for it cannot be quiet."[17] Matthew's Gospel says that the crowd came to the verge of rioting.[18] A gauge of the seriousness of the unrest is Pilate's alleged release of a violent rebel popularly known as Barabbas.[19] Apparently during major festivals Pilate had given special consideration to petitions concerning Jewish prisoners, but for him to relinquish a notorious cutthroat would have been an emergency measure comparable to the jettisoning of the ship's cargo in the Jonah story.[20]

Plumbing the Depths of the Abyss

The clue that drew our attention to the book of Jonah, the saying of Jesus about his spending "three days and three nights in the heart of the earth," leads to another identifier having to do with the curious "death" and "resurrection" Jonah experiences. The depths of the earth and of the sea become poetically interchangeable in Jonah's psalm. Jonah says, "The deep surrounded me," at 2:5 and then repeats the thought in the very next verse by saying, "The earth barred me in forever."

In the same way, the New Testament likens Jesus' death not only to a

---

16 Ps 44:23-24.
17 Cf. Luke 21:25; Jude 13.
18 Matt 27:24.
19 Mark 15:7; Luke 23:25; Barrabas means "son of the father" and may not have been his real name.
20 Jonah 1:5.

descent into the earth but also a descent into the "abyss" or the sea.[21] Being drawn out of the water is a figure of rescue from death in Psalm 18 and by implication also in Psalm 69, where the psalmist prays to be delivered "from my foes and from the deep waters." "May the flood of water not overflow me nor the deep swallow me up," he goes on, "nor the pit shut its mouth on me."[22] Here waters stand both for enemies plotting the psalmist's death and for death itself.

In saying that the grave threatens to "swallow" him, the psalmist uses the same Hebrew verb that describes the swallowing of Jonah by the fish. In Jonah's story the fish is an embodiment of the sea's deadly nature, which claims human lives through cold, through drowning or, rarely, through predators such as great white sharks, the largest specimens of which are capable of swallowing a man whole. The imagery is consistent with other passages in the Old Testament that associate dying with being swallowed.[23] The text at Isaiah 25:8 (quoted by Paul at 1 Corinthians 15:54) that says God will "swallow up" death forever is a play on words in which the "swallower" is swallowed, the destroyer finally destroyed.

Although Jonah was devoured he was not left in the fish, which he calls the "belly of Hades," just as Jesus would not be forsaken in "Hades," the realm of the grave.[24] An intriguing confirmation of this fulfillment occurs in Matthew, but before it can be understood we must go back to a point I raised briefly in Chapter 2 about the redemptive quality of Jesus' death. The claim that Jesus furnished a "ransom" or a price in blood to pay off the sin debt of mankind is one that secular people find grotesque. To many of them it smacks of the horrors of human sacrifice and seems to turn God into a bloodthirsty tyrant. While there is no pretending that the doctrine of the ransom is easy to come to terms with, it helps to realize that death for its own sake is not the object of Jesus' mission.

Instead of beginning with the idea of death, a better starting point is righteousness or obedience. In Biblical terms, perfect obedience to the

---

21 Rom 10:7; cf. Deut 30:13.
22 Ps 69:14-15; cf. Ps 124.
23 Exod 15:12; Prov 1:12; cf. Job 2:3, where the Hebrew reads "swallow him up without cause."
24 Jonah 2:3, LXX; Acts 2:31.

will of God is the condition, the "price" as it were, of everlasting life. Humans in general, subject as we are to frequent moral failure, cannot hope to pay that price. Assuming that someone could pay it, what would perfect obedience look like?

To obey only under favorable circumstances would fall short of perfection, which in the Biblical sense means "completeness." Obedience to be complete would have to be tested to the limit. That in turn can only mean obedience through temptation, distress, torture and death without the slightest moral failure. Death in that case would become a kind of seal, a certification that perfect obedience had been attained. This is what Jesus achieved according to apostolic teaching. "He humbled himself and become obedient as far as death," Paul says in Philippians, "death on a cross."[25]

According to the Scriptures the righteousness of Jesus up to death provided the basis for lifting the crushing burden of sin off humanity. "He himself bore our sins in his body on the tree, so that we might die to sins and live for righteousness."[26] At the same time Jesus' death constituted a different kind of price in that it entitled him to receive back his own life. Paul identifies the obedient death of Jesus as the basis for Jesus' exaltation by God at the resurrection.[27]

God says in Isaiah that he will award his servant "a portion among the great . . . because he poured out his life unto death."[28] The "life" said to be poured out here is actually the Hebrew word *nephesh*, "soul," which is symbolized by blood.[29] Hebrews 13:20 confirms that God brought Jesus back from the dead "through the blood of the eternal covenant," in other words, because of or by means of the perfect obedience represented by Jesus' shed blood.

With this "double price" in mind we can understand the incident recorded in Matthew. When Jesus comes to Capernaum, Peter is approached by men collecting the two-drachma tax for the maintenance of the temple in Jerusalem. The men ask Peter whether his teacher, Jesus, intends to pay the tax. When Peter next talks to him, Jesus comments

25 Phil 2:8.
26 1 Pet 2:24.
27 Phil 2:8-9.
28 Isa 53:12; cf. John 10:17.
29 Lev 17:11.

that members of the royal household do not have to pay taxes, implying that he as messianic king and the apostles as future rulers of Israel are not obligated to pay. Nevertheless, he tells Peter that to avoid giving offense they will comply by a decidedly unusual procedure. Peter is to go down to the water and throw in a fishing line. In the mouth of the first fish he catches Peter will find a stater coin worth four drachmas. "Take it and give it to them," Jesus says, "for my tax and yours."

Improbably, the coin comes out of a fish's mouth, but no more improbably than had the prophet Jonah. Jesus as the antitype of Jonah also comes out of the mouth of the fish, which pictures the grave according to Jesus' own words. The difference between Jonah and Jesus is that the Messiah came forth entitled not just to receive back his own life but to redeem sinful mankind, functioning as the price for both.

The coin out of the fish's mouth that pays alike for Jesus the sinless Son of God and for Peter the flawed human being, understood as a coded miniature, is no mere magician's trick. The symbolism is all the more appropriate considering the background of the temple tax. The tax was instituted as part of the Mosaic law at Exodus 30:12-16, where it is called a "ransom" for the soul of each man of Israel and as an "atonement" to prevent destruction from coming upon the nation. The corresponding Greek words from the Septuagint text of these verses, *lutron* and *hilaskomai*, are key words used of the redemptive value of Jesus' death in the New Testament.[30]

Jonah's Proclamation and the Gospel

The parallels between Jonah and Jesus do not stop at the resurrection. After his deliverance Jonah undertakes an unprecedented mission to Gentiles, preaching judgment to the infamously cruel Assyrians at Nineveh. Jesus, after his resurrection, delegates the disciples to preach in his name to the world, Gentiles included.[31] In both instances the goal of the preaching is repentance and the emphasis is on God's mercy toward those who have not known him.

When Jonah declares impending doom on Nineveh the Assyrians are

---

30 Mark 10:45; Heb 2:17.
31 Matt 28:19.

struck by his message, perhaps not least because a prophet is audacious enough to deliver it to their faces, and for a time they repent of their wickedness. The unnamed Assyrian king dresses in sackcloth and issues a proclamation commanding Ninevites to "call urgently on God" and "give up their evil ways and their violence" in the hope that "God may yet relent and with compassion turn from his fierce anger so that we will not perish."[32]

The language in the Septuagint text of this section of Jonah, which says that the people of Nineveh "turned each one," *apestrepsan hekastos*, from their "wicked ways," *poneras*, is followed closely in the book of Acts where Peter says to his listeners that Jesus wants to bless them by "turning each one of you," *apostrephein hekaston*, away from his "wicked ways," *ponerion*.[33]

We know from the book of Ephesians that it is appropriate to think of Jesus as preaching the message of God's grace to all people, Gentiles as well as Jews, even though he did so through representatives such as Peter and Paul. The second chapter of Ephesians introduces that thought by first referring to the sorry spiritual condition of the Gentiles before the message reached them. It reminds them that they were "separate from Christ, excluded from citizenship in Israel and foreigners to the covenants of the promise, without hope and without God in the world." The pitiable ignorance described in Ephesians 2:12 recalls God's description of the morally insensible Assyrians of Jonah's day, who "don't know their right hand from their left."[34]

Ephesians goes on to say that the Gentiles, who were once "far off" from God, have been brought near through the blood of Jesus. The catalyst for their repentance and reconciliation was evangelism, as it had been for the Assyrians. "He [Jesus] came and preached peace to you [Gentiles] who were far away and peace to those [Jews] who were near."[35] The great missionary effort among the Gentiles is attributed to Jesus as if he personally preached to them the way Jonah did to the Ninevites.

---

32 Jonah 3:8-9.
33 Acts 3:19, 26.
34 Jonah 4:11.
35 Eph 2:17.

With the outline of the fulfillment now clear, return to Jesus' statement that he would give no sign to his generation except his death and resurrection as typified by Jonah. I noted previously this saying must be weighed against Jewish hopes for a Messiah who would wield invincible power against the hated Roman occupation.

Exaggeration for emphasis also has to be considered where the context suggests it. For example, in Genesis God tells Jacob that "your name will no longer be Jacob, but Israel."[36] Actually, both Jacob and the nation of his descendants continued to be referred to occasionally by his birth name, but that name soon was overshadowed by the designation "Israel." By a similar hyperbole, when Jesus spoke about "no sign but that of Jonah" he may have meant that other works of his that might be called signs would pale next to his Jonah-like journey into and out of the grave. Here our study merges with the last chapter, where we saw that the fulfillment of the third sign of Moses, the pouring out of water and blood, would inspire belief where previous signs had not.

These suggestions as to how Jesus' comment was intended find support in a dialog from John's Gospel. Jesus' opponents try to trap him by asking, "What miraculous sign can you show us to prove your authority to do all this?" Jesus answers, "Destroy this temple, and I will raise it again in three days." The passage goes on to say that the "temple" Jesus refers to is his own body.[37] By refusing to recommend any sign to his antagonists except his coming death and resurrection, at the same time veiling his meaning thinly in a riddle, Jesus relies here on the same strategy he does in the Jonah saying of Matthew.

The passage in John is evidence that for all the peculiarities of the fourth Gospel the Jesus it portrays is the same one we meet in Matthew, Mark and Luke. Since John freely describes Jesus' supernatural works as "signs," we know that Jesus is not denying the significance of those works, but rather putting his crucifixion and resurrection in a special category. Later, the apostolic proclamation of the early church, the *kerygma*, will identify the death and resurrection of Jesus as the key miracle in the outworking of God's purpose. That central divine act gives sinful man the chance of entry into the kingdom of God. "I delivered to you as of first importance," Paul assures the Corinthians, "that Christ

---

36 Gen 32:28.
37 John 2:18-21.

died for our sins according to the Scriptures, and that he was buried, and that he was raised on the third day according to the Scriptures."[38] Every aspect of Jesus' statement about the sign of Jonah now makes sense.

Where Did the Jonah-Jesus Parallel Come From?

The similarity between Jonah's experiences and those of Jesus must have been orchestrated, but how and by whom? Consider the accounts in the Gospels of John and of Matthew. John most closely follows the actual language of the Greek Septuagint text of Jonah. Pilate's questions, "Where are you from?" and "What did you do?," in Greek *pothen ei su* and *ti epoiesas*, nearly duplicate those in Jonah, *pothen erche* and *ti touto epoiesas*, although they occur in a different order.[39] Matthew lacks these specific questions, but it contains an echo of Jonah not present in John, namely, Pilate's declaration of innocence regarding Jesus' blood.[40] If either of the two authors consciously imitated the other by basing part of his Gospel on Jonah, why would he leave out parallels the first already had established?

The Gospel of Luke compounds the difficulty. Like John, Luke lacks the declaration of innocence by Pilate and the earlier saying of Jesus that compares Jonah's three days in the fish with Jesus' three days in the grave. However, the episode of Pilate attempting to "sail" against the will of the Jewish crowd has more dramatic intensity in Luke than in the other Gospels. Luke compares the preaching of Jesus with that of Jonah more pointedly than does Matthew, saying that Jonah prefigured Jesus by becoming a "sign" to the people of Nineveh.[41] The verses in Luke regarding Jonah's preaching set the stage for the repeated post-resurrection commands to go and preach to Gentiles as recorded in Acts, the sequel to Luke's Gospel.[42]

Cosidering the different ways the Gospels reflect the Jonah storyline, how can literary borrowing explain its prophetic function? Imagine, for

---

38 1 Cor 15:3-4.
39 John 19:9; 18:35; Jonah 1:8, 10.
40 Matt 27:24; cf. Jonah 1:14.
41 Luke 11:30, 32.
42 Acts 1:8; 9:15; 10:34-35; 13:46-47; 22:21.

example, that the borrowing began with the writing of Mark, which is usually assumed to be the first Gospel and which has the simplest form of the Jonah motif. Even if the authors of Matthew, Luke and John all had access to Mark when they began writing, each of them would have to have recognized that Jonah was the "script" being followed by Mark's author. After making the discovery, each of them must have decided to expand the Jonah parallel in his particular Gospel version.

An astonishing degree of coincidence between the actions of the evangelists has to be accepted along with this theory, the purpose of which after all is to explain an otherwise unacceptable level of coincidence between Jonah and the Gospels.

The proposal that the evangelists simply appropriated plot elements from Jonah runs up against another obstacle because it assumes that they were free to invent the end of Jesus' biography. Clearly, that assumption is false. Certain beliefs about Jesus were widespread by the middle of the first century, well before any commonly accepted date for the writing of the Gospels. Among these was the teaching that he had been "crucified" by the "world rulers" of the time, the Romans.[43] But it was also thought that leading elements of Jewish society had called for Jesus' death.[44]

Other early beliefs were that Jesus rose from the dead on the third day, that he understood his death to be necessary and accepted it voluntarily, and that his death has redemptive value.[45] Whether or not these beliefs are provable historically, there is no doubt that they were widely held by Christians from an early date. When the evangelists began to write their accounts of Jesus' life such traditions formed the boundaries they had to stay within if they wanted their writings to be accepted by believers. These constraints would have applied even under the most cynical theory of how the Gospels were composed.

It is not difficult to see how early traditions would guide, specifically, Gospel narratives about the events immediately preceding the crucifixion. In all the Gospels the priests condemn Jesus and bring him before Pilate, asking that he be put to death as a threat to public order. To Pilate's puzzlement Jesus offers no defense, yet Pilate hesitates to grant

---

43 1 Cor 2:8.
44 1 Thess 2:14-15.
45 1 Cor 15:4; Gal 1:3-4; Rom 5:8-9; 6:23.

the Sanhedrin's request. A partisan crowd incited by the Jewish leadership agitates for Jesus' execution until the Roman governor acquiesces.

Aside from certain details, an account substantially like this was demanded by the tradition that Jesus' enemies among his own people were
the driving force behind the crucifixion even though the Romans carried it out. Of indirect support are Christian traditions that Jesus
approved the paying of Roman taxes and opposed violent resistance toward the imperial regime, since a rabbi who took such positions would
not be a natural target for Roman repression.[46]

The enmity between Jesus and Jewish religious leaders evident in the
trial scenes of the Gospels is not depicted as a sudden development.
The Gospels uniformly teach that it was a consequence of Jesus' ministry. Jesus not only declined to submit to institutional religious
authority, he also leveled stinging accusations against both priests and
Pharisees. New Testament scholar Graham Stanton has pointed out that
a clash between Jesus and the Judaism of his day is the most natural explanation for the tensions that appear to have existed between Jews and
Christians as far back as available sources can take us and that reached
the "point of no return" in the late first or early second century.[47]

In light of early Christian tradition and the relationship between the
story of Jesus' condemnation and the rest of the Gospel narrative, it is
impossible to imagine that the evangelists manufactured the circumstances of Jesus' death to conform to a few verses in a minor prophetic
book of the Hebrew Bible. Equally inconceivable is the suggestion that
Christian tradition itself originated when certain Jews decided to project
the experiences of Jonah onto a Galilean peasant, paying little regard to
the actual circumstances of that man's life and death, and then began to
proclaim their "new Jonah" as the Messiah.

We began in Chapter 1 with a study about Jacob and have added several typological sketches to it. Before I add still other examples I will
consider in greater detail the question of typology and coincidence.

---

46 Rom 12:17-13:7.
47 Stanton, *Gospel Truth?*, 160-62.

6

Typology and Coincidence

Look at the following statement:

Justification entails sanctification unto salvation.

It conveys the idea that to be "justified" or found righteous before God requires being "sanctified," that is, being cleansed of sin in the hope of being saved from eternal death. The sentence also happens to be an acrostic in which the initial letters of the words spell out the name *Jesus*. If we ran across these words and then noticed the acrostic code, how could we tell if it was planned rather than accidental?

The Christian theme of the phrase would have to count as a clue, but it would not be decisive. The preposition "unto" is archaic and may have been chosen in order to form the acrostic, but equally it may have been used simply to evoke the diction of the King James Bible. We could determine by surveying reading material that the sequence of initial letters J-E-S-U-S is rare. Still, having before us nothing but the phrase itself we could do no better than to say it was likely that the acrostic was intentional.

Let's now imagine that we have read the phrase as part of a list of two or three dozen spiritual maxims. As we study the list we notice that many, though not all, are acrostic codes for Biblical terms such as "God," "Lord," "Christ," "redemption," "gospel" and "kingdom."

Suppose also that we found the list at the end of a treatise on Biblical doctrine, and that in the treatise it was stated that as an aid to memorization spiritual maxims might be composed as acrostics. Suppose the treatise even cited a few of the other maxims from the list and explained that they were acrostics. In that setting, could we reasonably doubt that the particular acrostic above for J-E-S-U-S was intentional?

Finding our acrostic under the circumstances just described would make the probability of its being intentional so great that we would be unlikely to consider another explanation. Not only would we have the rarity of the sequence J-E-S-U-S and a correspondence of the subject of the maxim with the name in the acrostic, we would have a rare degree of compatibility with the context. It would defy imposing odds for a spiritual maxim containing an acrostic to appear purely by chance in a document with the unusual—and appropriate—characteristic that it discusses maxims that contain acrostics.

Apart from the question of sheer probability, we would judge our acrostic to be intentional because of its functioning purposefully in its context. We could understand why a mind or minds would compose the maxim as an acrostic, list it with other similar maxims and include an explanation of the concept somewhere in the accompanying text.

This quality of purposefulness is an important means of separating coincidences from consciously created patterns. For example, plaques and posters have been produced for several decades listing what appear to be astonishing similarities between Abraham Lincoln and John F. Kennedy, two famous U.S. presidents both of whom were assassinated while in office. The correspondence between the two is an illusion, however, created by assembling every discoverable fact about each man and then selecting only those that agree. One similarity is that the names "Lincoln" and "Kennedy" both have seven letters. So many names have seven letters that it is one of the faintest parallels that could be drawn, but it is exactly by looking for any such resemblances, whether strong or weak, that an impressive list can be worked up.

Coincidence versus Purposeful Alignment

Take the two names "Gilbert" and "Sullivan." Besides being the names of two men who collaborated to compose light opera there would seem to be no other relationship between them. But look again. Each name contains five consonants (GLBRT and SLLVN) and the third letter of each name is L. It also happens that the last four letters of each name spell yet other names, the names "Bert" and "Ivan." Each of those names, in turn, contains a word within it: the word "be" in the first case and "van" in the second. Finally, when the two words are strung together in order they form yet a fifth name, the name "Bevan."

When I began writing the preceding paragraph I had no idea what points in common I could find between the names Gilbert and Sullivan; it was matter of surveying every possible characteristic and noting those that agreed. Do this with a large assemblage of historical facts and the appearance of a special pattern can be created, just as in the Lincoln-Kennedy parallel.

Even if we assume for a moment that there are in fact strange correspondences between Lincoln and Kennedy, how could we understand these to be purposeful? To what would we attribute the supposed relationship? Nothing suggests itself except "fate" or "destiny." Aside from the vagueness of an explanation such as "fate," notice its mindlessness. Believers in "fate" don't conceive of it as a person who consciously plans the scheme of future events. Presumably, fate is an uncanny force occasionally recognizable for the patterns it creates. But this is what blind circumstance does, producing patterns by coincidence with a certain frequency.

To resort to "fate" or to any other unthinking cause of a phenomenon is to abandon any claim to purposefulness, since that quality is inferred not just from events lining up in a surprising way, but to their lining up in a way that indicates rational intent. Say we were to pick up the telephone to call a friend and found that the friend was already on the line trying to call us at precisely the same instant. We might be amazed at the coincidence but we would hardly conclude that an intelligent agent had arranged it.

For a body of facts to be purposeful does not require that everything about it be understandable. Go back for a moment to our hypothetical treatise containing various acrostics, including J-E-S-U-S. To an atheist the theological treatise and its maxims would make little sense. But the atheist's inability to identify fully with the thinking of the author would not keep him from recognizing thought as the process that gave rise to the document.

The typological codes we so far have examined possess the crucial characteristic of purposefulness, both individually and collectively. Chapter 2 cited typological prophecies that are explicitly identified as such in John 3:14 and 1 Corinthians 10:4. Chapter 5 referred to another, Matthew 12:40. We could extend the list by adding Acts 2:29-31, 1 Corinthians 5:7, Galatians 4:22-26, Hebrews 7:1-3 and others.

The word *allegoreo* with the sense of "to represent typologically" is found in the New Testament, as are the words *tupos* and *antitupon* with the meanings "prophetic type" and "prophetic antitype."[1] Typological interpretation therefore is not an ad hoc method born of a search for Biblical curiosities.

It makes sense that the subject of coded portrayals is the redemptive work of Jesus, since the New Testament identifies Jesus as the focus of the sacred Hebrew writings.[2] Like our hypothetical treatise with maxims forming acrostics, the Scriptures contain not just encrypted prophecies but also an explanation of the concept accompanied by examples. To the four features of Biblical typology discussed in Chapter 2 we can now add a fifth and list them as follows:

1) General resemblance between sketches and fulfillments
2) Presence in the tradition of key symbol identifiers
3) Economy of distribution of typological material
4) Integration (interconnectedness) of coded sketches
5) Purposefulness of type coding within the tradition

If evidence continues to mount showing that Biblical coding has these five attributes, then the effort to explain it naturalistically will increasingly resemble an overloaded airplane trying to take off from a short runway. The last feature on the list, purposefulness, is especially

---

1   Gal 4:24; Rom 5:14; 1 Pet 3:21.
2   Luke 24:27.

telling. We have seen that its presence must flow from intelligence, and an Intelligence capable of orchestrating historical events over the course of centuries and millennia is one definition of "God."

Homer and Mark: Manufactured Correspondence

This does not mean that we are finished examining what accident combined with clever arrangement of material is capable of. It cannot produce a sound typological system, but it can produce a set of literary parallels that are easily mistaken for such a system. An example is found in the book, *The Homeric Epics and the Gospel of Mark*, by Dennis MacDonald, a member of the Jesus Seminar.[3]

MacDonald speculates that the author of Mark's Gospel created episodes for Jesus' life based on events from the *Iliad* and the *Odyssey*. He observes that in the first century Homer's epic tales were used universally to teach the Greek language, so everyone who could read and write Greek was familiar with them. It was also a literary fashion of the day to borrow plot elements or characters from Homer and disguise them to create new stories. Mark did this, MacDonald theorizes, in order to make Jesus seem equal if not superior to Homer's widely admired hero Odysseus.

MacDonald finds it necessary to show that Mark had access to Homer's epics and that borrowing from them was common among contemporary authors. His only evidence of actual borrowing from Homer by Mark, however, is resemblance. Besides setting certain episodes side by side to show their similarity, he points out unusual words or aspects of narrative style that in his view reinforce the proposed derivations.

MacDonald presents his argument well and succeeds in convincing many of his readers. What he does not do is acknowledge how easy it is to use his technique to create the appearance of Homeric inspiration in other material. I set out to produce sets of parallels between the *Odyssey* and literature that by no reasonable judgment was derived from it. Within a short time I had produced two such parallel studies. The first example correlates the episode of Odysseus and the sorceress Circe with

---

3   Dennis MacDonald, *The Homeric Epics and the Gospel of Mark* (New Haven: Yale University Press, 2000).

the Old Testament narrative of Saul and the Witch of Endor from
1 Samuel 28. The second study correlates the same section of the
Odyssey to an online version of the Grimm fairytale, "Hansel and
Gretel."

When I showed the first of these parallel studies to an atheist ac-
quaintance who had read McDonald's book, he responded that perhaps
1 Samuel 28 is an imitation of the Odyssey! However, the books of
Samuel are part of a thoroughly Hebrew tradition likely to be as old as
the Homeric epics. From a secular perspective, it may be an open question whether Greek myth exerted a broad influence on early Hebrew
narratives, but not that sequential, item-for-item literary copying took
place across such formidable barriers of language, geography and culture. MacDonald himself stresses that borrowing from Homer may be
alleged only where it is historically plausible, a requirement that cannot
be satisfied for the books of Samuel as it can be, arguably, for the
Gospels.

The flaw in MacDonald's approach is its deceptive elasticity. Narrative elements that do not contribute to a fit between compared passages
are skipped over, regardless of their prominence in context. Once a
rough correspondence is constructed any further shared characteristics
are expounded. Dissimilarities are rationalized as changes the borrowing
author made to accommodate the original story to his own purposes.

This is not to say that a general likeness between literary texts is of no
use in determining whether one is the source of the other, merely that
the value of resemblance alone, even when punctuated by a few oddly
similar details, is limited. That is why symbol identifiers are so important
in Biblical typology. The resemblance of "Hansel and Gretel" to the
Odyssey and of the patriarch Jacob to Jesus are by themselves little more
than curiosities. Nowhere in the Odyssey or in Grimm's Fairy Tales, for example, do we find even a veiled identification to back up a proposed
parallel between Odysseus' band of men and Hansel and Gretel.

As we have seen in previous chapters, when it comes to coded
prophecies relating to Jesus we have more than lists of resemblances.
Outside the coded narratives themselves we find links between the
Messiah and Jacob, for example, and between the Messiah and Moses.
The need to establish such a prophetic rationale combined with specific
identification of symbols imposes a discipline on typological decryption

that is not present where similarity alone is the standard. Anyone who doubts this is free to set up parallels between narratives using, say, the tales of Chaucer as the source text and the plays of Shakespeare as the target text. He then can attempt to create a set of coded relationships verified by symbol identifiers using the same documents. Afterward he can judge for himself the relative difficulty of the two exercises.

How Flexible is Typological Coding?

Biblical type coding has so far held up well under scrutiny. Two possible objections still need to be addressed, however. The first is that more than one symbolic association is sometimes available for a given type, allowing the interpreter to mold the resulting meaning to suit his own taste.

We have seen, for example, that water may symbolize God's Spirit and such manifestations as divine law, divine teaching and miracle-working. Water may by contrast represent crowds of violent people as well as death or the grave. In typological interpretation a choice must be made between these, but the choice is not arbitrary. The sketches we have examined in which water is one of the symbols all contain clues as to whether water is taking on a positive or negative connotation. The distinction between water for quenching thirst and the threatening waters of a storm-tossed sea is so easy to draw that it can hardly be called subjective.

In practice Biblical symbols are too limited in their range of meanings to be made to tell any story we want them to. Only certain meanings make sense in combination with each other. The telephone keypad helps to illustrate. Each of the numerals 2 through 9 of the keypad is assigned three or four letters of the alphabet so that any word can be coded into numbers as a marketing tool and memory aid. A given combination of numbers therefore may encode several words, but the degree of flexibility is easy to overestimate.

Look at the keypad layout for two short words related to the subject of Biblical theology, "God" and "Lord":

4	6	3		5	6	7	3
<u>G</u>	M	<u>D</u>		J	M	P	<u>D</u>
H	N	E		K	N	<u>R</u>	E
I	<u>O</u>	F		<u>L</u>	<u>O</u>	S	F

Few other words can be deciphered from the same number sequences, and none of them form a related pair comparable to our
original two. The odds would be long against these number sequences
occurring together by chance in a document, such as this chapter, that
discussed keypad coding of theological terms.

The keypad exercise shows that even when a symbolic system is relatively elastic, creating thematic agreement between arbitrarily chosen
groups of symbols is difficult. To turn this around, when we find that
by choosing between symbol meanings we can achieve adherence to a
pre-selected theme, as we can with coded sketches in the Bible, the odds
are overwhelming that the coherence was built to the text from the
start. If the potential for different meanings really were great enough to
let the interpreter fashion them at will, it would not be as difficult as it is
to find coded systems in non-Biblical literature.

The second objection is the same one I discussed briefly in the last
chapter regarding typological alignment between what befell Jonah and
the trial, execution and resurrection of Jesus. What would prevent sectarians in Jesus' time from interpreting stories from Hebrew Bible
symbolically and then concocting the fulfillments? The first of many
problems with this theory is that stories and identifiers would already
have to exist by pure chance in order for such a scheme to be carried
out. Then, to exploit this extraordinary circumstance, our hypothetical
sectarians must have been exceptionally organized and deceitful.

Conspiracies, as I noted in the last chapter, tend to fail as historical
explanations because they tend to fail, period. But a conspiracy is what
we are left with, putting aside supernatural explanations. The conspiracy
must have embraced Christian writers living in different areas and working during different decades between the middle and end of the first
century.

How, exactly, are we to envision a plot on this scale, carried on by
such articulate proponents? The conspirators could not have been mis-

led by rumor and exaggeration about Jesus or even false reports of miracles generated by religious hysteria. Having dedicated their lives to what they knew to be a fraud, they nevertheless produced a system of fulfillments both dizzyingly complex and disarmingly subtle. The scheme would have been diabolical not only because it betrayed the truth it claimed to uphold but because of the pathological ingenuity required to carry it out.

A theory so laden with implausibilities falls short of a sound naturalistic explanation. It has no equivalent in our experience. It defies what we know of psychology and religious history. It proposes a daunting improbability regarding the Hebrew Bible and joins it to a literary crime so perverse and yet so artful that no one who reads the New Testament with anything approaching objectivity will find it credible. The case for Biblical inspiration—or for something equally removed from natural causes—looks increasingly formidable. Still, it depends upon the presence in the Scriptures of more coded sketches of the kind we have already examined. That, in turns, leads us back again to the young man Jacob and his interest in sheep.

7

Watering the Sheep

In Chapter 1 I examined the coded relationship between a story about Jacob and the ministry of Jesus. In the last chapter I referred to evidence outside the story itself showing that Jacob or Israel serves as a prophetic type for the Messiah. Isaiah 49:3-6, for example, says that God's Servant, Israel, will gather back the tribes of Jacob. "Gathering" in verse five of this passage is rendered in the Septuagint by the Greek word *sunago*, the same word from which "synagogue" is derived.

According to the Gospels, Jesus, like the messianic servant of Isaiah, began a gathering work. "He who does not gather [*sunago*] with me scatters," he tells his disciples.[1] "The fields," he says, "are white for harvesting. Already the reaper is receiving wages and gathering [*sunago*] fruit for everlasting life."[2]

The Gospels also indicate that the faithful would carry on the "harvest" or gathering of followers even after Jesus' death. The process began among the Jews but was to widen out to Gentiles in order to create a spiritual nation, what Paul calls the "Israel of God."[3] Another gathering is described in the New Testament as well, the assembling of believers at the end of the age. In Matthew Jesus says that when he returns with power and glory his angels "will gather [*episunago*] his elect from the four winds, from one end of the heavens to the other."[4]

---

1   Matt 12:30.
2   John 4:35-36
3   Gal 6:16.
4   Matt 24:31.

2 Thessalonians 2:1 advises Christians not to be misled by sensational predictions about the imminence of "the coming of our Lord Jesus Christ and our being gathered [*episunagoge*] to him."

Both gatherings are alluded to in the first chapter of Acts, where Jesus speaks to the apostles immediately before his ascension. The apostles expect to be fellow rulers with Jesus in his kingdom, so they ask him if he is going to assume power over the world immediately.[5] In answer, Jesus says that he will not provide them with a timetable, but that they must complete a worldwide mission before the kingdom is ushered in. "You will receive power when the Holy Spirit comes on you," he says, "and you will be my witnesses in Jerusalem, and in all Judea and Samaria, and to the ends of the earth."[6] Effectively the disciples get a "no" to their question. They had hoped for an early arrival of the apocalyptic gathering and were told to carry forward with the evangelistic gathering instead.

Jesus says that the first gathering will begin in "Jerusalem and in all Judea," the homeland of the Jews. It will extend afterward to Samaria, home of the mixed-race remnant of the northern kingdom of Israel, and finally to the vast Gentile population that stretches out to the "ends of the earth." These instructions mark a departure from Jesus' own ministry, which with few exceptions was directed toward Jews, and from the restriction he had placed on the early work of his apostles.

In Matthew's Gospel Jesus tells the twelve that they should not preach to Gentiles or Samaritans but only to "the lost sheep of Israel," meaning Jews.[7] This command, which contrasts with the later injunction to preach to the world, nevertheless identifies the same ethnic-spiritual divisions of mankind as does the first chapter of Acts, namely, Jews, Samaritans and Gentiles.

Besides dividing humanity into the same three categories we find in Acts, the passage from Matthew 10 incorporates the metaphor of sheep. The sheep image occurs again in a similar context in John's Gospel, where Jesus says that he has "other sheep" than those to whom he is presently ministering. "They too will listen to my voice, and there shall

---

5   Cf. Matt 19:28.
6   Acts 1:8.
7   Matt 10:5-6.

be one flock and one shepherd."[8] With these words Jesus predicts the transition from a Jewish ministry to worldwide evangelism. The sheep from different ethnic groups or sheepfolds, once divided, will unite. If we blend Matthew 10:5-6 with John 10:16, we see three divisions of mankind represented as three pens or flocks of sheep prior to their being gathered into a single church body.

Gathering the Sheep to be Watered

In Acts 1:8 Jesus says that this gathering of symbolic sheep is to begin "when the Holy Spirit comes on you," the Spirit being "the gift my Father promised" (v. 4). Acts goes on to describe the receipt of the "gift" at a worship service in Jerusalem when the apostles and a few dozen other disciples experience a miraculous manifestation of divine power, including the ability to converse with Jewish pilgrims in languages from the far corners of the Roman empire.[9] Peter, acting as the apostles' spokesman, addresses the Pentecost festival crowd and argues that Jesus was executed unjustly but in accord with God's plan for salvation, and that the miracle the crowd beholds among the small group of disciples is only possible because Jesus has been raised from the dead and seated at the right hand of God. Peter also invokes Old Testament prophecy that God would one day "pour out" his divine Spirit:

> "Fellow Jews and all of you who live in Jerusalem, let me explain this to you; listen carefully to what I say. These men are not drunk, as you suppose. It's only nine in the morning! No, this is what was spoken by the prophet Joel:
>
> 'In the last days,' God says, 'I will pour out my Spirit on all people. Your sons and daughters will prophesy, your young men will see visions, your old men will dream dreams. Even on my servants, both men and women, I will pour out my Spirit in those days.' "
>
> —Acts 2:14-18

Joel 2:28-29, the passage quoted by Peter, is not the only one where the pouring out of the Spirit is mentioned. "I will pour out water on the

---

8   John 10:16.
9   Acts 2:1-11.

thirsty land," God promises at Isaiah 44:3, "and streams on the dry ground; I will pour out my Spirit on your offspring." Based on the "pouring" terminology in Acts and Joel, we are justified in concluding that in these passages, as in Isaiah 44, the Spirit implicitly is being compared to water, and we could add that metaphor to those of the gathering of Jewish, Samaritan and Gentile "sheep."

I considered the use of water as a symbol for God's Spirit earlier, in Chapter 2. There I referred to a passage from John's Gospel that seems especially significant in connection with the metaphor of a shepherd caring for sheep. The setting is a visit by Jesus to Jerusalem during the Festival of Booths, a time of general celebration during which the people constructed temporary shelters out of leafy branches and fronds.[10] The "booths" were a reminder of God having led the nation through the desert "like a flock" after the exodus.[11] To commemorate the miraculous provision of water "from the rock,"[12] the priest would draw water from the spring-fed Pool of Siloam and carry it to the temple, where he poured it into a receptacle leading to the base of the altar.

On the final day of this festival, according to John 7:37-38, Jesus stood up and called out that anyone who was thirsty could come to him for water, and that streams of living water would in turn flow from anyone who believed in him. In verse 39, John explains that Jesus' invitation had to do with the Spirit the disciples would later receive. "Up to that time the Spirit had not been given," John adds, "because Jesus was not yet glorified."

The passage in John not only confirms the Spirit/water symbolism seen elsewhere in the Scriptures, it compares receiving the Spirit to drinking in order to relieve thirst. The setting is a festival that reminded Israel of how God, like a compassionate shepherd, had provided water for his flock. John further says that the Spirit will not be present, at least not in the manner needed to spur the growth of the church, until Jesus has been "glorified." We saw in Chapter 2 that water cannot flow from the rock until it is struck, that is, until Jesus has been killed. Jesus' death is only the initial stage of a process that includes his lying in the grave and then being resurrected on the third day. When later in John's

10 Lev 23:41-43.
11 Ps 78:52.
12 Ps 78:20.

Gospel Jesus tells his disciples that the coming of the Spirit must follow upon his departure, he must be referring not merely to death but to death followed by resurrection.[13]

John 7:39, in speaking about Jesus being glorified, is using resurrection language like that of Paul when he says, "The body that is sown is perishable, it is raised imperishable; it is sown in dishonor, it is raised in glory."[14] The connection between the resurrection of Jesus and the pouring out of the Spirit brings us back once again to Acts 2. Peter says of himself and the small group of believers with him that "we are all witnesses of the fact" that God raised Jesus to immortal life. "Exalted to the right hand of God," Peter continues, "he has received from the Father the promised Holy Spirit and has poured out what you now see and hear."[15]

Aligning the Symbols with a Hebrew Narrative

We now have the ingredients for a coded narrative. Through his resurrection Jesus, the good Shepherd, makes the "water" of the Spirit available to quench the spiritual thirst of Jewish, Samaritan and Gentile "sheep" gathered through evangelism. Peter invites his Jewish listeners to repent, be baptized and "receive the gift of the Holy Spirit," which he says is not intended for them alone but also for "all those who are far off—for all whom the Lord our God will call."[16] Acts later describes the conversion of Samaritans and their receipt of the Spirit upon being visited by a delegation of apostles. After that event, the admission of Gentile believers into the church begins with the Roman centurion Cornelius.[17]

The only item lacking from this motif of the gathering and watering of sheep is an appropriate symbol for Jesus' resurrection. In Christian tradition the resurrection is closely associated with the "empty tomb" that once held Jesus' body. Some scholars doubt the authenticity of the

---

13 John 16:7.
14 1 Cor 15:42-43.
15 Acts 2:32-33.
16 Acts 2:38-39.
17 Acts 8:14-17; 10:1-48.

tomb story because it is not mentioned in Paul's letters, which are widely considered to be the earliest Christian documents. However, Paul does not mention specific episodes from Jesus' ministry, either, or for that matter that Jesus even engaged in a ministry, though Paul cannot have been ignorant on that score. In favor of the story is the prominence it is given in the Gospels, all of which relate it in similar terms. At the least, we know the belief that Jesus' tomb was found to be empty occurs early and emphatically in Christian history.

As a concrete object, the tomb cannot be identified as a symbol in the sense of its being a metaphor, but it does function as an emblem of Jesus' resurrection. To be precise, however, the first indication that Jesus had been raised was not the unoccupied slab where his body had been laid but the displacement of the stone that sealed the entrance to the sepulcher. The "rolling away" (according to some scholars, "sliding away") of the stone was the first hint of something extraordinary having occurred and is noted in all four Gospels.[18] Mark, which gives the most graphic description, says that the women who come to the tomb ask themselves who will "roll away," in Greek *apokulindo*, the "stone," *lithos*, which is "large in the extreme," *megas sphodra*.

In view of its importance in the resurrection story, we would hardly be surprised to find the rolling away of the stone used to represent Jesus' rising from the dead. We might be surprised, though, to see it so used in the prophetic narrative we have been progressing toward, which is from Genesis:

> Then Jacob continued on his journey and came to the land of the eastern peoples. There he saw a well in the field, with three flocks of sheep lying near it because the flocks were watered from that well. The stone over the mouth of the well was large. When all the flocks were gathered there, the shepherds would roll the stone away from the well's mouth and water the sheep. Then they would return the stone to its place over the mouth of the well.
>
> Jacob asked the shepherds, "My brothers, where are you from?" "We're from Haran," they replied. He said to them, "Do you know Laban, Nahor's grandson?" "Yes, we know him," they answered. Then Jacob asked them, "Is he well?" "Yes, he is," they said, "and here comes his daughter Rachel with the sheep." "Look," he said, "the sun

---

18 Matt 28:2; Mark 16:4; Luke 24:2; John 20:1.

is still high; it is not time for the flocks to be gathered. Water the sheep and take them back to pasture." "We can't," they replied, "until all the flocks are gathered and the stone has been rolled away from the mouth of the well. Then we will water the sheep."

While he was still talking with them, Rachel came with her father's sheep, for she was a shepherdess. When Jacob saw Rachel daughter of Laban, his mother's brother, and Laban's sheep, he went over and rolled the stone away from the mouth of the well and watered his uncle's sheep. —Genesis 29:1-10

Here we see the symbolic elements we have been discussing: a gathering of sheep, their need for water and the provision of water by means of the rolling away of a large stone. Before we explore the parallels further, note that the passage contains what appears to be superfluous dialog about what should be done with the sheep given the time of day.

The biography of Jacob calls at this juncture for Jacob to find his uncle and encounter his cousin Rachel, whom he will fall in love with and marry. Genesis need only say that Jacob finds shepherds at a well, questions them about Laban and then helps Rachel water her sheep. Editing out verses seven and eight, from "Look" through "Then we will water the sheep" would improve the story's focus and eliminate an unnecessary discussion in which the verb "gather" is used in confusingly different ways. Jacob says that it is too soon to "gather" the sheep, meaning to bring them to a place of shelter for the night, and says that they should be watered instead. The shepherds respond that to water the flocks they must "gather" them. The awkwardness over the word "gather" is present in the original text, since in both cases it translates the Hebrew *asaph*.

Verses seven and eight of Genesis 29 might be taken as an insignificant snippet of patriarchal lore if not for the critical part these verses play in the coding of the episode. The question of what kind of gathering of the sheep should take place at midday corresponds to the subject of Jesus' exchange with the apostles in Acts 1. Jesus indicates that the Gospel Age, which at 2 Corinthians 6:2 is called the "day" during which salvation is freely offered, is not yet far enough along for the supernatural gathering of the church to occur. Instead, Jesus says, people to the ends of the earth, the sheep of three ethnic-spiritual flocks, must have the opportunity to hear the gospel message and be "watered" with

God's energizing Spirit. Until the coming of Jesus, the flocks of mankind had been waiting for spiritual water that became available only through the "rolling away of the stone," just as in Genesis 29.

In Acts the small group of apostles and disciples who meet together in Jerusalem are the first to experience the outpouring of the Spirit. It is only after the "little flock" of original believers are "watered" that the Spirit is made available publicly to anyone within the category first of Jews and later of Samaritans and Gentiles.[19] This corresponds in Genesis with the watering of Rachel's sheep. As a young shepherdess, unmarried and probably no older than her early teens, Rachel would have had charge of a relatively small number of sheep, which were the first to receive water as the well was uncovered. The story implies that the three larger flocks received water afterward.

Jacob not only provides water but says that after they are watered the flocks should be pastured. Jesus takes up this metaphor too with respect to the early church. "Feed my sheep" is Jesus' post-resurrection command to Peter.[20] After receiving the Spirit, the first congregations needed continuing education in the word.[21]

Still more evidence of a coded alignment between Genesis 29:1-10 and the birth of the church as described in Acts is provided by original language terms. The Septuagint text of Genesis, which predates the New Testament by more than three centuries, uses the verb *apokulindo* for the rolling away of the stone just as do the Synoptic Gospels. The stone, *lithos*, is large, *megas*, as in Mark's Gospel. The "watering" of the sheep is translated with a form of *potizo*, the same verb Paul uses at 1 Corinthians 12:13 to say that believers "drink" the holy Spirit. As we would expect, "gathering" is rendered as *sunago*.

Confirming Jacob as a Messianic Type

I have repeatedly mentioned that the scriptures provide a basis for believing that Jacob would prefigure the coming Messiah. According to Genesis, the man Jacob was given the alternate name "Israel" as a sign

---

19 Luke 12:32.
20 John 21:15-17.
21 Acts 9:31; 15:32-35.

of God's blessing. Jacob eventually fathered and led a clan consisting of his twelve sons and their families.

The Bible therefore uses the names "Jacob" and "Israel" both for the man Jacob and for the nation of his descendants, with context determining whether we should understand the terms in the individual or collective sense. The book of Isaiah calls Israel "the servant of Yahweh" and introduces a third sense in which we the terms "Jacob," "Israel" and "Yahweh's servant" ought to be understood. Besides referring to the patriarch Jacob and the nation he fathered, they may designate a future leader who would perform works appropriate to the coming Jewish king, the Messiah. This leader or shepherd would gather back the tribes from their dispersion, atone for Israel's sins and teach justice to the nations of the earth.[22]

Some commentators see all of Isaiah's "servant" passages as referring to Israel collectively rather than to a promised Messiah. In certain verses it is not easy to tell whether the "servant" language is being used of the nation, of the Messiah as the nation's representative or in a dual sense. Still, several of these passages make no sense if applied to Israel collectively. Isaiah 11:10 and 53:2 both call this messianic figure a "root," *sores*, but 11:10 is more specific in saying a "root of Jesse." Jesse was the father of David, the founder of the nation's dynasty, consequently the "root" must be an offshoot or descendant of royal lineage, not the nation as a whole.

This royal heir would be given the assignment of regathering the nation from its places of exile, something that could not be done by the nation itself. Nor could the nation atone for its own sins, considering that the sinners who need the servant's intercession, the "we" of Isaiah 53:4-6, are in the immediate context the people of Israel.[23] The Messiah as distinct from the Israelite people does, therefore, bear the name of Jacob/Israel, pointing toward a prophetic resemblance between the ancestral founder of the nation and its Regatherer.

---

22 Isa 11:4, 10-12; 42:1; 49:5-6; 52:13-53:12; 55:4.

23 Isa 53:8 says that the servant dies "for the transgression of my people," which indicates that Israel's transgressions are immediately in view, and those of Gentiles only by extension.

It is a measure of the neglect of typological study that casual readers and seasoned scholars alike routinely overlook the exquisite example of foreshadowing from Genesis 29. Concealed only by its unpretentious setting, the typological portrayal in retrospect appears too obvious to be missed. Scanning the entries in a Bible concordance under the word "roll" reveals that occurrences of the unusual phrase "roll away the stone" hint at a possible link between Genesis 29 and the Gospels. Anyone who doubts that the story is intended prophetically should attempt to create a coded episode of his own, couched within a larger story, in which so many symbolic elements are arranged so masterfully.

The stock explanations of skeptics become so self-evidently inadequate in the face of this caliber of evidence that I need not review them again. Those objections that have not yet been mentioned for the most part take the form of diversions. I have been told, for example, that no conclusions may be drawn about the typological significance of given narratives without looking at what related literature has to say. What is the spiritual significance of Genesis 29:1-10, if any, according to the Talmud? What are the comments of church fathers and other commentators from the second century onward?

Ancient commentary is of historical interest but it cannot tell us whether or not the text is prophetically coded. That determination, in the present instance as in others I have examined, must be based on the Scriptures under discussion. Whatever speculation the Talmud or other ancient Jewish sources contain regarding Genesis, we can be confident that they do not interpret the stories about Jacob as prophetic of New Testament events. What, exactly, does that have to do with our study here? It is no more important than the absence of information in the Talmud regarding the discovery of penicillin or of the planet Neptune.

Humans have the ability to uncover truth and accumulate knowledge, a capacity the Bible says is God-given.[24] It would make little sense for God to provide a book as challenging as the Bible unless he intended prayerful study of it to yield new insights with the passing of time. That is not to say that the meaning of the Scriptures is buried deep beneath the surface and reserved for the sophisticated few; one of the functions of typological prophecy is to confirm the divine character of a message that is open to all.

---

24 Prov 2:3-6.

We have seen how episodes in the life of Jacob encode Jesus' ministry, his resurrection and the bestowal of the Spirit. Jacob is far from being the only Old Testament character who prefigures the Messiah, however. He is not even the foremost of these—that distinction belongs to David, to whom we turn our attention next.

8

The Shepherd King
Ungirds for Battle

The Christian writer C. S. Lewis was fond of saying that we live in rebel-controlled territory. If the Bible is to be believed, the war caused by this rebellion has been underway for thousands of years. Turning the tide of battle required the Son of God to come down from heaven to engage the enemy on the plane of human existence. Neither the Son's descent at the incarnation nor his ascent after his resurrection is simply a change in physical location, as though "heaven" were to be found at some astronomical distance from earth. "Descent" and "ascent" are necessary ways of depicting the transition between one phase of reality and another.[1]

The ideas of the incarnation and spiritual warfare may seem quaint, even childish, to those of us with secular perspective, but it is not necessary at this stage for anyone to accept them as true—only to understand in some measure what they imply. We will see shortly how these concepts underlie the famous Biblical narrative of David and Goliath.

If the "David and Goliath" story as such is not associated with Jesus, the link between David's kingship and the Messiah is familiar to anyone who has read the Old Testament. It contains the promise that one of David's descendants would be Israel's greatest king.

---

1   For a discussion of the subject, see C. S. Lewis, *Miracles* (NY: HarperCollins, 2001), 107ff.

The Messiah is even called by David's name: "I have exalted a young man from among the people," God says in the Psalms. "I have found David my servant; with my sacred oil I have anointed him. My hand will sustain him; surely my arm will strengthen him."[2] In Ezekiel God says that one day he will place over his people "one shepherd, my servant David." He continues, "I the LORD will be their God, and my servant David will be prince among them."[3]

In Jewish tradition the Messiah has long been called the son of David. That description is applied to Jesus several times in the Gospels, and Jesus himself calls attention to it in his final debate with the Pharisees.[4] Although on its face the term refers simply to davidic ancestry, it suggests as well the resemblance a son often bears to his father. When Jesus praises a repentant tax collector named Zacchaeus by saying of him, "this man, too, is a son of Abraham," he is referring not to the man's fleshly ancestry but to his having proven at long last to be a man of integrity like Abraham.[5]

Conversely, when Jesus says that his enemies among the Jewish leadership have the devil as their father, he is talking about the wickedness of heart that they share with Satan. By the same rule, the Hebrew verses that refer to the Lord's Anointed as David or David's son imply a similarity between David and Jesus the Messiah. Might this resemblance have to do not just with David's godliness in general but with his outstanding act of heroism?

The Bible recounts many events in David's life, including his trials as a fugitive from jealous king Saul, his ascension to the throne of Israel, his sin with the woman Bathsheba and later repentance and his desire to build a temple for Yahweh. Above all it is the epic duel with Goliath, however, that defines David as an archetype.

Psalm 89, quoted above, recalls David's designation as the future king of Israel when he was youthful, vigorous and innocent. He was the youngest of several brothers and the one to whom fell the lowly task of caring for the family's sheep. The anointing took place through the

---

2   Ps 89:19-21.
3   Ezek 34:23-24.
4   Matt 1:1; 22:42; Mark 10:47; Luke 1:32.
5   Luke 19:9.

prophet Samuel at the home of David's father Jesse.[6] Shortly afterward David slew Goliath.

Setting the Stage for a Duel

The narrative about the encounter with Goliath occupies the entire seventeenth chapter of 1 Samuel, and begins by describing the setting of a battle about to take place between Israelites from the Judean highlands and their long-time enemies from the coastal plain, the Philistines. The two armies survey each other from the high ground on either side of a valley near Socoh, twenty-six kilometers southwest of Jerusalem. While each side waits for an opportunity against the other, a Philistine champion named Goliath taunts the Israelite king Saul and his soldiers from the valley floor: "Choose a man and have him come down to me. If he is able to fight and kill me, we will become your subjects; but if I overcome him and kill him, you will become our subjects."

Goliath is a battle-hardened warrior of impressive size, clad in primitive mail armor and carrying a spear with an iron point as heavy as a grapefruit-sized boulder. None of the Israelite soldiers is brave enough to take up the challenge until David arrives to deliver food to his older brothers in Saul's army. Goliath's mockery angers David, who appears before king Saul after he learns that a reward is offered to the soldier who defeats the Philistine. Saul holds out little hope for David's success and tries to improve the shepherd's chances by giving him Saul's own body armor, helmet and sword. David is unpracticed with these weapons and finds them awkward, so he removes the armor and lays aside the sword. Instead, he arms himself only with his shepherd's staff and the sling he uses to protect his father's sheep from predators.

When Goliath sees David running to meet him holding a staff, he contemptuously asks if David regards him as a dog to be chased away with sticks. Goliath then curses David by his gods. David replies that unlike the Philistine, who comes heavily armed, David has come "in the name of the LORD Almighty, the God of the armies of Israel, whom you have defied." He declares, "All those gathered here will know that it is not by spear or sword that the LORD saves, for the battle is the LORD's, and he will give all of you into our hands."

---

6   1 Sam 16:1-13.

David then takes a stone from his pouch and slings it at Goliath. It hits the Philistine in the forehead and caves in the front of his skull. David runs over to the fallen champion and beheads him with his own sword in front of the Philistine army, which draws back in surprise and fear. The army of Israel then attacks and wins a great victory. David carries the head of Goliath to Jerusalem, near his home village of Bethlehem. Later David donates Goliath's sword to Yahweh's sanctuary but keeps the rest of Goliath's weapons as prizes of war.

The parallel between David and Jesus is first suggested by the incongruous picture of young David charging at the enemy carrying a shepherd's staff instead of traditional weapons. The Gospels present Jesus in the same way. "I am the good shepherd," he says, defying expectations that the Messiah will introduce himself as a warrior prince.[7]

Yet Jesus acknowledges that he is engaged in a fight. When Jewish religious teachers accuse Jesus of using the power of the devil, "Beelzebub," to perform exorcisms, Jesus replies that it would make no sense for Satan to attack himself. Jesus then relates a parable about two warring opponents. He observes that it is impossible to enter the house of a strong man and seize his belongings without "tying him up," which would require subduing him in a struggle.[8] The obvious meaning is that Jesus himself is able to free people from the control of the devil, the "strong man," only by invading Satan's domain and overcoming him in spiritual combat.

How does this invasion of the enemy's "house" take place? When we look back at the story of David at 1 Samuel 17, we find that the young shepherd has to descend from a hill to the valley floor to fight Goliath. The Bible doesn't say this directly, but we can infer it from the descriptions and dialog. The army of Israel, like that of the Philistines, camps on high ground. "The Philistines occupied one hill and the Israelites another, with the valley between them."[9] Goliath stands in the valley between the armies in order to bellow his threats. Choose a man to represent Israel, Goliath demands, and let him "come down to me."[10]

---

7   John 10:11; cf. Matt 2:6; Mark 14:27; Luke 15:2-4.
8   Matt 12:24-29; Mark 3:22-27.
9   1 Sam 17:3.
10 1 Sam 17:8.

In the Septuagint Bible, Goliath says to let a man "descend," using the Greek verb *katabaino*. King Saul and his Israelite soldiers cower at Goliath, and every day for more than a month the Philistine taunts Israel with impunity from from the battleground between the camps. It is to this low place, effectively claimed by Goliath as his own territory, that David must come in order to answer the Philistine's challenge.

The Descent of the Hero

The opening verse of the Gospel of John says that in the beginning someone called "the Word" was with God and shared God's very nature. Jesus confirms that he existed with the Father before his birth, calling himself the one who "descended [*katabaino*] from heaven."[11] It also happens that angelic spirits are divided up into two armies or camps in the Bible. On one side are those who are loyal to God while on the other are those who rebelled, the "wicked spirits in the heavenly places," chief among whom is Satan.[12] Further, Jesus calls Satan the "ruler of this world," indicating that Satan claims the earth, the realm of mankind, as his own territory.[13] We begin to see that the setting of David's duel was orchestrated to encode something greater than a tribal skirmish in the Judean countryside three thousand years ago.

Because martial imagery is prominent the "David and Goliath" narrative, some background information on the subject is helpful here. The armies of ancient nations and city-states were often under the control of a leading general who answered to no one but the king. The Hebrew term for this commander-in-chief, whose power in many respects was equal to that of the king, is *sar tsaba*, "prince of the host." The corresponding Greek terms found in the Septuagint Bible are *archistrategos* and *archonton tes dunamis*. In Genesis, when a coastal chieftain comes to conclude a treaty with Abraham, he and his *sar tsaba* speak with a single voice.[14] When the prophet Elisha wants to do a favor for a hospitable Canaanite woman, he asks if he can speak on her behalf to the king of

---

11 John 3:13.
12 Rev 12:7; Eph 6:12.
13 John 12:31; 14:30; 16:11.
14 Gen 21:22-23.

Israel or to the prince of the host.[15] The names of kings and their commanders were closely linked: Abimelech and Phicol, Jabin and Sisera,
Hadadezer and Shobach.[16]

When the line of dynastic succession was broken, it was likely to be
the commander of the army who ascended the throne. The northern
kingdom of Israel saw the accession of at least two commanders, Omri
and Jehu. The first such commander in Israelite history to do so was
David. As result of his exploits David became *sar tsaba* briefly before
falling out of favor with King Saul. David subsequently assumed the
throne after Saul's death.[17]

Two Biblical passages, Joshua 5:13-15 and Daniel 8:11, 25, refer to a
sar tsaba who governs the angelic armies of God. In Joshua the heavenly
commander appears girded for battle with a sword in his hand as the
Israelites enter the Promised Land. Daniel chapter eight prophesies that
an evil dictator will appear and exalt himself against the "Prince of the
host," whom it also calls the "Prince of princes."

It is sometimes argued that the *sar tsaba* of Daniel 8 is God the
Father, but verses such as Daniel 9:9-13 show that author was familiar
with earlier Hebrew Scriptures and their terminology. Though Daniel
8:11 says that God's temple belongs to the "Prince of the host," at
Malachi 3:2-3 the temple is said to belong to the "messenger of the
covenant," the coming Messiah, leaving open the possibility that the
two titles refer to one and the same figure.

In the book of Revelation the armies of heaven are commanded by
the risen Jesus, who is pictured as riding a white horse and bearing a
sword that issues out of his mouth.[18] Revelation blends imagery from
Psalms 45 and 110, where the Messiah charges into battle against the
enemies of God, with Isaiah 49:2, which says that his mouth is made to
be a sharp sword. These passages combine to portray the Son of God as
residing at the right hand of the Father, wielding universal power and
giving commands for the destruction of God's enemies.

The Gospels provide support for the identification of Jesus as Prince
of the heavenly host. A Roman officer who requests that Jesus heal his

---

15 2 Kgs 4:13.
16 Judg 4:2; Ps 83:9; 2 Sam 10:16.
17 1 Sam 18:5; 2 Sam 5:2.
18 Rev 19:11-15.

sick servant implies that Jesus can command supernatural agents the way he, the officer, directs his soldiers. "I myself am a man under authority, with soldiers under me," he says. "I tell this one, 'Go,' and he goes; and that one, 'Come,' and he comes. I say to my servant, 'Do this,' and he does it."[19] Further confirmation comes from Jesus himself on the night of his arrest. When Peter strikes out with a sword, Jesus tells him to put it away, adding that if he wanted to resist he had "twelve legions of angels" at his disposal.[20]

The portrait of the divine Son as heavenly Commander, invested with supreme power and bearing the sword of justice, allows us to understand the curious way in which David prepares for battle with Goliath. David, as we saw earlier, is at one point outfitted with the armor of King Saul and given Saul's own sword. He then has to take the armor off and lay aside the sword before descending to the valley to face the Philistine. Paradoxically, David must ungird before going into battle.

What David was forced to do ingeniously pantomimes what the Son of God did in the process called the incarnation. The Son, the "Logos" or Word "in whom all the fullness of the Deity resides," left his place beside the Father and emptied himself of supernatural power in order to partake of human fragility.[21] David briefly had been made the image of Saul, the king of Israel, from his armor and sword to the helmet on his head.[22] The Son likewise is called the image of God, who is the true King both of Israel and the universe.[23] The Son's divestiture of heavenly power and glory is described in Philippians:

> Have this attitude in yourselves which was also in Christ Jesus, who, although he existed in the form of God, did not regard equality with God a thing to be grasped, but emptied Himself, taking the form of a bond-servant, and being made in the likeness of men.
> —Philippians 2:5-7, NASB

---

19 Matt 8:9.
20 Matt 26:53.
21 John 1:1-14; Col 2:9.
22 1 Sam 17:38-39.
23 Col 1:15.

"Form" in the phrase "form of God" translates the Greek *morphe*. Contrary to the way some English-language Bibles render this word, it refers not to the inner aspect of a thing but to its outward appearance. A passage from the Septuagint will serve to illustrate. The book of Judges tells the story of Gideon, who freed Israel from oppression by eastern marauders, the Midianites. After routing Midianite forces, Gideon pursues and finally captures two of their chieftains, Zebah and Zalmunna. He then questions them to learn the identity of some Israelite men whom they earlier had killed. When they answer that each of the men was like Gideon, having the "form" of a "king's son," Gideon realizes that the victims are his own brothers.[24]

The standardized Septuagint text uses the word *homoima*, "likeness," to describe the appearance of the men, while the Alexandrine text has *morphe*.[25] It is apparent that the "form" of the men refers, not just to their faces, but to the clothing and armor that distinguished them as men of prominence from Gideon's own clan and family. In the same way, David's wearing of Saul's garments and armor gives him the "form," *morphe*, of the king. David relinquishes this form and, by putting on his ordinary clothing and picking up his staff, takes that of a common herdsman. David's appearance is so youthful and unwarrior-like that it elicits contempt on the part of Goliath.[26]

A Soldier without a Sword

A key element of this coded sketch is David's laying aside of the sword. I noted previously that Jesus commanded Peter to put the sword away. Jesus indicated that the nature of his mission would not allow him at that time to unleash cosmic forces against his enemies—forces that the sword aptly represents. The same stance can be seen in an earlier event, Jesus' sermon at the synagogue in his home town of Nazareth.

As Luke tells it, Jesus opens a scroll and begins with a reading from the Hebrew Bible. The passage he chooses is from Isaiah 61:1-2, where the messianic Servant of Yahweh says that God's Spirit has moved him to preach good news and to proclaim liberty to the poor, the afflicted

---

24 Judg 8:18-19.
25 Phil 2:7 confirms the synonymity of *homoima* and *morphe* by parallel usage.
26 1 Sam 17:42-44.

and the captives. He concludes with the phrase, "to proclaim the favorable year of the Lord," but conspicuously stops short of the final words from the quoted passage, "and the day of vengeance of our God."[27] Vengeance and retributive justice are frequently associated with the sword.[28]

In his Nazareth sermon Jesus lays aside the "sword" by declining to pronounce immediate condemnation. His message as a whole does declare a judgment, of course, but a judgment in the future that leaves a precious interval for response to divine grace, the "favorable year of the Lord." "Favorable" translates the Greek *dektos*, which emphasizes potential acceptance by God as in Isaiah 49:8, LXX: "In an acceptable [*dektos*] time have I heard you, and in a day of salvation have I succored you."[29] Another way of expressing this act of laying aside the sword in favor of the shepherd's staff is found at John 12:47: "For I did not come to judge the world, but to save it."

David's ungirding and putting down the sword allows him to enter Goliath's territory, the "house" of the "strong man" in Jesus' related parable. As we have seen, the world of mankind into which the Son descends through the incarnation is rebel-occupied territory claimed by Satan. When Jesus squares off against the devil at the beginning of his ministry, Satan shows him in vision all the kingdoms of the world and says, "I will give you all their authority and splendor, for it has been given to me, and I can give it to anyone I want to."[30] Jesus refuses the devil's offer, telling him instead to "Go away."[31]

It is not just Satan's claim on the world that it is significant here, but the geographical setting of the confrontation. Jesus has been led by God's Spirit into the Judean desert, symbolically speaking the lair of Satan. I noted in Chapter 3 that Jesus compares evil spirits to snakes and scorpions, which are portrayed in the Scriptures as primarily desert-dwelling animals.[32] Jesus says that a demon wanders through "arid

---

27 Luke 4:18-19.
28 Deut 32:41; Jer 46:10; Rom 13:4.
29 Cf. 2 Cor 6:2.
30 Luke 4:6.
31 Matt 4:10.
32 Deut 8:15.

places" when not in possession of a victim.[33] Before Jesus cures a
Gadarene man under demonic oppression, one of the ways the spirits
torment the man is by periodically driving him into the "wilderness,"
that is, the Judean desert.[34] The Old Testament, too, identifies deserts as
the dwelling places of evil spirits.[35] Jesus' foray into the desert at the beginning of his ministry is an invasion of the devil's domain, the
equivalent of young David's boldly running toward the Philistine.

The ensuing battle is not only on the enemy's turf but on the enemy's
terms as well. "Give me a man," Goliath demands.[36] If our interpretation is correct, Goliath represents Satan and his challenge is diabolical.
As the Bible portrays him, the devil is anxious to have access to those
who claim to serve God in order to expose their faith as shallow and
self-serving. In the book of Zechariah, Satan is pictured as trying to
bring a case against Joshua the son of Jehozadak, a leading figure in
restoring temple worship after the return of the Jews from Babylonian
exile.[37] On the night of his arrest Jesus tells Peter that the devil has demanded the chance to test the disciples.[38] Revelation calls Satan the
unrelenting accuser of God's servants.[39] The most detailed depiction in
this regard, however, is in the book of Job. Job deserves examination
because in it Satan, like Goliath, asks that a man be given to him for a
contest.

As the book of Job opens, the angels are assembled before God.
Satan enters among them and says that he has been scouting out the
earth. Soon the subject turns to the man Job, living in western Arabia,
whom God calls the most outstandingly righteous of men. Satan accuses
God of bribing Job with material wealth and shielding him from life's
troubles. Satan demands access to Job in order to test him with disaster,
poverty and illness. Satan tells God that if suffering overtakes Job, "he
will surely curse you to your face."[40]

---

33 Matt 12:43.
34 Luke 8:29.
35 Isa 13:19-22; cf. Rev 18:2.
36 1 Sam 17:10.
37 Zech 3:1.
38 Luke 22:31.
39 Rev 12:10.
40 Job 2:5.

Job is a rich and esteemed judge of his Edomite clan, revered for his justice and compassion and seemingly invulnerable to temptation. In the midst of his affliction Job will look back and say that he had once dwelt like "a king among his troops."[41] In these respects he makes an ideal representative of the Son who resides "in the bosom of the Father," the Prince of the heavenly host, who shares the Father's own glory and authority. No one else would seem so secure in his relationship with the Father and so insulated from harm.

Other noteworthy resemblances exist between Job and Jesus. Job loses his wealth, prestige and children and endures a bout of agonizing sickness at the hands of Satan. Later Job is restored and granted blessings beyond those he originally enjoyed. This sequence of initial glory, humiliation and then exaltation corresponds to what the Son of God experienced. In the Gethsemane prayer found in John's Gospel Jesus asks the Father to restore to him the heavenly glory he originally possessed.[42] That glory is likened to wealth by Paul when he says of God's Son that "though he was rich, yet for your sakes he became poor."[43]

When Job is suffering, three outwardly pious associates turn against him and allege that his trials are a punishment for secret sins, just as the elders of the Jewish nation bring accusations against Jesus. When Job is restored, God condemns Job's former friends and counsels them that their only hope of forgiveness lies in Job's intercession on their behalf.[44] With Jesus' resurrection and ascension, he in a similar way becomes sole mediator and intercessor for the purpose of obtaining divine forgiveness, including forgiveness for those who condemned him.[45]

Abandoned into the Hand of the Enemy

The fleshly vulnerability assumed by Jesus at the incarnation therefore is represented both by young David divesting himself of armor and by the man Job being stripped of possessions and divine protection. Yet

---

41 Job 29:25.
42 John 17:5.
43 2 Cor 8:9.
44 Job 42:7-8.
45 Acts 3:17-19; 4:12.

another image in this regard is found in the regimen of animal sacrifices prescribed by the Mosaic Law. In terms of maintaining the spiritual standing of Israel before Yahweh, the most important of these sacrifices were the bulls and goats offered on Yom Kippur, the annual Day of Atonement. Two goats were selected: a "goat for Yahweh" and a "goat for Azazel."[46] The first of these was slain and its blood was carried by the priest into the Holy of Holies, the inner compartment of the temple, to be presented before God in expiation of the sins of the people. The New Testament book of Hebrews says that the sacrifice of the first goat along with the bull offered at the same time typify Christ's death in obedience to God's will.[47]

The "goat for Azazel," often referred to as the "scapegoat," was not killed outright but was released into the wilderness where it died of exposure or was devoured by wild animals. One theory is that this goat represents wicked people who are driven away from the presence of God. Another interpretation sees it as representing the criminal Barabbas, who was released to continue in his evil course when Jesus was condemned to die. A close look at the language of Leviticus shows instead that this goat, too, must represent Jesus. Like the other animal victims, the scapegoat was said to be for the purpose of "making atonement" before God.[48]

The priest was to lay his hands on the head of the animal and confess over it all the rebelliousness and evil of the nation. The goat would then "carry," *nasa*, the "iniquity," *awon*, of the people away. What is said of the scapegoat is also said of the messianic servant of God. According to Isaiah, God would lay the sins of the people "upon," *al*, his servant just as the priest put them "upon," *al*, the goat. The Messiah then would "bear," *sabal*, and "carry," *nasa*, both the sorrows of the people and their *awon*, their "iniquity."[49]

Some scholars have seen *azazel* as meaning "removal," since the sins of Israel were symbolically removed when the goat was banished to the desert. More likely though more troublesome for interpreters is that Azazel is a name meaning "strong one." Jewish tradition portrays Azazel

46 Lev 16:6-28.
47 Heb 9:7-14.
48 Lev 16:10.
49 Isa 53:5-6, 11-12.

as a desert-dwelling demon. In the *Apocalypse of Abraham*, from the late first or early second century, Azazel is the leader of fallen angels and wields power over his chosen abode, the earth.[50]

"Azazel" as a name meaning "strong" has a connotation of ferocity, as can be seen by comparing the related Assyrian verb *ezezu*, "to be furious."[51] This background allows us to understand better the references to Satan as a "strong man" and the additional detail from Luke that he aggressively "guards" his property.[52] The resemblance between Azazel and Beelzebub/Satan is even closer than it appears in translation, since the Greek for "strong man," *ischuros*, actually is a one-word qualitative noun, "strong (one)."

The way the emphasis on the enemy's strength relates to the typological significance of David and Goliath is obvious. 1 Samuel takes pains to depict the Philistine's size and power. Ancient sources vary somewhat on the figure for Goliath's height, but it must have been imposing. Our oldest manuscript containing 1 Samuel 17:4, 4QSam(a) from the Dead Sea Scrolls, is also the most conservative and puts him at 6-1/2 feet (2 meters). A tall man by any standard, Goliath would have been a giant in an era of low protein consumption and small average stature. For him to carry the heavy armor and weapons described in 1 Samuel 17:5-7 he must have been as bulky as he was tall, weighing 250 pounds or more.

The Hebrew narrative refers to Goliath as a Philistine "champion" and a "man of war."[53] He is also called a *gibbor*, meaning "mighty one" or "strong one."[54] The Septuagint uses the Greek word *dunatos*, "powerful one" to describe Goliath.[55] *Dunatos* in this context is synonymous with *ischuros*, the word Jesus uses of Satan.[56]

The Gospels further link Goliath with Satan by using the name "Beelzeboul" or "Beelzebub" in the passages concerning the "strong

50 James H. Charlesworth, ed., *The Old Testament Pseudepigrapha*, Vol. 1 (NY: Doubleday, 1983), 684.
51 *The New Brown-Driver-Briggs-Gesenius Hebrew and English Lexicon* (Peabody, MA: Hendrickson, 1979), 783.
52 Luke 11:21.
53 1 Sam 17:4, 23, 33.
54 1 Sam 17:51.
55 1 Kgdms 17:4, 23, 51, LXX (1 Sam 17:4, 23, 51, MT).
56 See 1 Cor 1:26-27, which parallels *dunatos* with *ischuros*.

one." A deity with a nearly identical name, Baal-zebub, meaning "Lord of the flies," was worshiped by Philistines at the city of Ekron.[57] Similar appellations were used by the inhabitants of Canaan and Phoenicia, such as Zebul Baal ("Exalted Lord"), and Beelzeboul/Beezeboul ("Lord of the house" or, mockingly, "Lord of dung"). Baal was a traditional Canaanite deity who stood in opposition to Yahweh. Goliath cursed David "by his gods," which may have included Baal-zebub and in any case represented demonic lordship.

We have supplemented the image of an all-but-unarmed young shepherd pitted against the deadly weapons of a murderous enemy with two others: the man Job beset by an invisible opponent who bludgeons him with successive disasters and the scapegoat left to certain death on a harsh landscape. All three illustrate the uneven contest entered into by the Son of God through the incarnation. They also prod us toward an appreciation of why nothing else could settle fundamental questions about nature of man and the goodness of God's creation.

Up until the coming of Jesus, the Bible says, every human who ever lived fell short of moral perfection. Even a man such as Job was righteous only comparatively, for "there is no one who does not sin."[58] Is sin a corruption of the human mode of existence or a necessary consequence of it? "Skin for skin," Satan quips, "and everything a man has he will give in exchange for his life."[59] The argument implies that even the Son of God, the supreme example of loving union with the Father, if exposed to the same physical and psychological pressures as humans could be made to curse the Sovereign. "Give me a man—any man—and unshackle me from every restriction on the force I can apply, and I will destroy his love for God," appears to be the devil's boast.

The challenge to God over his human creatures requires further investigation, as do the typological features of the David and Goliath narrative. We have already located identifiers relating David to the Messiah and the descent of David to the descent of the Son from heaven. We found that Biblical imagery allows us to connect David's laying aside the armor and sword of the king to the Son's relinquishing divine glory and

---

57 2 Kgs 1:2-8.
58 1 Kgs 8:46.
59 Job 2:4.

foregoing the sword of retribution. I also demonstrated that Goliath, the opponent of David, is an appropriate representative of Satan, the prime adversary of Jesus. In the following chapter I will probe the story further.

9

The Son of David Triumphant

"I come to you in the name of the LORD of hosts, the God of the armies of Israel, whom you have taunted."[1] With these words David runs toward what bids to be certain death at the hands of a huge Philistine soldier. As if in response to the unfolding action God says in the book of Proverbs, "If you are wise, my son, you will gladden my heart, and I will be able to rebut him who taunts me."[2] The object of this exhortation, written long after the time of David, is another son who must confront an an even greater adversary, one who may be defeated only through godly wisdom.

In the last chapter we saw that the circumstances surrounding the duel between David and Goliath encode those of the incarnation of the Son of God. The taunts of Goliath coincide with those of the devil himself, who boasts that any human delivered into his hands can be broken. Such a challenge was issued over the man Job, who in spite of great suffering never cursed God as Satan claimed he would. The devotion of Job, however, was alloyed with the sinful weakness common to humans generally.[3]

---

1 1 Sam 17:45, NASB.
2 Prov 27:11, *New American Bible.*
3 Job 14:17.

In addition, a restriction was placed on Satan that he could not take Job's life.[4] In literal terms he was to "be careful" of Job's "soul." Besides meaning that Job was not to be killed, Job's inner being was not to be subjected to unlimited anguish.[5]

For the devil's challenge to be answered, a perfectly sinless human would have to be completely abandoned into his power and yet remain faithful. Satan would have to be free to direct energies both visible and invisible at his victim without interference from God. Even the Hebrew Scriptures give us an indication that this was to be the fate of God's unique Son. In contrast to Job, whose soul was not to be touched, the Messiah would have to "pour out his soul to death."[6]

In the third chapter I noted that as punishment for its sins the nation of Israel was delivered into the hand of warlords such as Sargon of Assyria and Nebuchadnezzar of Babylon, and that these tyrants, like Goliath, were fitting representatives of Satan. Further, the New Testament says directly that incorrigible sinners are left to the dubious kindnesses of the devil and his world.[7] In the last chapter we examined verses from Isaiah 53 that say that the messianic servant would bear the people's sorrow and iniquity. One of these, verse 5, says specifically that the "punishment" for the nation's sins would fall upon him. Since this punishment meant being delivered into the hands of the enemy—ultimately, the devil—the implication again is that the Messiah would be left utterly to Satan's devices.

In keeping with these prophecies, on the night of his arrest Jesus says to those who seize him, "This is your hour, when darkness reigns."[8] Ostensibly the mob that comes to Gethsemane is led by the traitor Judas Iscariot. John's Gospel adds that the real master of ceremonies is Satan, who enters into Judas in order to put the night's events in motion.[9] When Jesus sees Judas at the head of the priests and temple guards, he makes a comment that is rendered as either "Friend, do what you came

---

4   Job 2:6.
5   1 Cor 10:13.
6   Isa 53:12.
7   1 Cor 5:5; 1 Tim 1:20.
8   Luke 22:53.
9   John 13:27.

for," or "Friend, why are you here?"[10] The second translation, a question similar to God's question to Satan, "Where do you come from?" is probably the correct one, and may be Jesus' way of acknowledging the presence of the chief adversary.[11]

In the hours following his arrest, Jesus is convicted of blasphemy, repeatedly beaten with fists, given a brutal flogging, denied sleep and apparently food and water as well, then forced to carry the horizontal beam of a heavy wooden cross. Injured and exhausted to the point of collapse, he at last is hung from the cross to die in agony. His body weight depends brutally from nails driven between the bones of his hands or wrists and through his feet. The upright perhaps is fitted with a small cleat for him to "sit" against so that death does not come too quickly. Even when Jesus cries out under this agony, having been stripped of all divine protection, he does not repudiate his Father.[12]

The Serpent's Tooth

Archaeological findings help us to better understand Jesus' ordeal. As we saw in Chapter 3, the skeleton of a man named Jehohanan, executed by the Romans, was part of a monumental find made in 1968. The most grisly part of the victim's remains is a heel bone skewered by a jagged nail. The probability is overwhelming that, as in the case of Jehohanan, Jesus' feet were nailed through the heels, not through the arches as pictures usually show. The placement of the nails not only caused torturous muscle spasms and overwhelming pain, it fulfilled yet another Old Testament prediction concerning the battle between the Son of God and the devil.

The prediction is the first prophecy in the Bible, found at Genesis 3:15. God promises there that a "seed," or offspring from the family of mankind, will battle the "serpent." "He will crush your head," God says to the serpent, "and you will strike his heel." The defeat of Satan is here foretold, since unlike a foot wound, a wound to the head ordinarily would be fatal. The image evoked is that of a man who smashes the head of a snake with his foot but is bitten in the process. The detail of

---

10 Matt 26:50.
11 Job 2:2.
12 Matt 27:46.

the non-fatal heel wound was not fulfilled upon David, but it well could symbolize the sufferings of Jesus, who although he was killed was restored to life by resurrection.

The promise of a seed of deliverance is not limited to Genesis 3. It is part of God's covenant promises to Abraham and, much later, to David.[13] The word "seed," *sperma* in the Greek of the Septuagint, is used of offspring in the plural when God says he will greatly multiply the seed of Abraham and David.[14] In 2 Samuel 7:12-13, the seed of the covenant appears with the singular pronoun, referring simultaneously to David's son Solomon and to a future heir whose reign, unlike that of Solomon, would endure forever.

The New Testament reconciles plural versus singular uses of "seed" in the context of God's unfolding covenant. Paul says that the *sperma* is primarily Jesus and secondarily the congregation of all believers.[15] If Jesus is the seed of promise then he is the one who, according to Genesis 3:15, crushes the head of the serpent. At this juncture the prophecy about the seed converges with our story of David and Goliath. The young shepherd slings a stone at Goliath that not only strikes him but sinks into his forehead, necessarily fracturing the Philistine's skull.[16] David, representing the "seed," crushes the head of Goliath, representing Satan the "serpent."

Goliath's connection to the satanic snake or dragon was verified in the eyes of ancient rabbis by the Philistine's scale armor. We know that such armor was made at the time by sewing rows of small bronze plates to a leather tunic. Other than where it denotes fish scales, the Hebrew word for Goliath's body armor, *qasqeseth*, elsewhere is used only to describe the reptilian monster to which Egypt is likened at Ezekiel 29:3-4.

We turn now to the symbolism of the stone that David uses to strike down Goliath, a stone that acts as an extension of David himself. Jesus is likened to a stone in two different ways. The first is by his becoming the cornerstone of the spiritual temple.[17] The second is by being a destructive stone that smashes all opposition to God. The Gospels

---

13 Gen 3:15; 2 Sam 22:51.
14 Gen 15:5; Jer 33:22.
15 Gal 3:16, 29.
16 1 Sam 17:49.
17 Mark 12:10; Eph 2:20.

combine these senses. As related in Matthew and Luke, Jesus quotes Psalm 118:2 concerning the cornerstone and then alludes to Isaiah 8:14-15 and Daniel 2:34-35. Isaiah says that unfaithful Israelites will be broken against the divine stone, while Daniel says that the stone will crush Gentile powers that stand in the way of God's kingdom. Leaving no doubt that the Messiah is an agent of demolition as well as of construction, the Gospels warn that "he on whom [that stone] falls will be crushed."[18]

Stones, Weapons and Spoils of War

Identifying Jesus not just with David but with the sling-stone that brings down Goliath raises a further question. Just before he runs out to meet Goliath, David chooses five smooth rocks from a creek bed and places them in a pouch he carries. He loads his sling with one of these stones as he draws near Goliath and hits his mark on the first try. Various commentators have suggested that David chose five stones because Goliath was one of five great champions, the "descendants of Rapha," who fought for the Philistines of Gath.[19] There is no mention of other Philistine heroes in the account about Goliath, however, either in the events leading up to the duel or in the ensuing battle. The Scriptures say that the champions of Gath were killed one by one in various skirmishes over the course of many years. Only by a stretch can they be related to the five stones in David's bag.

To interpret the five stones typologically I must analyze the function of the stones and the pouch that held them. Sling-stones became potentially lethal projectiles, missiles of warfare shot at great speed. David's bag, *keli* in Hebrew, was probably a leather receptacle used for personal items. On the occasion of the duel, this receptacle was transformed into an ammunition pouch. The bag became like a quiver, which is a leather container to hold another ancient type of missile, the arrow. A quiver, for which the Hebrew term is *aspa*, could be classified generally as a container, *keli*, made of leather, *or*.[20] The significance becomes clear when we find that the messianic servant of God is likened to an arrow

---

18 Luke 20:18.
19 Cf. 2 Sam 21:16-22; 1 Chron 20:4-8.
20 Lev 11:32.

concealed in a quiver.[21] In a similar expression from the Psalms, a man's sons are compared to arrows that go forth against his people's enemies. "Blessed is the man whose quiver is full of them."[22]

We do not in the case of David's stones have a precise identifier, but there is a close conceptual link. If arrows can stand for sons in a man's family, and if we generalize arrows in a quiver to missiles in an ammunition pouch, then the implication is easy to see. Five sling-stones in David's bag, the first of which fells the enemy, points to the Messiah being the firstborn of five sons in a family from the line of David. That is exactly what the Gospels say of Jesus. "Isn't this Mary's son and the brother of James, Joseph, Judas and Simon?"[23]

The speculative identification of the five stones will become less doubtful if we can establish even more solidly the typological character of the story. In the last chapter I noted similarities between the David and Goliath narrative and a brief parable of Jesus. Jesus compares himself to someone who invades the house of a strong man, overcomes him and then takes his possessions. In Matthew and Mark, the Greek word for these possessions is *skeos*, meaning "equipment" or "articles" in a broad sense. When we return 1 Samuel we find that Goliath's belongings are seized as are those of Jesus' "strong man": "[David] put the Philistine's weapons in his own tent."[24] In the Septuagint, what David takes is not specifically the weapons of Goliath, as in the Hebrew text, but simply the warrior's *skeos*, "equipment."

Even putting aside the clue from the word *skeos*, we can learn the nature of the strong man's possessions by turning to the version of the parable contained in Luke's Gospel. "When a strong man, fully armed, guards his own house," Jesus says in Luke, "his possessions are safe. But when someone stronger attacks and overpowers him, he takes away the armor in which the man trusted and divides up the spoils."[25]

Here we see plainly stated what we already had inferred. The strong man is indeed a heavily armed warrior like Goliath. The articles taken from him are his *panoplia*, armor in the sense of an arsenal of weapons in

---

21 Isa 49:2.
22 Ps 127:4-5.
23 Mark 6:3.
24 1 Sam 17:54.
25 Luke 11:21-22.

which he had trusted for his security. In this regard David says to Goliath, "You come against me with sword and spear and javelin, but I come against you in the name of the LORD Almighty, the God of the armies of Israel, whom you have defied."[26] The declaration implies that, while David trusts in Yahweh, Goliath trusts in his weaponry. "All those gathered here will know that it is not by sword or spear that the LORD saves; for the battle is the LORD's, and he will give all of you into our hands."[27]

What, exactly, are represented by the weapons of the strong man? The comparison may extend to tactics of the devil, such as deception and disguise, which Jesus exploits by exposing them to the light of truth. Specifically, however, the weapons are people over whom the devil exerts control. Jesus' reason for giving the parable in the first place is to defend his power of exorcism, which frees people from outright enslavement to the demons. Beyond exorcism, all of Jesus' activity is directed against the devil's influence. "He went around doing good and healing all who were under the power of the devil."[28] "The reason the Son of God appeared was to destroy the devil's work."[29]

The Gospel of Luke is not the only place where we find that human beings under the devil's control are represented as weapons or articles of value. We find the same comparison in a passage from Isaiah:

> Thus says the LORD:
> Can booty be taken from a warrior?
> or captives be rescued from tyrant?
> Yes, captives can be taken from a warrior,
> and booty rescued from a tyrant;
> Those who oppose you I will oppose,
> and your sons I will save. —Isaiah 49:24-25, *New American Bible*

The imagery is the same as that used by Jesus. In Isaiah the immediate application is to Jewish exiles in Babylon who God says will be freed to return to the land of Israel. The verse puts "booty" in parallel with "captives." The process of liberating Israelites in bondage is compared

---

26 1 Sam 17:45.
27 1 Sam 17:47.
28 Acts 10:38.
29 1 John 3:8.

to overcoming a powerful enemy and carrying off plunder. The word for "warrior" here is actually *gibbor*, "mighty one," the Hebrew term used of Goliath. The Greek text of these verses is fascinating to compare, since it calls the enemy a "strong one," *ischuros*, and a "giant," *gigantos*. The combined information from both the Hebrew and Greek texts echoes the story of David and Goliath by describing an adversary of exceptional size and strength. At the same time, by revealing that the booty taken from the enemy actually consists of captives it points forward to Jesus' victorious campaign to free people from satanic domination.

The Septuagint version of Isaiah 49:24-25 is of added interest because for "spoils" is has the Greek *skulon*. This word occurs just once in the entire New Testament, in Luke's version of the "strong man" parable. In that passage Jesus says that the "spoils," *skulon*, will be divided by the one who emerges from combat as the strong man's superior, that is, by Jesus himself.[30] The same thing is said of the suffering messianic servant described in yet another passage of Isaiah. In the previous chapter we saw that this mysterious servant would "bear" the sins of the people the way the scapegoat did on Yom Kippur, the Day of Atonement. In return for suffering death to remove the people's guilt, the servant gains a reward: "He [the servant] will apportion the spoils [*skulon*] of the strong [*ischuros*]."[31]

David's Reward

Thus far I have compiled an assortment of distinctive, shared elements relating Jesus to David in terms of the encounter with Goliath. It is conceivable that the Gospel writers drew inspiration from the story and interpreted Jesus' ministry as a spiritual version of David's famous duel. What is not conceivable is that the various circumstances of that duel, including the unlikely way David prepares for battle, should line up with the what the New Testament says about the incarnation. Nor is it likely that in context Goliath would so precisely reflect Satan's power and ambition, even as far as the diabolic accusation regarding human weakness. Insofar as David's experience portended the work of God's

30 Luke 11:22.
31 Isa 53:12.

Son in ways that neither manipulation nor coincidence can account for, we have already met any reasonable burden of proof. We are not finished with the story, though. At least one feature still remains to be investigated.

We have seen that David's victory over Goliath allows him to appropriate the Philistine's weapons as spoil. Other prizes are at stake also. When David first arrives at the Israelite encampment and hears Goliath's taunts, he inquires about a reward for the man who answers the challenge. He is told that indeed the king is offering a reward in three parts. First, the victor will receive riches from the king. Second, he will receive the king's own daughter as his wife. Third, his father's house, the family estate of the victor, will be "set free" or redeemed.[32] If the narrative is prophetic of Jesus, we might expect this reward to reflect what Jesus gains as a result of defeating Satan.

The first prize Jesus received after his death was resurrection to immortal life and enthronement at the right hand of the Father. In Chapter 6 I examined the way this process is summarized at John 7:39, which says that Jesus would be "glorified," and at 1 Corinthians 15:43, which says that Jesus was "raised in glory." Other texts, such as Hebrews 2:9, use similar language: "But we see Jesus, who was made a little lower than the angels, now crowned with glory and honor because he suffered death."[33] Jesus having received glory as a reward is important to our study because "glory," in Greek *doxa*, is equated with riches, *ploutos*, in three separate New Testament passages. Romans 9:23 and Ephesians 3:16 both refer to the "riches of God's glory," while Colossians 1:27 speaks about the "riches of the glory" of the hope believers have through Christ.

Ploutos happens to be the word used for the first part of David's reward in the oldest Greek version containing 1 Samuel 17:25, the Alexandrine Text. The identifiers in Romans, Ephesians and Colossians prove that glory may be regarded as a form of wealth. We have still more evidence in Paul's statement that though Christ had been "rich," *plousios*, "he became poor" in order to bring salvation.[34] The Son of God had to lay aside his divine glory in order to share in humanity. Not only

32 1 Sam 17:25.
33 Cf. Rom 8:17; 2 Thess 2:14; 1 Tim 3:16; 2 Pet 1:17.
34 2 Cor 8:9.

is this implied as well by what Paul says in Philippians about the Son having "emptied himself," it is referred to directly when Jesus asks to receive once again the glory he enjoyed alongside the Father "before the world existed."[35] Multiple identifiers demonstrate that the first part of David's reward, riches from the king, is an appropriate symbol for glory bestowed on Jesus by the King of the universe.

The second part of Jesus' reward is his joyful union with the members of his church when he returns at the end of the present age. The Gospels contain many references to the "marriage feast" that will take place at the Second Coming and otherwise employ the image of Jesus as a bridegroom and the church as his betrothed.[36] "I promised you to one husband, to Christ, so that I might present you as a pure virgin to him," Paul tells the Corinthians.[37]

Ephesians says that " 'a man will leave his father and mother and be united to his wife, and the two will become one flesh.' This is a profound mystery—but I am talking about Christ and the church."[38] The New Testament teaches that believers are in a covenant with Jesus, much as an engaged woman is with a man, and will enjoy the privilege of administering the earth as his partners during the coming age.[39]

In Revelation an angel says to John, "Come, I will show you the bride, the wife of the Lamb." John is next shown the church, represented as the idealized city of Jerusalem.[40] Revelation carries forward the Old Testament figure likening God's people to a woman, the "daughter of Zion" or "daughter Zion." The Gospels of Matthew and John, quoting Zechariah 9:9, apply this term to the followers of Jesus who hailed him upon his entry into Jerusalem: "Do not be afraid, O Daughter of Zion; see, your king is coming, seated on a donkey's colt."[41] The "daughter," *thugater* in Greek, who is promised in marriage to Jesus relates directly to the daughter of the king of Israel promised as the second item in David's reward.

---

35 Phil 2:7; John 17:5.
36 Matt 9:15; 22:2-13; 25:1-10; Mark 2:19-20; Luke 5:34-35; 12:36; John 3:29.
37 2 Cor 11:2.
38 Eph 5:31-32.
39 Luke 22:29-30; 1 Cor 6:2; Rev 2:26-27; 5:10.
40 Rev 21:9-10.
41 John 12:15.

The third part of the reward for vanquishing Goliath is a grant of liberty to the family estate, exempting it from royal levies. Even before a formal civil tax was established in Israel that consumed a tenth of the land's produce, the king could demand a portion of goods or services including grain, oil, wine, fruit, livestock and the labor of servants.[42] One clue as to the typological meaning is the word that describes this debt relief, *hopsi* in Hebrew, meaning "set free." The corresponding term in the Greek text of 1 Samuel 17:25 is *eleutheroo*, and we find this word applied in the New Testament to the recovery of the universe itself through the ministry of Christ and his glorified church.

In Romans Paul reflects on the newness of life Christians enjoy through the operation of God's Spirit, the same Spirit that accomplished the resurrection of Jesus.[43] In the future, Paul says, the people of God will be glorified as joint heirs with Christ.[44] As we have just seen, the first two parts of David's reward are symbolized by these very events, namely, the resurrection of Jesus to glorified existence and his being united with the faithful. Paul next contemplates a third event, the glorification of the physical world:

> The creation waits in eager expectation for the sons of God to be revealed. For the creation was subjected to frustration, not by its own choice, but by the will of the one who subjected it, in hope that the creation itself will be liberated [*eleutheroo*] from its bondage to decay and brought into the glorious freedom of the children of God.
> —Romans 8:19-21

The "sons of God," believers, are "revealed" as co-rulers with Jesus at the time of his return, inaugurating an age of universal renewal.[45] At Matthew 19:28 this transformation of the material world is called the *palingenesia*, the "regeneration." In Acts Peter calls it the restoration of "all things," *panta*, as foretold by the Hebrew prophets.[46] "Behold, I am making all things new," God says at Revelation 21:5. We know from the New Testament that a house, *oikos* or *oikia*, is an appropriate symbol for

---

42 1 Sam 16:18-22.
43 Rom 8:11.
44 Rom 8:17.
45 Col 3:4.
46 Acts 3:21.

"all things" comprising the universe. Ephesians says that God through Christ will reconstitute "all things" in heaven and earth by means of an *oikonomia*, literally a "house administration."[47] "Every house [*oikos*] is built by someone," the author of Hebrews observes, "but God is the builder of everything [*panta*]."[48] *Oikos* in our story from 1 Samuel, meaning as it does not just the dwelling but the land and everything associated with it, is especially well suited to represent creation both animate and inanimate.

In Chapter 1, when we examined the story of the band of debtors David gathered around him during his exile, we saw that sin is likened in the Scriptures to indebtedness. The same concept is at work in third part of David's reward. The creation labors under the debt of sin just as every estate in Israel carried the royal levy. The created world "groans in pain" under this burden, Paul says, in the same way each of us groans in a body vulnerable to old age, disease and death.[49] The fall of man into sin meant the fall of the rest of material creation along with him. Understanding the nature of the fall is therefore important to grasping all that is involved in reversing it.

According to Genesis, God prepared the universe in successive steps until, with the creation of man, it at last began to reflect the divine image. It is apparent, however, that while God completed his own part of the project, he intended further progress to be made by man himself. God put all creation in subjection to man and woman, and we tend to assume, incorrectly, that this refers to the power human intelligence has always afforded man over his environment.[50] Instead, the Bible says that the mandate over creation has never been carried out except as Jesus is poised to exercise it.[51]

Having creation in subjection means more than tinkering clumsily with the created order as man does now, often with destructive results. Paul in Philippians says that Jesus will transform the bodies of believers to be like his own "by the exertion of the power he has even to subject

---

47 Eph 1:10.
48 Heb 3:4.
49 Rom 8:22-23.
50 Gen 1:28; Ps 8:6.
51 Heb 2:8-9.

all things to Himself."[52] Holding creation in subjection means being able to glorify it, having the means to alter physical reality from the inside out in ways undreamt of by man in his present state.

From the beginning man was intended to have the powers we glimpse, for example, in the miracles of Jesus. With rebellion against God man's potential to develop these powers, along with the effects they were intended to have on creation, was lost. Like a rose bud bitten by frost just as it begins to open, the created order was crippled before the beauty implanted in it by God could unfold. To beings who have known nothing else, a stunted and dying world looks natural, looks in fact as if it were the only kind of world possible. A transformed world can be imagined only through metaphor, in the same limited way that a person born deaf might try to imagine a world of sound. It is exactly that—a transfigured world—that is promised as the eventual result of Jesus' victory on the cross.

Epilogue to a Duel

With its last component in place the triple reward shimmers as the prophetic jewel of the David and Goliath narrative. Not only do the three elements correspond in their basic import with the reward of Jesus, their order reflects the sequence in which the fulfillments occur. To make the case airtight, the identifiers for the symbolism include key words found in the Greek text of 1 Samuel: *ploutos*, "riches"; *thugater*, "daughter"; *eleutheroo*, "liberate"; *oikos*, "house." In terms of typological prophecy the reward of David is capable of standing on its own, but as we have seen it is part of a narrative that portends the work of Jesus in other respects.

I noted several chapters ago that no illustration can represent its subject perfectly. The mechanical limitations of the David and Goliath narrative still allow for an ingeniously elaborate collection of figures. When Jesus evokes David's triumph in his brief parable about the "strong man," his application is better served by putting the enemy in a house (a palace in Luke) rather than on a battlefield. But even this revised imagery corresponds to the story in that the territory Satan claims

---

52 Phil 3:21, NASB.

is the created world humans inhabit, exactly what is represented by the family "house" mentioned in connection with the reward.

Inevitably there is roughness in equating a physical victory such as David's with the moral and spiritual victory Jesus gained on the cross. The defeat Jesus administered to Satan does presage the actual destruction of the great adversary. The Son of God shared our humanity, Hebrews says, "so that by his death he might destroy him who holds the power of death—that is, the devil."[53] But that destruction is reserved for an unknown time in the future. This two-stage campaign against Satan does not lend itself to portrayal in terms of a single episode, but it is hinted at in the narrative. David "kills" Goliath with a stone in that he deals him a mortal blow, but it is when David stands over the Philistine and beheads him with his own sword that Goliath definitely is put to death.[54]

In another event from the conclusion of the story, David takes Goliath's head to Jerusalem.[55] Doubt has been raised about this claim on the grounds that at the time of the duel with Goliath Jerusalem was in the hands of another hostile people, the Jebusites. The criticism is unwarranted. The Jebusites controlled the "stronghold" or fortified portion of the city, not necessarily the entire area.[56] A custom of the time was to exhibit body parts of prominent adversaries as trophies.[57] It would have been typical for David to hang the head of an enemy champion in plain sight of the Jebusites, who lived near his home town of Bethlehem and who probably exchanged taunts with their Israelite neighbors regularly.

Historical background aside, the messianic imagery is obvious. The future reign of Jesus is closely associated with Jerusalem. In the book of Revelation, the vision of Jerusalem in splendor in chapter twenty-one follows closely the death blow dealt to Satan in chapter twenty.

If typological foreshadowing runs through "David and Goliath" from beginning to end, the New Testament writers appear oblivious to it. Because his version of the "strong man" parable portrays Jesus as

---

53 Heb 2:14.
54 1 Sam 17:51.
55 1 Sam 17:54.
56 2 Sam 5:6-9.
57 1 Sam 31:8-12; 2 Sam 4:8, 12.

overcoming a heavily armed warrior, Luke comes closest to openly suggesting a link to the story. But consider how many elements are lacking from Luke's writings. He does not speak explicitly about the preexistence of the Son nor about him having laid aside his divine grandeur in order to descend into the world; these must be referenced in John's Gospel and the letters of Paul. Nor does Luke ever associate "riches" with "glory," as would be natural if he saw David's reward as predictive of Christ's.

What is true of Luke is true of every other New Testament writer inasmuch as no single source contains more than a partial list of the symbolic elements we have reviewed. Instead, the fulfillment of "David and Goliath" is a mosaic discernible only when we expand our field of vision to take in the entire New Testament. If Christian teachings about Jesus were invented in order to correspond to David's heroics, then the project somehow was coordinated among writers working at different places and times, just as in the other examples we have examined.

Having explored the link between David and Jesus, it is time now to turn to another character who, like David, was a young man of promise.

10

The Son of Joseph

There is a strain of Jewish tradition, dating back at least to the early second century, that predicts two Messiahs, a victor called the son of David preceded by a martyr called the son of Joseph. To appreciate the logic of a double Messiah, it helps to understand the dual nature of Israel itself during the Biblical period.

When Jesus lived there were two rival peoples, consisting of the Jews, whose homeland was Judea, and the Samaritans, who inhabited the district just north of Judea and south of Galilee. Before there were two peoples, there were two Israelite kingdoms, the nation of Judah with its capital at Jerusalem and the nation of Israel with its capital at Samaria. Before there were two kingdoms, there were two tribal factions within a single nation: a federation in the north led by the large tribes of Ephraim and Manasseh existing uneasily alongside the "super tribe" of Judah in the south. Long before that, as the book of Genesis tells it, there was a festering rivalry among the sons of Jacob who fathered the tribes. The division within Israel goes back farther yet, however.

At its root, the bifurcation of the Hebrew people arose from two circumstances. The first was a trick played on Jacob by his uncle Laban. Return for a moment to the Genesis narrative that was the subject of Chapter 7. The story tells how Jacob arrives in Syria to stay with his relatives and first meets his cousin Rachel when he waters her sheep.

Jacob falls in love with Rachel and agrees to serve her father Laban seven years in order to marry her. When the time is up, Laban cynically forces Jacob to marry Rachel's older, less attractive sister Leah at the same time.

And so Jacob comes to have as wives two sisters who are bitter rivals and whose ill feelings by various turns come to be reflected in their children. The strife-prone triangle left its mark in the Mosaic Law, which forbids a man ever again to marry both a woman and her sister.[1] It also left a legacy of internecine conflict between the descendants of Leah's most prominent son, Judah, and those of Rachel's firstborn, Joseph.

The other circumstance contributing to factionalism within Israel is the natural division between the farmlands and pastures along the northern banks of the Jordan river and the slightly drier, less accessible hill country to the south. Over time the identities of tribal groups settling in these areas were reinforced by geography. "Judah is to remain in its territory on the south," Joshua 18:5 intones, "and the house of Joseph in its territory on the north."

The symmetry of the division can be seen in the location of patriarchal shrines. Abraham set up altars at Shechem and Bethel in the north and at Hebron and Moriah (at or near Jerusalem) in the south.[2] The tabernacle, the precursor of Yahweh's temple, possibly resided first at Shechem near Mt. Gerizim and then for generations at Shiloh midway between Bethel and Shechem in the territory of Ephraim. Eventually the tabernacle was relocated permanently to Jerusalem, the capital of Judah and of Israel as a whole prior to the division of the kingdom.

Brothers Against Brother

The way this rivalry played out among the sons of Jacob is well known from the story of Joseph, which takes up the last third of the book of Genesis. Joseph, born late to Jacob's beloved but long-childless wife Rachel, becomes Jacob's personal favorite, provoking resentment among the older sons. Most directly threatened is the fourth oldest, Judah, who stands to become the family leader as a result of Reuben, Simeon and Levi each having forfeited the birthright through miscon-

---

1   Lev 18:18.
2   Gen 12:6-7; 12:8; 13:3-4, 18; 22:2, 9.

duct. The hatred of the older brothers toward Joseph is so intense that they plan his murder, but later decide to sell him as a slave to traveling merchants instead. The brothers then lead Jacob to believe that Joseph has been killed and dragged off by wild animals.

Joseph is resold as a slave in Egypt, where his divine gift of prophecy allows him to rise above hardship and imprisonment and become civil administrator at the right hand of Pharaoh. After several years a great famine arises, a famine that Joseph has foreseen and for which he has prepared Egypt. Jacob's sons travel to Egypt to buy grain and have an audience with Joseph, unaware of his identity. Joseph secretly tests the attitude of the brothers toward his younger brother, Rachel's second son Benjamin. Under Judah's leadership, the men demonstrate that they have put aside their jealousy toward Rachel's children. Joseph is reconciled with his brothers and arranges to bring them, their families and his father Jacob to Egypt to live.

Joseph's Long Shadow

Points of resemblance between Joseph and Jesus quickly become apparent. Both men are marked early as sons of destiny and both arouse deadly opposition from their associates. Joseph is not put to death literally, but death is evoked repeatedly in connection with his enslavement. The brothers had originally planned to kill Joseph, and are sure that by selling him they are rid of him forever. They later claim that he is dead, and Jacob believes him to be dead. They eventually speak about their accountability for their brother's blood as if their crime is tantamount to murder.[3]

When Joseph reveals himself, it is as if he has returned from the grave. Not only is Joseph "resurrected" in relation to his family, at the same time he is found to be deputy ruler of the leading world power of the day, Egypt, and the one who holds the key to the survival of his brothers. These events correspond to the New Testament gospel message, which says that the resurrected Jesus has been enthroned at the right hand of God as divine arbiter of life and death.

When we examine the alignment closely, the resemblances become more intricate. In Genesis Joseph reveals himself privately to his eleven

---

3   Gen 42:22.

brothers.[4] In the gospels, it is only when the resurrected Jesus is about to appear to the eleven remaining apostles that he refers to them as his brothers.[5]

The reason for eleven brothers being present is different in the Gospels than in Genesis, resulting from the defection of Judas Iscariot. It is unlikely that the Gospel writers would resort to a device as elaborate as Judas' betrayal solely to create the numerical agreement. Nor does it seem artificial that the disciples are frightened and must be reassured by Jesus that it is really him standing before them, yet this likewise mirrors what takes place between Joseph and his brothers. Until Joseph makes his identity plain, his brothers fail to "recognize him," *epignosan auton*, just as Jesus' disciples do not "recognize him," *epignonai auton*, until he allows them to do so.[6]

Before Joseph makes himself known to his brothers, he partakes of a special dinner with them. The steps taken in advance of the meal are described in the Septuagint at Genesis 43:16-25. Joseph tells his "house steward," *to epi tes oikias auto*, to slaughter, *thuo*, animals for a feast. The steward must "make preparation," *hetoimazo*, because Joseph soon will eat with the men from Canaan.

The eleven brothers are conducted to the house in advance of Joseph, who is to join them when the feast begins. Water is brought so that their feet can be washed. The brothers themselves also "make preparation" by setting out delicacies they have brought as gifts. Several foods including meat are on the menu, but when Joseph calls for food he mentions only the staple of every meal. *Parathete artous*, Joseph commands his servants, meaning, "Serve bread."[7] Despite having domestics to attend his every wish, Joseph serves his brothers out of his own portion. The men also "drink freely" together, and from the verb used in the Hebrew text of these verses we know the beverage was wine.

Compare Joseph's banquet to the "Last Supper" that Jesus holds with his apostles the night before his death. The account, as found at Mark 14:12-25 and in the other Gospels, begins on the day when lambs are "slaughtered," *thuo*, for the Passover feast. Jesus tells two of his disciples

---

4   Gen 44-45.
5   Matt 28:10; John 20:17.
6   Gen 42:8, LXX; Luke 24:16; cf. John 20:14.
7   Gen 43:31, LXX.

to follow a man carrying a jar of water until he enters a house. They are to ask the "house steward," *oikodespotes*, on Jesus' behalf about a room where he and those with him can eat the Passover. When they do as instructed, the steward conducts them to a room that already been "prepared," *hetoimos*. The two disciples themselves then "make preparation" in advance of Jesus' arrival.

We may assume that lamb is eaten when Jesus comes, but it is never actually mentioned. As the meal proceeds Jesus takes water, perhaps from the jar delivered earlier, and washes the apostles' feet. Judas Iscariot quietly leaves, so that eleven men remain with Jesus. It is at this point that Jesus takes bread and gives it to the disciples, followed by a cup of wine, as signs of spiritual communion.

The apostles, chosen both to represent a faithful remnant within fleshly Israel and to lay the foundation for a spiritual nation, were Jesus' brothers in a special sense. More broadly, all Jews alive in Jesus' day, including his enemies, were his "brothers."[8] What Joseph says to his brothers as he reveals himself to them bears comparison to what the Jews in general are told by Jesus' representatives after his resurrection. Joseph discloses that he is the one whom his brothers "sold into Egypt," but then consoles Judah and the others that God has brought a good result out of their sinful act. "Do not be distressed and do not be angry with yourselves for selling me here," he says, "because it was to save lives that God sent me ahead of you."

Peter's appeal regarding Jesus, as recorded in Acts, is similar to that of Joseph. After accusing Jews at the temple of having delivered Jesus into the hands of Pilate and disowned him as worthy of death, Peter says, "Now, brothers, I know that you acted in ignorance, as did your leaders. But this is how God fulfilled what he had foretold through all the prophets." Jesus, whom Peter calls the "author of life," now can wipe away the sins of his Jewish brothers and bless them with "times of refreshing" from God if they turn to him.[9] God has made Jesus Lord, Peter says, echoing Joseph's words to his brothers, "God has made me lord of all the land."[10]

---

8 Heb 2:11.
9 Acts 3:17-19.
10 Acts 2:36; Gen 45:9, LXX.

The salvation Joseph provides for his brothers comes in the form of bread, *artos*, to sustain them and the choicest land, *ge*, to live on as their inheritance.[11] Alluding to images found elsewhere in the Scriptures, Jesus promises the "bread [*artos*] of life" to those who come to him for salvation along with a renewed "earth," *ge*, as an inheritance.[12] The plea of the masses who come to Joseph is, *dos hemin artous*, "Give us bread." A virtually identical request, *dos hemin ton arton*, is made of Jesus by the crowds that throng to him.[13] In order to be given bread by Joseph, those who come to him must "do [*poeio*] whatever [*ho ean*] he tells you." In order to receive wine from Jesus at a wedding feast, the attendants must "do [*poeio*] whatever [*hoti an*] he says to you."[14]

The order in which lives are saved by Joseph also has a spiritual fulfillment. At the start of the famine he begins offering stored grain for sale, but the narrative does not immediately speak about lives being saved. When Joseph's brothers come from Canaan, he gives them grain and land "to save your lives by a great deliverance."[15]

As the famine deepens, the people of Egypt run out of money to buy from the royal granaries. Joseph agrees to continue supplying them on the understanding that everything they own, including their very lives, now belongs to Pharaoh; when the land again produces, a fifth will be given to Pharaoh in token. The Egyptians agree to Joseph's terms while declaring, "You have saved our lives."[16] In this way the family of Jacob is saved first, and afterward the people of Egypt.

Jesus, like Joseph, ministers salvation first to the "family of Jacob," the Jews. When a Greek-speaking Syro-Phoenician woman asks Jesus to cure her daughter, he initially refuses, saying that it is not proper to take the bread of the "children," meaning the Jewish people, and give it to the "dogs," that is, Gentiles. The woman persists, reminding Jesus that pet dogs eat the children's leftovers in the form of crumbs that fall from the table. Jesus rewards the woman's tenacity by healing her daughter.[17]

---

11 Gen 45:18; 47:11-12, LXX.
12 John 6:35 cf. Isa 55:2-3; Matt 5:5 cf. Ps 37:11.
13 Gen 47:15, LXX; John 6:34.
14 Gen 41:55, LXX; John 2:5.
15 Gen 45:7.
16 Gen 47:25.
17 Matt 15:22-28.

The incident with the Gentile woman highlights the principle found repeatedly in the New Testament that salvation is offered "to the Jew first and also to the Greek," "Greek" here standing for "Gentile."[18] Apart from this order of Jew first and then Gentile, "the same Lord is Lord of all and richly blesses all who call on him."[19] The order is reflected as well in the Bible text, with the Hebrew books of the Old Testament (and minor portions of certain books in Aramaic) coming before the Greek Septuagint version and the Greek writings of the New Testament.

The priority of Jews over Gentiles is acted out even within the Jewish population of the early church. Christian widows in Jerusalem who converse primarily in the Gentile language of Greek, as opposed to Hebrew or Aramaic, at first fail to receive their daily allotment of food. Greek-speaking ministers are appointed to correct the inequity in a manner reminiscent of the way Greek-speaking missionaries such as Paul will later take the gospel to the Gentiles.[20] The metaphorical significance of food is apparent here as it is in Jesus' remarks to the Syro-Phoenician woman, in which the food is specifically said to be bread. This is an identifier for the coding in the Genesis narrative, where "grain" and "bread" are used interchangeably to describe Joseph's provisions for the people.[21]

The Exaltation of Christ in the Joseph Story

If, as already seems apparent, Joseph encodes Jesus as Christ, then God is typically represented by Jacob in the first part of Joseph's story and by Pharaoh in the last part. Joseph is Jacob's best-loved child, the "son of his old age"; Jesus is the "beloved Son" of Yahweh, the Ancient of Days.[22]

Joseph's favored status provokes resentment on the part of his brothers, who cannot speak peaceably to him. In one instance, he brings his

---

18 Rom 1:16, NASB.

19 Rom 10:12.

20 Acts 6:1-6; 9:29; 21:37.

21 Cf. Gen 41:54; 42:2.

22 Gen 37:4; Mark 1:11; Dan 7:9; David, too, was the son of an aged father according to 1 Sam 17:12.

father a bad report about them after tending sheep in their company. When Joseph goes on to tell his brothers about dreams in which he sees them bow down to him, their jealously becomes murderous. Jesus, like Joseph, testifies against the teachers of the law that they have not cared properly for the "sheep" of Israel.[23] The elders of the Jewish Sanhedrin finally deliver him up for execution "out of envy," their jealousy piqued by Jesus' declarations that they must do him honor and that they will see him exalted at the right hand of God.[24]

When we turn to Pharaoh, the typical portrayal of God involves both close resemblance and specific identifiers. Pharaoh is the sovereign of Egypt, the leading power of the time. When Joseph interprets Pharaoh's dreams as predictive of a coming famine, he is made second in command of the empire. The term "second" is somewhat misleading, however, because he wields the full power of the monarchy. Everyone in the royal palace and all Egyptian officials must submit to Joseph, in the same way that the "angels and authorities and powers" of heaven are made subject to God's Son.[25] By this directive Pharaoh sets Joseph "over my house," *epi to oiko mou*, as God sets Jesus "over his house," *epi ton oikon auto*.[26] Then the narrative says that Pharaoh "appoints him over," *katestesen auton eph*, the whole land of Egypt, as the New Testament says of Jesus that God "appointed him over," *katestesas auton epi*, all of creation.[27]

Pharaoh gives Joseph a name denoting his exalted status and assigns heralds to make proclamation before him. The word the heralds use, *avrekh*, seems to be an order for those along Joseph's route to "bow the knee" or otherwise gesture their submission.[28] In Philippians Paul says about Jesus that "God exalted him to the highest place and gave him the name that is above every name, that at the name of Jesus every knee should bow."[29] Joseph refers to his high station as his "glory," *doxa*,

---

23 Gen 37:2; Matt 10:12-14; Luke 15:1-5; John 10:8-13.
24 Mark 14:62; 15:10; John 5:23.
25 Gen 41:40; 1 Pet 3:22.
26 Gen 41:40, LXX; Heb 3:6.
27 Gen 41:43, LXX; Heb 2:7.
28 Gen 41:43.
29 Phil 2:9-10.

again paralleling Jesus.[30] Pharaoh further gives Joseph the daughter of an Egyptian priest as his wife in the same way that Jesus is given a bride in the form of the church, just as we saw in the last chapter concerning David.[31]

"Only with respect to the throne," Pharaoh says to Joseph, "will I be greater than you." Yet according to the Hebrew text, Judah when speaking to Joseph implores, "Do not be angry with your servant, though you are equal to Pharaoh himself."[32] The same balance is reflected in New Testament concerning the Son. Paul says that everything and everyone in the universe is under Jesus' authority with a single exception: "It is clear that this does not include God himself, who put everything under Christ."[33]

Paul goes on to say that even the divine Son defers to God the Father. At the same time, when asked by the apostle Philip to "show us the Father," Jesus replies, "Don't you know me, Philip, even after I have been among you such a long time? Anyone who has seen me has seen the Father."[34] The positions of Joseph and Pharaoh are as finely calibrated to those of Christ and God the Father as can be expected from an illustration.

Were the New Testament writers influenced, on either the conscious or subconscious level, to shape their image of Jesus to conform to that of Joseph? Even if they were, it is puzzling that identifiers would turn up in such diverse books as the four Gospels, Acts, Philippians and Hebrews. More puzzling still is that such a fixation on Joseph would generate so few explicit references to him—less than a half dozen in the entire New Testament.

Whatever the likelihood or unlikelihood of a "Joseph obsession" among New Testament authors, it would fail to explain the identifiers present in the Psalms, Isaiah and other books of the Hebrew Scriptures. The symbolic alignment between Pharaoh and God, for example, is demonstrated by an unusual oath Joseph takes when he demands that the older sons of Jacob return with their youngest brother, Benjamin.

---

30 Gen 45:13, LXX; John 17:24.
31 Gen 41:45.
32 Gen 41:40; 44:18.
33 1 Cor 15:27-28.
34 John 14:9.

"As surely as Pharaoh lives," Joseph says, "you will not leave this place unless your youngest brother comes here." He repeats the oath twice in as many verses.[35]

Swearing by the life of God, of a pagan deity or even of a human being is common in ancient extra-Biblical literature and occurs in many variations. In the Hebrew Bible, however, the forms the oath takes are limited. Rarely, the speaker swears by the life of someone else in the second person: "As surely as you live, O king, I don't know."[36] In a few more cases, God is invoked and then a prominent individual, again in the second person: "As surely as the LORD lives and as you live, there is only a step between me and death."[37]

The vast majority of occurrences are third person references to God: "As surely as the LORD lives, if you had spared their lives, I would not kill you."[38] The Israelites of the northern kingdom are condemned for using the formula to swear by gods other than Yahweh.[39] Joseph's unique use of this oath invoking Pharaoh in the third person, without a hint of censure, is evidence for the coding of the narrative.

Joseph-Jesus Typology in the Psalms

We have seen that the correspondence of Jesus to Joseph entails a representation of God by Pharaoh in the last part of the Joseph narrative. We can further establish the Pharaoh-God equivalence by comparing the Genesis narrative with a poetic reference to Joseph in the Psalms and then following the same language through to the book of Acts. In Genesis chapter forty-one, as we saw earlier, Pharaoh sets Joseph over his palace (or, "house") and over all Egypt. In Genesis chapter forty-five, Joseph says that it is God who has made him ruler of Pharaoh's house and lord of all Egypt, with Pharaoh serving as an instrument of God's will. In the Psalms Pharaoh is described so as to make him difficult to distinguish from God. The entire section is worth examining:

---

35 Gen 42:15-16.
36 1 Sam 17:55.
37 1 Sam 20:3.
38 Judg 8:19.
39 Amos 8:14.

> He sent a man before them,
> Joseph, who was sold as a slave.
> They afflicted his feet with fetters,
> He himself was laid in irons;
> Until the time that his word came to
> pass,
> The word of the LORD tested him.
> The king sent and released him,
> The ruler of peoples, and set him free.
> He made him lord of his house
> And ruler over all his possessions.
> To imprison his princes at will,
> That he might teach his elders
> wisdom. —Psalm 105:17-22, NASB

Here the "king," like God himself, is the sovereign "ruler of peoples" who appoints Joseph as lord over all his house and possessions. The word in this passage for "possessions" also happens to be the word for "creation," both in the original Hebrew and in the Greek of the Septuagint. No one except Yahweh, the rightful ruler of all humankind, could fulfill these words in the absolute sense by awarding rulership over all creation.

Besides reinforcing the symbolism regarding Pharaoh and God, the section as a whole may be taken as a poetic summary of what the New Testament says about Jesus. In certain respects it is more appropriate to Jesus than to Joseph. Joseph was thrown in prison after being falsely accused by the wife of his Egyptian master and within a short time was made trustee with broad responsibility over other prisoners. Genesis says nothing about him being restrained with iron—a metal not smelted in patriarchal times—much less about his feet being injured in the process.

Nor did Joseph's testing in prison end as soon as "his word came to pass," since even after he successfully interpreted the dreams of two fellow prisoners he waited years until Pharaoh summoned him. It was rather Jesus who was hobbled brutally to a beam with iron nails and who was delivered out of death on the third day when his own words were fulfilled.

The Genesis narrative is equally silent about Joseph imparting wisdom to Pharaoh's "elders" or overseers. The New Testament, by contrast, is straightforward about Jesus being able to infuse the shepherds of the church with divine insight once he has been raised from the dead. Jesus says that it is only after he goes his way to the Father through death and resurrection that the Spirit of truth will be available to his disciples.[40] I reviewed this point in some detail in Chapter 7. The "Spirit of truth" provided by the resurrected Jesus is called at Ephesians 1:17 the "Spirit of wisdom."

Verse 20 of Psalm 105 says that the king "released" Joseph. The Septuagint here uses the Greek verb *luo*, "to loosen." But this word is not used in the Genesis narrative to describe Joseph's release from prison. Rather, *luo* is used by Peter to describe the release of Jesus from the "pangs" of death in the same sermon in which he declares that God has "made him Lord and Christ."[41] The verb alludes to the expression "cords of Sheol" and "cords of death" in Psalms 18:4 and 116:3.

The translators of the Septuagint chose to render "cords," *hebel* in Hebrew, with the Greek *odin*, "pangs," but the image lingered of ropes tightening around a victim. A similar metaphor associating death with constraint lies behind the Biblical expressions, "gates of Sheol," "gates of death" and "gates of Hades," which suggest walls and iron-clad doors like those of a dungeon.[42] We encountered that imagery in Chapter 5 in Jonah's words, "the earth barred me in forever," as if a crossbar or bolt prevented Jonah's escape.[43]

We can confirm prison as a symbol of death when we look at Israel's history. The return of Jews from exile is foretold in Ezekiel's vision of a valley full of dry bones that miraculously come to life.[44] A parallel prophecy in Isaiah says instead that the people will be freed from pits and prisons.[45]

If being dragged to a dungeon in chains and then released may be likened to death and resurrection, then Psalm 105 functions in every de-

---

40 John 14:25; 16:7.
41 Acts 2:24.
42 Job 38:17; Isa 38:10; Matt 16:18.
43 Jonah 2:6.
44 Ezek 37:1-14.
45 Isa 42:22; 43:4-14; cf. Ps 107:10-16.

tail as a symbolic portrayal of Jesus. The death-like imprisonment of Joseph is preceded by the humiliation of being sold as a "slave," *doulos*.[46] Traveling merchants purchased Joseph from his brothers for twenty pieces of silver, and presumably made a profit by selling him in Egypt for thirty or forty pieces. Jesus' life, according to Matthew's Gospel, was traded to his enemies by Judas Iscariot for thirty pieces of silver, the price of an able-bodied male slave at the time.[47]

Apart from that monetary transaction, Philippians says that through the incarnation God's Son accepted the form of a "slave," *doulos*.[48] Philippians 2:6-11 as a whole offers a strong parallel to Psalm 105:17-22.

The Death and Resurrection of the Envied Brother

So far, there are at least two ways in which the death-and-resurrection theme can be found in the Joseph narrative. First, Joseph is lost to his family as if dead, only to be reunited with them later. Within this long span of events Joseph experiences another type of journey into and out of death when he is unjustly thrown into prison, then released and exalted by Pharaoh. Look further at what happens to Joseph and yet another portrayal of death and resurrection becomes apparent.

The stage is set when Jacob sends the young man Joseph from Hebron north to Shechem where his older brothers are pasturing sheep. When he arrives in the area someone asks him what he is seeking and Joseph replies that he is "seeking," *zeteo*, his brothers.[49] Here we can make a connection to Jesus, who says that he has come to "seek," *zeteo*, and to save that which was lost, meaning the nation of Israel and along with it all of mankind.[50]

In Matthew Jesus says that a good shepherd who loses one of his sheep will "seek," *zeteo*, until he finds it. So, Jesus says, if your brother sins against you go and make him aware of his fault. If he listens to you, "you have gained your brother."[51] The course of action Jesus advocates

---

46 Ps 104:17, LXX (Ps 105:17, MT).
47 Matt 26:14-15.
48 Phil 2:7.
49 Gen 37:16, LXX.
50 Luke 19:10.
51 Matt 18:11-15.

is the one he himself follows. By coming to seek his brothers for their salvation Jesus enacts in a spiritual way the mission of Joseph at Shechem, but neither Joseph nor Jesus is favorably received.

The elders of the Jewish nation conspire against Jesus, following the pattern of Jacob's older sons. When the sons see Joseph coming from Hebron in obedience to their father, they plot to do away with him. They talk about throwing his body into a pit such as a cistern or sink hole and then telling Jacob that he has been killed by wild animals. As the plan unfolds, Reuben and Judah urge the other brothers not to go as far as murder. Joseph is thrown into the pit alive and then sold to merchants who are on their way to Egypt.

The Hebrew word for "pit," *bor*, is frequently used for a cistern or well, but it is also a synonym for the place of the dead. "For the grave cannot praise you," Hezekiah says to God in prayer, "those who go down to the pit [*bor*] cannot hope for your faithfulness."[52] In Joseph's case both meanings are present, since the abandoned well into which he is thrown is initially intended as his tomb.

The narrative contains an intriguing detail about this pit: "Now the pit was empty, without any water in it."[53] Water, as discussed in previous chapters, can symbolize the Spirit of God, one of the functions of which is to impart and sustain life.[54] In Ezekiel's vision of a valley of bones, the bones are said to be "very dry" to emphasize their lifelessness.[55] A dark hole without any life-sustaining moisture is an appropriate symbol of death, as are the depths of the ocean where, conversely, there is no air to breathe.

The waterless pit shows up again in the Hebrew Bible in a messianic prophecy from the book of Zechariah. In chapter nine of that book the "daughter of Zion" is told to rejoice because her king is coming, riding upon a donkey. Wars will cease and his rule will extend to the ends of the earth. Through the "blood of the covenant" God will set free the prisoners of the "pit without water." He will appear above his people and "blow the trumpet" to give them final victory over their enemies.[56]

---

52 Isa 38:18.
53 Gen 37:24, NASB.
54 Job 33:4; John 6:63; 2 Cor 3:6.
55 Ezek 37:2.
56 Zech 9:9-17.

The "prisoners of the pit" were probably understood at the time to be deportees who had never returned to Israel, including Joseph's descendants from the northern kingdom who were resettled by the Assyrians far to the east, in Media.[57]

Neither the Bible nor secular history records a formal return of Samaritan exiles (so named for Samaria, the political capital of the northern kingdom), and it is unlikely that more than a small number ever made the long journey home. The prophecies about Joseph's progeny returning to Israel from the "land of the enemy" never saw more than a token fulfillment.[58] Instead, the New Testament implies that hidden in the story of Israel's captivity and restoration, compared as we have seen to death and resurrection, is a sign of the actual resurrection of the dead at the return of Christ.

Jesus paraphrases language from Ezekiel's vision of the valley of bones when he describes the resurrection of the dead in the coming age.[59] Paul borrows imagery from Zechariah nine by saying that Jesus will descend with "God's trumpet" to gather his people, transforming those who are alive and raising those who are dead.[60] For Paul, then, the "pit without water" is not just a condition of exile but the grave itself, and the "land of the enemy" is the land of the "last enemy," death.[61]

Clearly, being cast into the waterless pit and then raised out again is one of three depictions of death and resurrection contained in narrative about Joseph. When traders bound for Egypt fortuitously appear and Joseph is sent with them, Jacob's eldest son Reuben is absent from the group of brothers. Not knowing what has transpired, Reuben later comes to the pit hoping to rescue Joseph only to find it mysteriously empty. "The boy isn't there! Where can I turn now?," he cries in anguish.[62] In an odd conjunction with the Gospels, his words are echoed by Mary Magdalene when she finds Jesus' tomb to be empty. "They have taken the Lord out of the tomb," she says to Peter and John, "and we don't know where they have put him!"[63]

To say it was Jesus' tomb that was found empty is true in a practical

---

57 2 Kgs 17:6; Zech 10:6-9.
58 Jer 31:16-18; Amos 9:14-15.
59 John 5:28-29.
60 1 Thess 4:16-17.
61 1 Cor 15:26.
62 Gen 37:30.
63 John 20:2.

but not in a legal sense. All four Gospels say that the tomb belonged to
a disciple, Joseph of Arimathea. In the first century Arimathea was a
"city of the Jews," but historically it had been the Israelite town of
Ramathaim-zophim (Haramat) in the "hill country of Ephraim."[64]
Arimathea was one of three "toparchies" or districts taken from Samaria
and annexed to Judea by Seleucid ruler Demetrius II Nicanor in 152
BC.[65] Joseph the disciple, appropriately enough, came from territory
once part of the "house of Joseph." The name Arimathea means "high
place" or "the height." Joseph's tomb, a cavity hewn out of rock, was a
type of pit, and may alternatively be decoded as "the pit of Joseph from
the place on high," that is, the pit into which the "Joseph" from heaven
was cast.

The tomb of Joseph/Jesus puts us on the track of another identifier
that turns on a double meaning. In Chapter 8, while analyzing the designation "son of David," I noted that Jesus makes a play on words when
he calls the repentant tax collector Zaccheus a "son of Abraham" because Zaccheus exhibits faith like that of Abraham.[66] Jesus does the
same in his remarks about the scribes and Pharisees who oppose him.
He says his enemies adorn the tombs of the prophets, and claim that if
they had lived in the days of their forefathers they would not have
joined efforts to kill the messengers of God. "You testify against yourselves," he continues, "that you are the sons of those who murdered the
prophets."[67]

In his comment about the sons of the killers of the prophets Jesus
once again exchanges the definition of "son" as a natural descendant for
that of someone who bears a resemblance to another as a son does to a
father. These different but sometimes coincident meanings of the word
explain, for instance, why Jesus is never called the "son of Judah" even
though his ancestry is traced through Judah. Genesis tells us that Judah
overcame the ill will he felt toward Joseph and became a just and compassionate man. But Judah never withstood the harrowing trials or
performed the heroic feats that would invite comparison of him to the
Messiah, as did his descendant David and his younger brother Joseph.

The potential for the word "son" to have more than one meaning is

---

64 Luke 23:51; 1 Sam 1:1.
65 1 Macc 10:30, 38; 11:34; Josephus, *Antiquities* 13.4.9.
66 Luke 19:9.
67 Matt 23:31, NASB.

important to our current study because Jesus was known as the "son of Joseph."[68] The miraculous conception of Jesus, famously reported in Matthew and Luke, does not affect his legal status as the son of the carpenter from Nazareth. Jesus was raised by Joseph as one of his own children.[69] Even Jesus' disciples acknowledge his legal parentage: "We have found the one Moses wrote about in the Law, and about whom the prophets also wrote—Jesus of Nazareth, the son of Joseph."[70]

Jesus' family designation when decoded identifies him as "a man like Joseph." Did God ordain that the man who raised Jesus and the man in whose tomb Jesus was buried both would be named Joseph? The occurrence of the same name in either instance could be coincidental. What is outlandishly unlikely is that by chance that particular name would connect Jesus with someone whose life circumstances are so elaborately aligned with his own.

Skeptics might try to sidestep the relationship between Jesus and Joseph by invoking a combination of literary influence and conspiracy. They may say it is natural that the memorable story of Joseph would echo in various ways through subsequent Hebrew writings. It is equally natural that the evangelists would attempt to present Jesus as heir to the legacy of Joseph. Is this a sufficient explanation?

As noted above, if the earliest Christians as a group were willing to falsify Jesus' life to make him more "Joseph-like," then they constituted a "Joseph cult" as much as a "Jesus cult," and we would expect the New Testament to draw considerably more attention to Joseph than it does. The theory also falls prey to the objection raised in Chapter 5 that the evangelists were bound by early traditions that cannot have been dictated by a single story from the Hebrew Bible. One of these traditions tells of the antipathy between Jesus and the Jewish religious leadership. Another describes the Eucharistic meal of bread and wine Jesus instituted among his disciples. Yet another testifies to Jesus' death, resurrection and exaltation.

Even where specific allusions to the Joseph story occur in the Gospels, the difficulty remains. For example, Luke's account of the crucifixion has one of the two criminals executed with Jesus repenting and

---

68 Luke 3:23.
69 Matt 13:55.
70 John 1:45.

being told by Jesus that he will enter Paradise.[71] The narrative calls to mind Joseph's experience with two of his fellow prisoners in Egypt. The similarity of the two situations and of the dialog, which focuses in either case on a request for remembrance, has long been remarked upon.

In theory, Luke could have invented these details because he saw a likeness already existing between Jesus and Joseph. Neither Christian nor secular scholars, however, believe that Luke wrote the first Gospel or that he could have invented the key features of Jesus' life that connect him to Joseph in the first place. In a later chapter we will learn why Luke especially would have appreciated anecdotes and reminiscences linking Jesus to Joseph. If there was a conspiracy to create a "greater Joseph," it must have begun long before Luke, and stretched across decades of time and wide expanses of geography.

Conspiracy theories aside, an appeal to cultural or literary influence relies upon a uselessly broad generalization. An example of this kind of reasoning would be to say that since every five-year-old child possesses a unique combination of talents, a kindergärtner who can perform the piano concertos of Rachmaninoff is "not unusual." The argument is flawed because even though each child is unique, the talents of young children ordinarily fall within a limited range. Likewise, the influence we might expect the Joseph to have on later writers from the same tradition is not enough to explain the appearance of type coding. Nor does it account for the cumulative weight of several coded narratives, most of which are not about Joseph.

Jacob moves a stone from the mouth of a well to water some sheep. Joseph rises from slavery to glory in Egypt and feeds his brothers. Jonah is expelled from the gut of large fish and preaches to the Assyrians. While it is safe to assume that a shared culture shaped the narratives, their similarities are too meager for us to see these events as closely related to one another, much less as versions of a single story. Their obvious differences notwithstanding, each of them encodes the resurrection of Jesus and the outpouring of the holy Spirit. The accounts are tied to Jesus by more than wispy strands of imagination, as we have seen. Not only do specific identifiers link type and fulfillment, in each case the episode is part of a larger story that itself is connected to Jesus by language and symbolic imagery.

---

71 Gen 40:13-15; Luke 23:40-43.

I began this chapter by observing that Jewish tradition came to include speculation about a suffering Messiah called the "son of Joseph." It is not hard to understand why, given the historical circumstances of the late first and early second centuries. The Jewish nation suffered catastrophic defeats by the armies of Rome in AD 70 and AD 132. Judeans by the thousands were either slaughtered, driven into exile or dragged into slavery as Joseph himself had been.

For some Jews, at least, it became as easy to identify with a Messiah who suffered at the hands of Israel's enemies as with one who strode effortlessly to victory. The patriarchal hero Joseph, wrongfully accused and imprisoned by Gentiles in Egypt, seemed a good model for such a figure. Nonetheless, Joseph was delivered to the Gentiles by his own brothers. It was his brothers who judged Joseph as a pretender to greatness whose self-exaltation, apart from violence or dishonesty, made him deserving of death in Gentile captivity. More than the Jewish people as a whole, one Jew in particular fulfilled the pattern set by Joseph—Jesus of Nazareth.

We have examined enough typological episodes to establish a pattern of foreshadowing of Jesus in the narratives of the Old Testament. These narratives were recorded either directly by the Hebrew prophets or by scribes who acted as editors and custodians of the prophetic tradition. If the prophets were destined to foretell in various ways the coming of Jesus, might their mission itself be encoded? That is the next question I will try to answer.

11

The Burden Bearers

To skeptics who find the Bible to be filled with absurdities, two of the silliest-sounding episodes have to do with donkeys. In the first of these, a donkey holds a conversation with a prophet named Balaam. In the second, the Israelite hero Samson slays a thousand Philistines with a donkey's jawbone.

To these we might add Matthew's narrative of the triumphal entry of Jesus into Jerusalem. Because Matthew says that a donkey colt and its mother were brought for Jesus to ride on, some early Christian pictures of the event show Jesus awkwardly astride both animals at once. Typological study reveals that these three donkey tales, though seemingly as comical as the long-eared beast itself, have a serious significance.

The story of Balaam unfolds as the nation of Israel, after wandering in the desert of Sinai for forty years, prepares to enter the land of Canaan from their encampment at Moab east of the Jordan. Even though the Israelites have taken no hostile action against the local Moabite and Midianite tribes, the Moabite king, Balak, begins plotting against them. Hesitant to engage them militarily, he sends for Balaam, a famed prophet and diviner. Balak's emissaries tell Balaam that he will be paid handsomely if he will come and place a curse on Israel.

Balaam is acquainted with Yahweh, the God of the Hebrews. When the prophet is alone Yahweh informs him that because Israel enjoys his blessing Balaam is forbidden to go with Balak's men.

The next day Balaam tells the emissaries that he cannot do what they ask, but within a short time a new delegation arrives from Balak with an even more tempting offer. Balaam seeks another answer from God, though Yahweh has already made his wishes clear. Balaam now is told to go with the men, but also is sternly warned that he will not be allowed to thwart Yahweh's will.

To understand what happens to Balaam on his journey to Moab, it is necessary to know the conclusion of the story. Three times Balaam will look upon Israel from a high elevation, make sacrifices and attempt to curse the people. Each time God will cause him to bless Israel instead, much to the consternation of Balak, who has no intention of paying Balaam for an unsuccessful mission.

Balaam then will counsel Balak to send out Midianite women to seduce Israelite men into illicit sex and idolatry, apparently realizing that Yahweh is a jealous God who will punish Israel for its sins. Many Israelites will succumb to temptation, bringing upon themselves a plague. Israel will respond by executing its own offenders and by striking out against the desert tribes with a terrible slaughter. Eventually, Balaam himself will be caught and killed for his part in the conspiracy.

The outcome of Balaam's journey proves that even though he professes a desire to do what Yahweh commands, from the start the prophet nurses a determination to get his hands on the reward offered by Balak. Seeing what is in Balaam's heart, God sends an angel to resist the prophet as he makes his way toward the plains of Moab. The angel stands in the road unseen by Balaam but visible to Balaam's donkey, which turns off the road twice to avoid the danger.

Balaam beats his mount to force her back on the path, but at last the angel stands where the road narrows, with a wall on either side. Unable to turn away, the donkey lies down in the road. When Balaam beats the donkey severely, God miraculously causes the animal to speak and ask Balaam why he is mistreating her. Balaam says that his frustration is such that he would kill her if he could. She answers by reminding him that she has always served him well.

Balaam is then allowed to see before him Yahweh's angel holding a sword of destruction in his hand. The angel tells Balaam that God is displeased with him and that the donkey has saved his life. The prophet is permitted to continue on with Balak's men only after he receives from the angel a final warning about opposing God—one that he foolishly refuses to heed.

Balaam and Israel

The New Testament cites Balaam as an example of the greed and covert rebellion manifested by insincere, licentious Christians. Balaam is listed alongside Israelite rebels who followed the clan leader Korah in an attempt to oust Moses, as told in another part of the book of Numbers. The association of Balaam with unfaithful Israelites leads to the discovery of parallels between the rogue prophet and the early Israelite nation.

Balaam and Israel alike set out on a journey across the desert that leads to the plains of Moab. The journey in either case has been authorized by God on the condition of strict obedience to his voice. But as they travel toward their destination the majority of the Israelites "go astray," *planao*, in their hearts in the same way that Balaam and those like him "wander off," *planao*, into sin.[1] God knows that the acquisitive attitude of the majority of Israelites will become apparent with time, as it does with Balaam: "When I have brought them into the land flowing with milk and honey, the land I promised on oath to their forefathers, and when they eat their fill and thrive, they will turn to other gods and worship them, rejecting me and breaking my covenant."[2]

A little digging turns up more specific resemblances between Israel and Balaam. As the Israelites approach the region east of Jordan, they request safe passage through Edomite and Amorite territory. They offer assurances to the local people by saying that they will "not go through any field or vineyard," meaning they will pass by such properties without disturbing them and will not steal water from local wells. "We will travel along the king's highway and not turn to the right or to the left until we have passed through your territory."[3]

The phrasing in these verses anticipates what happens just two chapters later as Balaam, riding on his donkey, passes by first a field and then a vineyard. It is where the road winds along the vineyard that "there was

---

1   Ps 94:10, LXX (Ps 95:10, MT); 2 Pet 2:15.
2   Deut 31:20.
3   Num 20:17.

no room to turn, either to the right or to the left."[4] Curiously, Balaam must carry on his journey in a manner that reflects the way Israel has been marching. This description of travel, combining the Hebrew words for "field," "vineyard," "turn," "right" and "left," occurs in no other passages of the Hebrew Bible.

Identical terms link Israel's professed intention to obey Yahweh and the same profession on the part of Balaam:

> The people all responded [*anah*] together, "We will do [*asah*] every-thing [*kol eth*] the LORD [*Yahweh*] has said [*dabar*]."
> —Ex. 19:8, cf. 24:3, 7

> Balaam answered [*anah*], "Did I not tell you I must do [*asah*] whatever [*kol eth*] the LORD [*Yahweh*] says [*dabar*]?" —Numbers 23:26

In the narrative in Numbers, God's angel goes forth to resist Balaam by "standing," *natsav*, with a sword in his hand. The angel positions him-self where the road narrows, literally in a "troublesome" place, *tsar*, ready to "slay" the prophet, *haragh*.[5] We encounter these terms again when in later history God "stands" as a "troubler," *tsar*, or adversary of Israel and "slays" them by the armed might of the Babylonians.[6]

When Balaam is viewed as a type of wayward Israel, something fasci-nating is revealed about his donkey's behavior. By seeing danger ahead that Balaam cannot and by attempting to divert him away from it, the donkey functions as did the prophets of Israel. The Hebrew Scriptures sometimes refer to the prophets as "seers," since by divine power they could see what was in store for the nation.[7] What lay ahead was the prospect of divine punishment if Israel continued down the path of unrighteousness:

> They worshiped idols, though the LORD had said, "You shall not do this." The LORD warned Israel and Judah through all his prophets and seers: "Turn from your evil ways. Observe my commands and decrees,

---

4   Num 22:22-26
5   Num 22:22-23, 26, 32-33.
6   Lam 2:4.
7   1 Sam 9:9.

in accordance with the entire Law that I commanded your fathers to obey and that I delivered to you through my servants the prophets."

But they would not listen and were as stiff-necked as their fathers, who did not trust in the LORD their God. They rejected his decrees and the covenant he had made with their fathers and the warnings he had given them. —2 Kings 17:12-15

Balaam's donkey tries to save her master by "turning aside," *shuwb*, from an encounter with the avenging angel, although the prophet drives her back onto the road once more. God would later say that his people, like Balaam, refused to alter their course. "Again and again I sent my servants the prophets," he says, "But they did not listen or pay attention; they did not turn [*shuwb*] from their wickedness or stop burning incense to other gods."[8]

Balaam's donkey is miraculously empowered to speak in order to call Balaam to his senses, just as the prophets were moved by the holy Spirit to utter God's messages.[9] Balaam "was rebuked for his wrongdoing," 2 Peter says, "by a donkey—a beast without speech—who spoke with a man's voice and restrained the prophet's madness."[10] The donkey persists in trying to steer Balaam away from disaster even though its efforts earn it three beatings and the threat of death. The same kind of abuse was endured by the Hebrew prophets. Luke's Gospel represents the line of the prophets as three servants who, one after another, are beaten by those to whom they are sent.[11] Mark's Gospel gives no number for the prophets, saying only that "some of them they beat, others they killed."[12]

After revealing himself to Balaam the angel says, "The donkey saw me and turned away from me these three times. If she had not turned away, I would certainly have killed you by now, but I would have spared her."[13] A parallel occurs later in Israelite history when God sends a prophet from Judah north to Bethel to rebuke the new king of Israel,

---

8 Jer 44:4-5; cf. Ezek 33:11.
9 2 Pet 1:21.
10 2 Pet 2:16.
11 Luke 20:10-12.
12 Mark 12:5.
13 Num 22:33.

Jeroboam, for setting up idol shrines. The prophet disobeys the instructions God gives him and as a result he is attacked and killed by a lion as he travels. Strangely, however, the prophet's animal is left unharmed. "The lion had neither eaten the [prophet's] body," the narrative says, "nor mauled the donkey."[14] In both stories the donkey, faithful to its humble calling, cannot be faulted for taking its errant master where he insists on going.

The angel's words about sparing Balaam's donkey anticipate what God will later say about prophets who loyally discharge their duty. "If you do warn the wicked man to turn from his ways and he does not do so," God tells the prophet Ezekiel, "he will die for his sin, but you will have saved yourself."[15]

Carrying the Weight

Weaker than the ox and slower than the horse, the donkey is nevertheless unrivaled for its versatility in agragrian societies. It can carry a substantial load, be fitted with a yoke as a draft animal or serve as an even-tempered mount. In Biblical times, the donkey's lot always was to bear burdens of one kind or another. The first occurrence of the Hebrew word for "burden," *massa*, connects it with the donkey: "If you see the donkey of someone who hates you fallen down under its load [*massa*], do not leave it there; be sure you help him with it."[16] This posture, "fallen down," *rabats*, is the one Balaam's donkey is forced to assume.

The word *massa*, besides meaning a burden such as a donkey might transport, in a few Biblical instances means a burden of responsibility like that Moses carried in leading Israel.[17] The most common figurative meaning of *massa* in the Hebrew Bible, though, is "oracle" or "prophetic declaration." Entire books of prophecy, and sections of those books, are introduced with the word:

> The sayings of Agur son of Jakeh—an oracle [*massa*] . . .
> —Proverbs 30:1

---

14 1 Kgs 13:28.
15 Ezek 33:9.
16 Exod 23:5.
17 Num 11:17.

An oracle [*massa*] concerning Babylon that Isaiah son of Amoz saw . . .
—Isaiah 13:1

An oracle [*massa*] concerning Moab . . . —Isaiah 15:1

An oracle [*massa*] concerning Damascus . . . —Isaiah 17:1

An oracle [*massa*] concerning Egypt . . . —Isaiah 19:1

An oracle [*massa*] concerning Arabia . . . —Isaiah 21:13

"Say to them, 'This is what the Sovereign LORD says: This oracle [*massa*] concerns the prince in Jerusalem and the whole house of Israel who are there.'" —Ezekiel 12:10

An oracle [*massa*] concerning Nineveh. The book of the vision of Nahum the Elkoshite. —Nahum 1:1

The oracle [*massa*] that Habakkuk the prophet received.
—Habakkuk 1:1

An oracle [*massa*]: The word of the LORD to Israel through Malachi.
—Malachi 1:1

The prophets delivered condemnations of rapacious foreign nations and predicted that restoration for the Hebrew people would come only after catastrophe overtook the kingdoms of Judah and Israel. Such messages won little popularity for those who, in effect, had to carry them from Yahweh to their intended recipients.

Prophetic warnings were even more burdensome to deliver than they were to hear. Jeremiah was so weighed down by the task of calling Judah to account that at one point he longed to cease prophesying. "Whenever I speak," he laments, "I cry out proclaiming violence and destruction. So the word of the LORD has brought me insult and reproach all day long." But when he tried to hold back, the word became like a "fire in his bones" and he could not hold it in.[18] So, like heavily-laden donkeys, the prophets shouldered the weight of bringing God's

_____

18 Jer 20:8-9.

messages to the people and then "carried" the people themselves by enduring their complaints, insults and hostility.[19]

Donkeys are no longer a feature of everyday life in developed countries, but the English-language expression "donkey work" still refers to menial labor done by humans as well as animals. The servants or slaves who performed such labor in Biblical times, too, functioned as the human equivalent of donkeys. Returning to what 2 Peter says about Balaam's donkey speaking with a human voice, we find that the word used for the animal is not precisely the Greek word for ass or donkey, *onos*, but rather the word *hupozugion*.

Hupozugion is compounded from *hupo*, meaning "under" and *zugos*, meaning "yoke." Originally the word referred to any animal that could bear a yoke, but it came to be applied primarily to the donkey; in the Septuagint and the New Testament *hupozugion* is not used of any other animal. The status of slaves as "donkey workers" is evident from the fact that they, too, are spoken of as being yoke-bearers: "All who are under the yoke [*hupo zugon*] of slavery should consider their masters worthy of full respect."[20]

In keeping with the correspondence implied by donkeys and slaves both being under yoke, the Hebrew prophets are referred to as God's servants or slaves. In the verses quoted earlier from 1 Kings 17, in which God reminds the Israelites that he has warned them repeatedly to change their course, he says in verse 13 that his orders have been delivered "through my servants the prophets." In verse 23 God's "servants the prophets" are mentioned again. Though all Israelites were servants of God broadly speaking, the prophets in particular warranted that designation, as in these further examples:

From the time your forefathers left Egypt until now, day after day, again and again I sent you my servants the prophets. —Jeremiah 7:25

We have not listened to your servants the prophets, who spoke in your name to our kings, our princes and our fathers, and to all the people of the land. —Daniel 9:6

19 Num 11:12-14.
20 1 Tim 6:1.

> Surely the Sovereign LORD does nothing without revealing his plan to
> his servants the prophets. —Amos 3:7

The identification of prophets as God's servants or slaves occurs more than twenty times in the Old Testament and twice in the New. Besides the figurative yoke of servitude worn by the prophets, we find that a literal yoke was worn by one of them, Jeremiah. "This is what the LORD said to me: 'Make a yoke out of straps and crossbars and put it on your neck.' "[21]

Jeremiah is told to wear the yoke as a visible demonstration of the way Israel and the surrounding nations, if they are to avoid devastation, must submit to Babylonian rule as a discipline from God. When the false prophet Hananiah takes the yoke of wood off of Jeremiah's neck and breaks it in repudiation of the warning, God instructs Jeremiah to replace it with a yoke of iron. "For thus said the LORD, I have put a yoke [*zugos*] of iron on the neck of all the nations, that they may serve the king of Babylon."[22] By virtue of his status as servant/prophet, Jeremiah accepts a yoke fit for a donkey as a sign that the nation should accede to God's will.

Converging lines of evidence, therefore, establish the donkey as a code symbol of the Hebrew prophets. These including the double meaning of the word *massa* as "burden/oracle," the identifier formed by the term "under yoke" as applied to donkeys and servants, the fact that a donkey was used by God as a prophet and that a prophet was made to resemble a donkey.

Further evidence comes from the story of how God makes known his choice for Israel's first king, in 1 Samuel chapters nine and ten. A young man named Saul, the son of a prominent Benjamite, embarks on a search for several stray donkeys belonging to his father. Instead of finding the animals, Saul finds instead the prophet Samuel, who anoints him with oil to designate him as future king.

Saul then comes upon a band of lesser prophets, among whom he falls into an ecstatic trance. The donkeys are mentioned repeatedly in the course of Saul's journey. Saul is twice assured that the donkeys have

---

21 Jer 27:2.
22 Jer 35:14, LXX (Jer. 28:14, MT).

been safely found, first when he meets Samuel and again just before he meets the other prophets. By searching for burden-bearing animals, Saul finds those who bear the prophetic word concerning his own destiny and that of the nation.[23]

We have already seen how effectively the symbolism of the donkey as prophet functions in the story of Balaam. Identifying the symbol is of greatest value, however, in understanding Jesus' entry into Jerusalem on the back of a donkey. The Old Testament book of Zechariah contains a prophecy that Israel's king would come "gentle and riding on a donkey, on a colt, the foal of a donkey."[24]

The source of Zechariah's prophecy is the story of young Solomon's coronation as king of Israel. 1 Kings tells how Solomon's older brother Adonijah attempts to preempt Solomon's accession to the throne. Adonijah assembles his partisans in order to declare himself king while David lies on his deathbed. When David learns that a struggle for the kingship is underway, he hurriedly has Solomon installed on the throne and makes it clear that he, not Adonijah, is David's choice as successor:

> [David] said to them: "Take your lord's servants with you and set Solomon my son on my own mule and take him down to Gihon . . .
> So Zadok the priest, Nathan the prophet, Benaiah son of Jehoiada, the Kerethites and the Pelethites went down and put Solomon on King David's mule and escorted him to Gihon. Zadok the priest took the horn of oil from the sacred tent and anointed Solomon. Then they sounded the trumpet and all the people shouted, "Long live King Solomon!" —1 Kings 1:33, 38-39

Zechariah, recognizing Solomon as a model of the Messiah, sees his ride on the king's mule as a pattern for the way the Messiah would be introduced to Israel. Zechariah exchanges the mule for a donkey, perhaps because hybridization, no matter how widely practiced, was

---

23 The narrative of Saul's "donkey chase" calls attention to the prophets yet another way when it pauses to explain that Israelites used to consult "seers" because "he who is called a prophet now was formerly called a seer" (1 Sam 9:9).

24 Zech 9:9.

forbidden under the Mosaic Law.[25] As an animal associated with peaceful farming, the donkey also may have seemed appropriate to a king who would bring universal peace. Lastly, the substitution introduced a symbol of the prophets into the formal presentation of the Messiah to Israel.

All the Gospels portray Jesus as fulfilling Zechariah 9:9 by entering Jerusalem on Passover Week riding a donkey. Matthew, however, includes a detail omitted by the other three accounts by having the disciples borrow two animals from the city, a donkey colt and its mother. "They brought the donkey and the colt, placed their cloaks on them, and Jesus sat on them."[26] "Them" may refer to the donkeys or to the cloaks on one of the donkeys. According to some critics Matthew is suggesting, ridiculously, that Jesus somehow straddled both animals at once. They claim that the unintended comedy comes from a misunderstanding of the passage in Zechariah. Using a typical Hebrew parallelism Zechariah says that the Messiah comes riding "on a donkey, on a colt, the foal of a donkey." Matthew's author allegedly took this poetic repetition literally and so put Jesus astride a donkey and its foal.

Another explanation of Matthew's anecdote about the two donkeys, one more charitable to the intelligence of the evangelist, is evident from a detail left out by Matthew but included by Mark and Luke, namely, that the colt had never before been ridden.[27] An animal so young likely would still be with its mother, and the mother would try to follow the colt unless prevented from doing so.[28] Assuming the disciples did bring both animals, we would expect the Gospel writers to be interested mainly in the colt because it was the colt that Jesus actually rode, according to Mark and Luke (John says simply, "a donkey").

Matthew's phrasing is vague in a way seen elsewhere in the Bible. When in the book of Revelation, for example, Jesus talks about "sitting down with" his Father on his "Father's throne," we might picture either a throne that resembles a love seat or else Jesus sitting on his Father's lap, when all the verse means is that he was enthroned in a place of

---

25 Lev 19:19.
26 Matt 21:7.
27 Mark 11:2; Luke 19:30.
28 See note to Matt 21:7, *NASB Study Bible*.

honor near his Father.[29] Matthew, using similarly broad language, feels it
necessary to say that the mother donkey is present when Jesus rides into
Jerusalem, but why?

A Donkey Colt for the Messiah

If Jesus' ride on the donkey has a coded meaning, it must have to do
with the Hebrew prophets. We have seen that the prophets carried the
word of God to the people the way a donkey transports a burden. Jesus
is called the "Word of God," the living expression of God's mind, so
carrying Jesus to the people of Jerusalem was an appropriate task for an
animal that symbolized the prophetic office.[30] To see the full significance of Jesus' actions we must examine the history of the prophets.

The patriarchs are given the status of prophets in the Bible, but the
prophets as God's messengers to the Israelite people began with Moses
in second millennium B.C.[31] The last prophet, Malachi, finished his ministry around 430 B.C. Though Israel continued to have priests, scribes
and rabbis after that time, the nation recognized no one as an inspired
prophet. The Seventy-fourth Psalm laments, "We are given no miraculous signs; no prophets are left, and none of us knows how long this
will be."[32] Today we know that prophets would not be seen for over
four centuries.

It seemed as if the line of the Hebrew prophets had ceased for good
until, unexpectedly, "a voice of one calling in the desert, 'Prepare the
way for the Lord . . . ' And so John came, baptizing in the desert region
and preaching a baptism of repentance."[33] The Gospels say that the
Jews of the early first century recognized John the Baptist as a genuine
prophet.[34] Also according to the Gospels, John directs his disciples to
Jesus as a likely candidate for the Messiah.

While John does not announce Jesus as the Messiah in so many
words, he does say that his own ministry will pave the way for the

---

29 Rev 3:21.
30 John 1:1; Rev 19:13.
31 Deut 18:18.
32 Ps 74:9; cf. Amos 8:11.
33 Mark 1:3-4.
34 Mark 11:32.

anointed. Someone greater is coming, he says, who will "baptize with the Holy Spirit."[35] He tells of a miraculous vision of a dove descending upon Jesus at the moment of his baptism, and he calls Jesus "the Son of God" and "the Lamb of God" who will take away sin. John's words would have identified Jesus as the Suffering Servant of Isaiah, who would die a sacrificial death "like a lamb."[36] From what we know of first century Judaism, this figure was not generally recognized as the Messiah. But we have earlier noted that the scriptural case for such an identification is strong. In Luke's Gospel, shortly before his execution John from prison sends representatives to Jesus asking him to confirm that he is indeed the "coming one," the Messiah-King.[37]

"For all the Prophets and the Law prophesied until John," Jesus says in Matthew's Gospel, "And if you are willing to accept it, he is the Elijah who was to come."[38] Jesus does not hesitate to number John with the earlier prophets. The last prophetic book of the Old Testament, Malachi, closes by saying that the next messenger to come will be "Elijah," the name Jesus applies to John.[39] Jesus also claims that John's testimony about him confirms that Jesus has come from God.[40] By giving favorable witness to the point of encouraging at least two of his own disciples to follow Jesus, John in a sense brings Jesus to the Jewish people.[41] This function of bringing Jesus to the nation is performed in a literal way by the young donkey colt on Passover Week. Is the donkey a graphic token that Jesus has come in the authority of God as proclaimed by John the Baptist?

John's surprising appearance as a representative of the old and seemingly extinct line of the Israelite prophets has a parallel in the Messiah himself. Isaiah calls the Messiah a "shoot" that sprouts up "from the stump of Jesse."[42] The line of Davidic kings had been reduced to vassal

---

35 John 1:33.
36 Isa 53:7.
37 Luke 7:20.
38 Matt 11:14.
39 Mal 4:5.
40 John 5:31-35.
41 John 1:35-38.
42 Isa 11:1.

rulers with the death of Josiah near the beginning of the sixth century BC and had ceased altogether with the destruction of Jerusalem by the Babylonians in 586 BC. The apparently dead "stump" of the Davidic dynasty would, against all odds, produce a new seedling or royal heir after several centuries.

If the symbolism of the donkey were expanded in a similar way to portray the revival of the prophetic tradition, we would expect the new prophet to be pictured as a young donkey colt born to old female. That imagery reflects a typical Biblical metaphor in which a body of people, such as the population of Jerusalem, is represented as a woman, a female, while individual persons are called sons and daughters of the group as a whole.[43] It also would harmonize with passages demonstrating that the actions of Balaam's donkey—a female—parallel those of the prophets collectively during Israel's history.

John's personal background supports this analysis. Elizabeth, John's mother, did not conceive him until she was long past child-bearing age.[44] Elizabeth had seemed to be as incapable of producing a son as the prophetic legacy was of producing a new messenger worthy of being set alongside Isaiah, Ezekiel, and Malachi. Then Elizabeth's husband, a priest named Zechariah, was told that by a miracle his wife would become pregnant. Elizabeth herself is shown assuming a prophetic role by twice speaking under the guidance of God's Spirit, once about Jesus and once about her own son, John.[45]

When Jesus sends his disciples to fetch a colt and, in Matthew's telling, a mother donkey along with it, the owners of the animals release them when they are informed that "the Lord needs them." They recognize that the donkeys ultimately belonged to God and are at the disposal of the messianic heir. Ownership here has to do with authority. David made his personal mule available to Solomon in order to show that Solomon enjoyed his father's unqualified backing.

The narrative in 1 Kings repeats three times that it is David's own animal that Solomon rides to his coronation.[46] We may understand the scene of Jesus riding on the donkey colt with the mother animal in tow

---

43   Ezek 23:4, 10; Hos 2:2-4; Gal 4:25.
44   Luke 1:18.
45   Luke 1:41-45, 60-63.
46   1 Kgs 1:33, 38, 44.

as portraying that he has arrived not only with the support of a contemporary prophetic witness, John, but in fulfillment of what was spoken by God's personal servants in the prophetic tradition.

What we suspect about the meaning of the donkey incident is verified by an exchange between Jesus and his enemies shortly after his arrival in Jerusalem. When Jesus drives moneychangers out of part of the temple court and begins holding teaching sessions there, the priests and elders confront him and demand to know "by what authority" he dares to act as he does.[47] Jesus offers to answer if they first will answer a question of his: "John's baptism—was it from heaven, or from men? Tell me!"

The priests spurn John the Baptist, but they are afraid to voice a negative opinion about him in front of a Passover crowd that holds John to be a martyred prophet. The priests and elders decline to answer Jesus' question, so he says he will give no reply to theirs. In fact, Jesus shrewdly has answered their question while seeming to avoid it. By invoking the name and prophetic stature of John, Jesus reminds all those present that a credible witness has vouched for him.

Having deflected his enemies' challenge, Jesus now takes the offensive by telling them and the gathered festivalgoers the parable of the vineyard and the tenants. As we saw when we took up this parable in Chapter 2, it compares God's people collectively to a vineyard, the leaders of the nation to hired cultivators and the Hebrew prophets to servants of the vineyard owner. The servants, sent to collect the fruit on the owner's behalf, are beaten or killed, as we noted earlier in this chapter. "He had one left to send, a son," Jesus continues, "whom he loved. He sent him last of all, saying, 'They will respect my son.' "[48]

Instead of respecting the son, the cultivators kill him and in turn suffer destruction at the hands of the owner. The parable puts Jesus in the company of the servants, except that he is the ultimate emissary, from the Father's bosom and vested with his full authority.[49] By calling attention first to John the Baptist and then to the line of Hebrew prophets, Jesus puts into plain words what is implied symbolically by his arrival on a donkey colt with the mother in tow.

---

47 Mark 11:28.
48 Mark 12:6.
49 John 1:13.

Wielding the Words of the Prophets

The skirmish at the temple deepens the resolve of factions usually at odds with one another, including Pharisees, Sadducees, and Herodians, that the common threat represented by Jesus cannot be tolerated.

Jesus, it should be noted, is not without sympathizers even among the religious elites. We know about the Pharisee Nicodemus and the Sanhedrin member Joseph of Arimathea from the Gospels, but they cannot be unique. Eventually, numbers of Pharisees and Sadduccaic priests will become Christians.[50] John's Gospel says that during the days leading up to the crucifixion, however, those in positions of influence who incline toward Jesus are too cowed to support him openly.[51] Opposers of Jesus may be momentarily frustrated by his ready answers and his way with the festival crowd, but they have the institutional machinery on their side.

Even while puzzling over how to have him arrested without touching off a riot, his enemies regroup and approach him again in an effort to undermine his teaching authority. A party of Pharisees and Herodians asks Jesus whether it is "lawful" to pay taxes to the Roman Caesar. They know that if Jesus answers in a way that seems to approve of the Roman presence in Judea he will be branded by many in the crowd as a collaborator. On the other hand, if he publicly opposes paying taxes to Caesar, he will be subject to arrest by the Roman governor.

Jesus asks to see a Roman coin bearing Caesar's likeness and then issues the famous dictum, "Give to Caesar what is Caesar's and to God what is God's."[52] His answer, while endorsing the paying of Roman taxes, denies that paying them is an acquiescence in whatever Caesar does that opposes the will of God. By answering wisely, Jesus forces his enemies again to retreat.

The reasoning implied by Jesus' answer concerning payment of taxes, combined with his reference to Caesar's "image," *eikon*, on the coin, leads us to the Old Testament book of Daniel. The traditional Jewish classification of the Scriptures places Daniel in the "Writings" section of the Hebrew Bible rather than in the "Prophets," but the title character

---

50 Acts 6:7; 15:5.
51 John 12:42-43.
52 Mark 12:17.

functions as a prophet and Jesus refers to him as "Daniel the prophet."[53]

The book of Daniel begins by recounting the initial subjugation of Jerusalem by the Babylonian crown prince Nebuchadnezzar. Taken back to Babylon as exiles, Daniel and his three companions are recognized as educated scribes and impressed into the service of the Babylonian court. Daniel's first personal encounter with Nebuchadnezzar occurs when Daniel is the only adviser who can correctly relate and then interpret a dream that has troubled the Babylonian ruler.

The dream is a vision of a great statue or "image," *eikon* in the Septuagint, representing the march of empires down through history. Daniel says that Nebuchadnezzar, and by implication the Babylonian kingdom as a whole, is represented by the statue's gold head:

> You, O king, are the king of kings. The God of heaven has given you dominion and power and might and glory; in your hands he has placed mankind and the beasts of the field and the birds of the air. Wherever they live, he has made you ruler over them all. You are that head of gold. —Daniel 2:37-38

Daniel's circumstances as well as his words leave no doubt that God has permitted Nebuchadnezzar to dominate the world of his time. God has even given him control of Jerusalem and allowed him to plunder its treasury and the precious articles of the temple. Daniel and his companions obediently serve Nebuchadnezzar, not because he is more powerful than Yahweh, but because for the time being their God has granted secular power to Babylon. God's continuing claim to sovereignty is apparent from the end of the dream, in which the messianic kingdom is pictured as a stone that smashes the image to pieces and then fills the earth.

The question of "God's due" becomes more urgent in the episode immediately following that of the king's dream. Nebuchadnezzar assembles civil servants of certain ranks, including Daniel's three companions, and commands them to signify their loyalty by bowing down to an image of gold that he has erected. Although Daniel's friends serve their Babylonian master dutifully, they refuse to break the law of their God

---

53 Matt 24:15.

by engaging in idolatry. "We will not serve your gods or worship the image of gold you have set up," they tell the king.[54] Incensed at their refusal, Nebuchadnezzar attempts to execute the three Hebrews by having them thrown into a fiery brick kiln, but God miraculously preserves their lives.

The lesson of the first three chapters of Daniel is precisely the one summarized by Jesus in his answer to the Pharisees and Herodians. Earthly emperors wield their power only at God's leave. Whatever claim such authorities make on their subjects' money and physical labor, God's exclusive right to worship remains paramount. Caesar's profile stamped into silver, like the head of gold representing Nebuchadnezzar, is of temporary duration, fit to be returned to its issuer in the form of taxes but not fit for worship. Jesus has encapsulated a key teaching of one of the prophets, Daniel, to rout his opponents.

Little time passes before other antagonists come to do battle with the meddlesome rabbi from Galilee. This time it is a contingent from the priestly sect of the Sadducees with a loaded question concerning the resurrection. Jesus refutes them by quoting from Exodus, which is part of the Pentateuch (first five Biblical books) and therefore one of the few books accepted by the Sadducees. Large portions of the Pentateuch likely were written by the first and greatest of the Israelite prophets, Moses, and all of it carries his authority, a fact Jesus draws attention to by calling it "the book of Moses."[55]

While replying to yet another question, apparently posed by one of the Pharisees, Jesus cites something written by David. David's prophetic gift was expressed in songs or "psalms." Introducing a quotation by saying, "David himself, speaking by the Holy Spirit, declared . . . ," Jesus stresses that it was as prophet that David wrote the verse he is citing, Psalm 110:1: "The LORD [Yahweh] said to my Lord [the Messiah] . . . " "Speaking by the Holy Spirit" is the defining characteristic of prophetic utterance. "For prophecy never had its origin in the will of man," says 2 Peter 1:21, "but men spoke from God as they were carried along by the Holy Spirit."

Jesus argues that God's Spirit led David to acknowledge the coming

54   Dan 3:18.
55   Mark 12:26.

Messiah as the Lord and Master even of David himself. After this last reply of Jesus the crowd at the temple goes on listening to him "with delight," but his enemies are silenced and "from that day on no one dared to ask him any more questions."[56]

Samson on Jawbone Hill

The triumph of Jesus over his adversaries, accomplished by deploying the words of the prophets against them, brings us to our final donkey episode, concerning Samson. Samson is sometimes called the "Hebrew Hercules" because of the stories about his great strength told in the book of Judges. Nevertheless, Samson's exploits against Israel's warlike neighbors, the Philistines, are intended not just as entertainment but as a sign that Israel worships the only true God.

In one of the stories, Israelites intimidated by the superior weaponry and aggressive disposition of the Philistines agree to surrender their champion, Samson. As soon as Samson is in Philistine hands, "the Spirit of the LORD came upon him in power."[57] Samson breaks his bonds, reaches for something to use as a club, and ends up killing a thousand enemy soldiers.[58] Regardless of the precise number of men killed, the point of the narrative is that in God's strength Samson, armed only with a discarded animal bone, can overpower an entire war party of Philistines.

The passage from Judges recounting Samson's victory is written tersely, in language vague enough to make translation partly a matter of guesswork. It also relies heavily on Hebrew word play. The club used by

---

56 Mark 12:37; Matt 22:46.

57 Judg 15:14.

58 The number of a thousand killed on a single spot is hard to envision regardless of Samson's strength, but evidence exists for inflation of such numbers as this with manuscript transmission. In Chapter 8 we noted that the height of Goliath varies in the text tradition. The Philistine champion "grows" from six-and-a-half feet in the Dead Sea Scrolls to eight feet in the LXX to over nine feet in the Masoretic Text. Among other examples: seven hundred charioteers in 2 Sam 10:18 becomes seven thousand in the later account at 1 Chron 19:18; the number of casualties given at 1 Kgs 20:30 is so unrealistically large that it cannot be taken at face value. Moreover, large numbers at times are used for dramatic emphasis, e.g., 1 Sam 18:7.

Samson is the jawbone of a donkey, and after he strikes down the Philistines with it he describes what he has done poetically:

> With a donkey's jawbone
> I have made donkeys of them.
> With a donkey's jawbone
> I have killed a thousand men. —Judges 15:16

The play on words is in the first two lines, which literally read, "With donkey jawbone donkey donkeys," or by a different translation of the last two words, "With donkey jawbone heap heaps." Samson may be saying, as in the NIV rendering, that he has made donkeys out of the Philistines. Alternatively, he may be using a word for "heap" that is nearly identical to the Hebrew word for "donkey" to say that his slain enemies have fallen one upon another. Either way, the effect is to focus attention on the nature of the weapon. Further attention is drawn to it by the name of the place where the incident occurs, given in verse 14 as "Lehi," meaning "jawbone," and in verse 17 as "Ramath Lehi," meaning "jawbone height."

Since the jawbone is the part of the human skeleton articulated in speech, the metaphorical equivalence between donkey and prophet suggests that Samson's club, when viewed typologically, relates to the speech or words of the prophets. What happens next only deepens the connection to prophetic speech.

"When he finished speaking," the narrative says, "he threw away the jawbone." Samson's words have been uttered in the power of the "Spirit of the LORD," as indicated by their form and timing. The poetry is part of the victory, spoken while Samson still holds the jawbone with which he has vanquished the enemy. He puts the weapon aside when his inspired declaration ends, as if resting his own jaw and that of the donkey at the same time.

Judges additionally says about the jawbone that it is "fresh," from the rarely used Hebrew adjective *tariy*. The word actually means "dripping," and shows the jawbone to be moist whether or not it comes from a recently dead animal. Water can symbolize God's Spirit, so water being associated with the jawbone might serve to connect God's Spirit with what the jaw represents. This detail reinforces the conclusion that jawbone stands for prophecy, that is, for speech suffused with the divine Spirit. Samson's use of it anticipates the way Jesus defeats his spiritual opponents in Jerusalem. Jesus' weapon consists of the words of the prophets, for which the moist jawbone of a donkey makes a quirky but memorable symbol.

Once Samson relinquishes the jawbone, gone too is his miraculous strength. It is replaced by a thirst so severe that Samson feels himself suddenly near death. "You have given your servant this great victory," he cries out to God. "Must I now die of thirst and fall into the hands of the uncircumcised?"[59] Besides initiating prophecy, the Spirit of God sustains life.[60] Thirst, or lack of the Spirit as represented by water, is closely associated with death in the Hebrew Scriptures. In a message of judgment against unfaithful Israel, God says, "I will make her like a desert, turn her into a parched land, and slay her with thirst."[61] Job observes that as "a riverbed becomes parched and dry, so man lies down and does not rise."[62] In Ezekiel's vision of the valley of bones, representing the hopeless condition of Israel, the dryness of the bones demonstrates their utter lifelessness.[63]

In a curious juxtaposition of metaphors, the character who speaks in the Sixty-ninth Psalm says that the "floodwaters" of death have engulfed him, but then adds, "I am worn out calling for help; my throat is parched."[64] Like Samson, who also pleads with God for deliverance, the Psalmist suffers from a dryness that shows death is imminent. The New Testament applies various portions of this Psalm to Jesus, including verse 21, which says that the Psalmist's enemies "gave me vinegar for my thirst."[65]

The Gospel writers portray Roman soldiers as offering the crucified Jesus a sponge soaked in vinegar, a liquid that the soldiers may have had on hand as a condiment.[66] In the accounts of Mark and Matthew, the

---

59 Judg 15:18.
60 John 6:63; 2 Cor 3:6.
61 Hos 2:3; cf. Isa 5:13-14.
62 Job 14:11-12.
63 Ezek 37:2.
64 Ps 69:2-3.
65 Mark 15:36; cf. Ps 69:9a/John 2:17; Ps 69:9b/Rom 15:3.
66 Mark 15:36; cf. Ruth 2:14.

event occurs shortly after Jesus' plea, "My God, my God, why have you forsaken me?" In John's Gospel the offer of vinegar, which could only worsen the raging thirst of a man dying of trauma and shock, follows Jesus' exclamation, "I am thirsty."[67] If we combine these versions, Jesus says, "My God, my God, why have you forsaken me? I thirst!" The gist of Jesus' outcry is the same as that of Samson. After having employed the words of the prophets to achieve spiritual victory, Jesus nevertheless is forsaken into the hands of his enemies. Strength is withdrawn from him and a torturous thirst accompanies the approach of death.

God answers the anguished prayer of Samson by opening "the hollow place in Lehi," so that a spring of water comes forth. "When Samson drank," the narrative says, "his strength returned and he revived." The water seems to have come from a fissure created in the bedrock at the bottom of a gully. The account concludes by saying that the spring continues to be known as En Hakkore, meaning "the spring of him who called out."[68] The word for the "strength" that returned to Samson is actually *ruach*, the word "spirit." The word for "revived" is the word for "lived." Samson undergoes a kind of resurrection, a sudden return of life that had been ebbing away. There are only three literal resurrections recorded in the Hebrew Bible, and the wording of one of them corresponds closely to the description of Samson's experience:

> Then he stretched himself out on the boy three times and cried [*qara*] to the LORD . . . The LORD heard Elijah's cry, and the boy's life [*nephesh*, soul] returned [*shuv*] to him, and he lived [*chayah*].
> —1 Kings 17:22

> Because he was very thirsty, he cried out [*qara*] to the LORD . . . Then God opened up the hollow place in Lehi, and water came out of it. When Samson drank, his strength [*ruach*, spirit] returned [*shuv*] and he revived [*chayah*]. —Judges 15:18-19

Although *nephesh*, "soul" or "living being," and *ruach*, "spirit," are distinguished in some contexts, in these two accounts they refer in

---

67 John 19:28.
68 Judg 15:19.

common to the life force that is restored.[69] The Alexandrine Text of the Septuagint has a parallel in the Greek wording of these passages similar to that of the Hebrew. In addition, the Greek verb for "lived," *zao*, found in the Septuagint version of Judges 15:19 is used of resurrection in the New Testament at Revelation 20:4.

The close resemblance of Samson's experience to a resurrection is coupled with resurrection typology. Samson is revived by fresh drinking water provided by God. Water is already implicated here as a symbol for God's Spirit by its association with the donkey's jawbone. The role of the water in relieving Samson's thirst is a further clue. In Chapter 7, we noted that Jesus invites everyone who is "thirsty" to come to him for "living water," which is said to refer to "the Spirit."[70] In the everyday language of the time, "living water" could describe spring water, like the water provided to Samson, as opposed to the less refreshing still water from a cistern.

The agency of Jesus' own resurrection, according to the New Testament, was God's Spirit. "If the Spirit of him who raised Jesus from the dead is living in you," Paul says, "he who raised Christ from the dead will also give life to your mortal bodies through his Spirit."[71] The death-dealing thirst that overtakes Samson and the miraculous provision of water to restore his life encode the death and resurrection of Jesus.

The Heaviest Burden

The interlaced episodes we have studied concerning Balaam, Samson and Jesus have more in common than the figure of the donkey. They collectively focus on the critical period in Jesus' ministry known as the Passion Week. It begins with Jesus' arrival in Jerusalem on a donkey. Unlike Balaam, he is not at odds with his mount. Nevertheless, by encoding the prophetic mission to Israel the Balaam narrative underpins Jesus' actions both in choosing to enter the city the way he does and in appealing to the prophets for his legitimacy. Other circumstances attending his arrival leave no doubt about where geographically that appeal will be made.

---

69 Cf. Isa 26:9, where the words function as synonyms.
70 John 7:37-39.
71 Rom 8:11; cf. 1 Pet. 3:18.

One who is greeted with acclamations that he is the "son of David" (i.e., "new Solomon") can have only the Jerusalem temple, the spiritual and psychological heart of the city, as his ultimate destination. When his personal authority clashes as it must with the institutional authority centered on the temple, Jesus is propelled swiftly toward his execution and, according to the Gospels, his resurrection. The events at the start of the week lead seamlessly into the fulfillment of the Samson narrative, which also draws on the donkey metaphor.

So far the donkey has conveyed us from Jesus' triumphal entry to the empty tomb on resurrection Sunday, but along the way the "burden bearer" saw its ultimate fulfillment in Jesus himself. We have seen that Jesus is set apart from the prophets as a group. "The prophets were until John."[72] "In the past God spoke to our forefathers through the prophets," the author of Hebrews concurs, "but in these last days he has spoken to us by his Son."[73]

Yet, Jesus too was a prophet, the Prophet *par excellence*. The crowds and the disciples so describe him.[74] Jesus accepts the designation when he says that a prophet is not honored in his own territory and that it is not appropriate for a prophet to die anywhere but in Jerusalem.[75] In keeping with the servant status of prophets, Jesus is the Suffering Servant of Isaiah. In his own words, he comes to serve rather than be served, even to wash feet as would the household drudge. Like the lowly donkey, Jesus toils under the yoke of service and offers it to others: "Take my yoke upon you and learn from me, for I am gentle and humble in heart, and you will find rest for your souls. For my yoke is easy and my burden is light."[76]

Jesus' yoke, which is "easy" because he bears it with and for his people, is an instrument of torture, the cross. "If anyone would come after me," he says, "he must deny himself and take up his cross and follow me."[77] The cross here stands for self-sacrifice in a broad sense, but we cannot read the verse without picturing Jesus carrying his cross to the

---

72 Luke 16:16.
73 Heb 1:1-2.
74 Matt 21:11; Luke 7:16; 24:19; John 6:14.
75 Mark 6:4; Luke 13:33.
76 Matt 11:29-30.
77 Mark 8:34.

place of execution. "It is good for a man to bear the yoke while he is young" says the Old Testament book of Lamentations, and just two verses later, "Let him offer his cheek to one who would strike him, and let him be filled with disgrace."[78]

The "yoke" in these verses is directly associated with Jesus' pre-execution ordeal. It is necessary here to correct the misconception perpetuated by Christian art and movies that Jesus managed to drag the entire cross from Pilate's residence to the outskirts of Jerusalem. A timber of indigenous hardwood long enough to hold Jesus securely a meter or more above the ground would be too heavy to be carried by a healthy man, let alone by a victim of beating and scourging who could barely walk. Rather, what was carried was just the crossbar, a rough-hewn beam that weighed up to half as much as a man.

Judging from available sources, it seems that the crossbar of the executional stake was placed across the shoulders of the condemned prisoner with his arms draped over it.[79] The prisoner was then paraded through the streets and finally hoisted up on a standing post. In this way the prisoner was led to his death resembling a donkey wearing a wooden yoke or bar.[80] Making the victim look literally asinine was an appropriate prelude to crucifixion, which had as its purpose public humiliation as well as torture. According to Mark, the exhortation of Jesus to "take my yoke upon you" was graphically enacted by Simon of Cyrene, who was pressed into service to carry the bar when Jesus' physical stamina gave out.

The oldest known picture of the crucifixion, dating to the third century or earlier, is from the wall of a house found on the Palatine Hill in Rome. The crucified Jesus is crudely drawn as a man with the head of a donkey. A second figure, below, kneels in an attitude of reverence. The caption, a nearly illegible scrawl in Latin, reads, "Alexamenos worships

---

78 Lam 3:27-30
79 See for example the Roman playwright Titus Plautus (254-184 BC), *The Braggart Warrior*, lines 350-360.
80 "Crossbar" or "pole" is the basic meaning of *mowtah*, the Hebrew word describing the yoke worn by the prophet Jeremiah. One of the secondary meanings of the Greek word for "yoke," *zugos*, is the yardarm or horizontal bar that forms a cross on the mast of a ship.

God."[81] The subject's Greek name makes it probable that he was a slave. Alexamenos' Christian faith had made him the butt of blasphemous graffiti. As with the crucifixion itself, however, the attempt to heap ridicule on the person of Christ and on believers ended up bearing ironic witness to the "prophet like Moses."[82]

In the beginning of this chapter we focused on the prophetic imperative to turn Israel away from the path of destruction. The arduous labor of the "burden bearers," who with little effect had warned the Israelite people to reform their ways, did apparently bear fruit after the Babylonian exile. Under the leadership of Ezra and Nehemiah along with post-exilic prophets such as Haggai, the nation kept itself mostly free from idolatry and became zealous for the Mosaic Law. However, the sending of John the Baptist centuries later with a call to repentance betrayed an infection still growing beneath the surface. How is it that devotion to the law proved insufficient to restore Israel's spiritual health? That question brings us to our next story.

---

81 Michael Gough, *The Early Christians* (New York: Frederick A. Praeger, 1961), 83.

82 Acts 3:22.

12

The Repurchaser

Our last chapter began with the story of Balaam, who was called to curse the Israelites as they camped in the territory of Moab east of the Jordan River. Even though the events that followed sowed long-standing enmity between Israel and Moab, through the centuries individuals emigrated back and forth across the shared border. One of the heroes of David's refugee army, for example, is listed as a Moabite named Ithma.[1] David has other connections to Moab as well. The book of Ruth, named for David's great-grandmother, tells of an Israelite family that escapes from a famine in the Judah by taking up residence in Moab.

The father of the family, Elimelech, dies before he can return to his native country. More tragedy overtakes the family when Elimelech's two grown sons, Mahlon and Chilion, die in young adulthood, leaving as widows two Moabite women, Ruth and Orpah. Elimelech's widow, Naomi, impoverished and disconsolate, hears that conditions have improved in Judah and decides to return to the family's plot of land there. Her daughters-in-law offer to go with her but she urges them to return to their Moabite families.

1   1 Chron 11:46.

Orpah takes Naomi's advice. Ruth, on the other hand, refuses to leave Naomi, declaring, "Where you go I will go, and where you stay I will stay. Your people will be my people and your God my God."[2]

The women arrive in the vicinity of Bethlehem in Judah at the beginning of the barley harvest. Having no acreage of their own under cultivation and little or no money, the women must "glean" or gather leftover stalks of grain from fields being harvested. Naomi is incapable of hard physical labor, so the job falls to Ruth. By chance Ruth works in the field of a wealthy relative of Elimelech. The relative, named Boaz, notices Ruth and instructs his men to treat her with respect and make sure she has plenty of grain at the end of the day. Ruth returns and tells Naomi about Boaz's generosity.

In time Boaz desires to marry Ruth, but according to Israelite custom the obligation to perform "levirate marriage" with a childless widow of child-bearing age falls to the "repurchaser" or "kinsman-redeemer," the closest male relative of the dead husband. Since cessation of a man's family line is a catastrophe, the duty to take in a young widow and raise a child to bear the former husband's name is a serious one. The existing wife or wives of the male relative, along with children he already has, must make room for the widow's claim to part of his resources and physical attention. He assumes responsibility to pay off liens on the dead man's property and maintain it as an inheritance for children of the union. An Israelite widow denied such a marriage has the legal right to confront the derelict man in front of tribal elders and disgrace him by drawing off his sandal and spitting in his face.[3]

Boaz knows of a relative who is more closely related to Elimelech than he himself is. When Boaz approaches this relative about Ruth, the man says that concerns for his own family prevent him from fulfilling the duty. In a legal ceremony in front of village elders, the relative of Elimelech declines marriage to Ruth and allows the right of repurchase to devolve to Boaz. Boaz's willingness to undertake the obligation, coupled perhaps with Ruth's weak legal standing as a Moabitess, spares the male relative full public humiliation. Even so, the relative must remove his sandal in ritual acknowledgment that he has not upheld Elimelech's family name. Boaz and Ruth eventually have a son, Obed, who becomes the ancestor of David and ultimately of Jesus.

---

2   Ruth 1:16.
3   Deut 25:5-10.

Gentile Women in Need

Our first clue about the coded meaning of the story is an incident from Jesus' ministry. The Gospel of Mark tells about a Syro-Phoenician Gentile woman who comes to Jesus seeking a cure for her demonized daughter. Jesus learns about the woman's request from the disciples, and when she is brought to him she falls down and bows as she begs him for help.[4] Jesus advises her that he cannot take the "bread of the children," meaning the divine provisions intended for Israel, and "give it to the dogs," meaning non-Jews. The woman replies that the dogs do eat the crumbs that fall from the table of the children. Jesus expresses admiration for the woman's faith and heals her daughter.

The story from Mark's Gospel is reminiscent of Ruth's encounter with Boaz. Ruth asks Boaz's servants for permission to glean in their master's field. The servants then advise Boaz of Ruth's difficulties, and he tells her she is welcome to continue gathering leftover sheaves. He also praises her selflessness in caring for her aged mother-in-law. For her part, Ruth falls down and bows before Boaz, acknowledging his kindness in view of her being a foreigner. Boaz invites her to eat bread with his own servants before she returns home.

"Gleaning" means foraging for leftovers from the harvest, including stalks that happen to be dropped by the reapers. Dogs forage in the same way for crumbs that fall from the household table, as the Syro-Phoenician woman points out. The miraculous cure of the woman's daughter, although likened by Jesus and the woman herself to "crumbs off the table," qualifies as a generous helping of crumbs of the highest quality. Again, this follows the pattern set by Ruth. Ruth comes to salvage enough dusty gleanings to keep herself and Naomi alive, and is rewarded with a meal of bread and a portion of roasted grain in addition to the stalks she picks up. We know that she gathers quality stalks because Boaz instructs his harvesters to drop some of their own stalks deliberately so that Ruth can retrieve them.

The instruction Boaz gives his men neither to insult nor rebuke the Moabitess anticipates the way Jesus later will treat sympathetic Gentiles. The disciples want to send the Syro-Phoenician woman away, but Jesus

---

4   Mark 7:25; Matt 15:25.

gives her a hearing instead. Jesus also praises the faith of a Roman centurion and heals his servant. As we saw in the last chapter, when Jesus drives away the money changers apparently it is from the "court of the Gentiles," the only place on the temple grounds where Gentiles could gather and pray, because the justification Jesus gives is that the temple should be a "house of prayer for all the nations."[5]

Even the best gleanings are, however, still leftovers. The centurion, understanding his position as a Gentile, does not allow Jesus to come into his house, saying humbly, "I do not deserve to have you come under my roof."[6] The Syro-Phoenecian woman whose daughter is healed cannot expect to receive immediately all the covenant promises claimed by Israel. "First let the children [Jews] eat all they want," Jesus says, a rule that the woman asks him to bend, not break.[7]

The time for admitting Gentiles into a new covenant will come only after Jesus is rejected by fleshly Israel and fulfills the old covenant at the cross. We find this prophetically represented when Boaz tells Ruth that another relative has first right of repurchase and that this other man must give his response before Boaz can take any action himself. As it turns out, if Ruth were dependent solely upon this other relative she would find herself in dire poverty, because when asked he says that he cannot marry her.

The prophetic portrayal contained in Ruth now becomes apparent in its broad outline. Gentiles such as the Syro-Phoenician woman were excluded by the terms of the law, the charter of the Mosaic Covenant. That covenant was the first means given to designate a people for God and through that people to accomplish the blessing of all nations. Jesus, the greater Boaz, would become the repurchaser only after the Mosaic Law "had its say" on the subject of salvation. "For the law was given through Moses; grace and truth came through Jesus Christ."[8]

The first concern of the law was not the fate of Gentiles but the moral and spiritual purity of Israel. The law forbade intermarriage of Israelites with Canaanites because of their decadence, and its exclusionary tone discouraged marriage to foreigners in general. Early in Israel's

---

5   Mark 11:17.
6   Luke 7:6.
7   Mark 7:27.
8   John 1:17.

history what the law said about mixed marriages was frequently ignored to the nation's detriment. Gentile wives brought with them their idolatrous beliefs, and women married to Gentiles were unable to live according to the law's standards of purity.

After the return of Jewish exiles from decades of punitive exile in Babylon, their leaders had to make changes. The only chance the nation had of keeping foreign influences at bay was to erect high cultural barriers and deal harshly with any Israelite who breached them. Ezra, Nehemiah and other post-exilic leaders began a program of public education in the dictates of the law. They restored temple worship and enforced the Sabbath. Their campaign also included rancorous condemnation of marriage to foreigners. Ammonite and Moabite women were singled out as a threat.

As recounted in the book of Nehemiah, the Israelites learn about Balaam and the seduction of Israel on the plains of Moab. As a result, the people realize how great the danger is from marriage to Moabite women and from close contact with the peoples east of the Jordan. "When the people heard this law, they excluded from Israel all who were of foreign descent."[9] Upon finding Jews "who had married women from Ashdod, Ammon and Moab" and further seeing that half of the children of such women cannot even speak Hebrew, Nehemiah confronts the men. "I rebuked them and called curses down on them," he says. "I made them take an oath in God's name and said: 'You are not to give your daughters in marriage to their sons, nor are you to take their daughters in marriage for your sons or for yourselves.' "[10]

The Weakness of the Law

The bitter medicine administered by post-exilic leaders was needed to prevent the eventual dissolution of Israel. As he leads a public expression of repentance, the scribe Ezra recounts Israel's past adoption of the sins of the surrounding nations and then quotes from the law, "Therefore, do not give your daughters in marriage to their sons or take

---

9   Neh 13:1-3.
10 Neh 13:23-25.

their daughters for your sons." He continues by quoting from the account in Deuteronomy 23:1-6, which says concerning Moab and Ammon, "Do not seek a treaty of friendship with them at any time." Next, Ezra gives the reason for uncompromising separation: "that you may be strong and eat the good things of the land and leave it to your children as an everlasting inheritance."[11]

The reason Ezra gives for avoiding marriage to foreigners, including Moabites, is the same reason given by the male relative of Elimelech in the story of Ruth. Referring to Elimelech's estate and the obligation toward Ruth that goes with it, the relative tells Boaz, "I cannot redeem it for myself, because I would jeopardize my own inheritance."[12] The relative's property would be combined with Elimelech's, and any children Ruth bore could end up vying with the relative's other children for pieces of the estate.

The Hebrew word Ezra uses for inheritance is not the word used by Elimelech's relative, but the meaning is essentially the same. In the Greek of the Septuagint, Ezra 9:12 has the word *klerodoteo* while Ruth 4:6 has the related word *kleronomeo*. The need to protect a hereditary possession illustrates Israel's inability under the Mosaic Covenant to extend a helping hand toward the Gentiles without imperiling itself. The Jewish nation was like a man treading water in the open sea who is too hard pressed keeping his own nose above water to rescue someone drowning nearby.

By God's grace, the Gentiles were given sufficient gleanings to keep alive the hope of a blessing for them under the future reign of the Messiah. Yet they remained far off from God as compared with the Jews unless they became Jews themselves in every respect. That meant observance of burdensome dietary restrictions and other ceremonial purity laws, and for male Gentiles the painful ordeal of circumcision. After the death of Jesus and the outpouring of the holy Spirit, the apostle Peter argues against requiring Gentiles to become Jews before admitting them into the Christian church. Enslavement to the ritual regulations of the law is, he says, "a yoke that neither we nor our fathers have been able to bear."[13]

---

11 Ezra 9:12.
12 Ruth 4:6.
13 Acts 15:10.

If the law proved inadequate as a means of bringing the Gentiles to God, it offered only temporary reconciliation to Jews. A sacrificial goat figuratively could be made to carry the people's sins away, but it could not remove their sinfulness. The offering of an animal at the temple acknowledged that something must be repaid to God for transgression, but it could not make the giver capable of paying what God was actually owed—a life of perfect obedience to the law.

"The law," says the book of Hebrews, "can never, by the same sacrifices repeated endlessly year after year, make perfect those who draw near to worship. If it could, would they not have stopped being offered?"[14] The law was necessary for the curing of sin the way an electrocardiogram is necessary for curing a heart ailment. The diagnosis must be made and accepted by the patient before he will submit to further treatment. But, as we saw back in Chapter 1, a diagnosis by itself is not a cure.

The Mosaic Law Covenant was enacted with a certain ethnic group, the Hebrews, and the incapability of the law to remove sin, like the law itself, was passed down in a blood line from parents to children. Elimelech's family, too, is a blood line in which failure and incapacity are attached to every male. Elimelech himself dies as an exile before he can return to his allotment in Israel. His sons die in the prime of life, leaving no heirs. The unnamed male relative is unable to preserve Elimelech's family line by marrying Ruth. We are reminded of Paul's words when he writes about the law being "powerless to do" what was done eventually through Jesus.

It was not that the law was bad, Paul says, but that it "was weakened by the sinful nature" of those charged to keep it.[15] The Old Covenant amounted to a "ministry that brought death," he says, a ministry that "condemns men" by exposing their sinfulness while offering no means of permanent rehabilitation.[16]

The name of Ruth's late husband, Mahlon, denotes the incapacity characteristic of both the Mosaic Law and the males in Elimelech's lineage. The name is derived from the Hebrew *hala*, meaning "sick,"

---

14 Heb 10:1-2.
15 Rom 8:1-3.
16 2 Cor 3:7-9; cf. Rom 7:10.

"weak" or "afflicted." A passage showing that this word means specifically weakness as opposed to strength is part of the narrative of the capture and torture of Samson by his enemies.

Samson is a Nazirite, meaning one ceremonially dedicated to God, and is forbidden to cut his hair. He compromises himself by revealing the spiritual significance of his long hair to his lover Delilah, who is secretly in the pay of the Philistines. "If my head were shaved," he tells her, "my strength would leave me, and I would become as weak [*hala*] as any other man."[17] In the Septuagint, the word for "weak" here is *astheneo*, the same Greek word Paul uses at Romans 8:3 to say that the Mosaic Law is too weak to liberate mankind from sin and death.

Mahlon's weakness is apparent not just from his name and untimely death but from his failure to produce an heir. So joyful was the birth of a child to an Israelite family and so crucial was the handing down of the covenant promises from one generation to the next that birth became a metaphor for the final realization of God's blessing, and barrenness by contrast a figure of desolation. "We were with child, we writhed in pain, but we gave birth to wind," Isaiah laments. "We have not brought salvation to the earth; we have not given birth to the people of the world."[18]

Under the law, Israel failed to attain the divine glory that would have made her a source of blessing to all the nations. Post-exilic Israel, like Naomi, returned from its sojourn in a foreign land alive but spiritually childless.

"One Thing You Lack . . . "

Paul's writings as well as the Gospels refer to Israel's failure to become "a kingdom of priests and a holy nation."[19] "What Israel sought so earnestly it did not obtain," Paul says, in that Israel did not receive the blessing promised in the law as a reward for righteousness.[20] The experience of post-exilic Israel parallels that of a young Jewish noble who comes to Jesus imploring, "Good teacher, what must I do to inherit

---

17 Judg 16:17.
18 Isa 26:18.
19 Exod 19:6.
20 Rom 9:31; 11:7.

eternal life?" Jesus first corrects him by asking, "Why do you call me good? No one is good—except God alone."

What appears to be a quibble on Jesus' part is a means of framing the discussion that follows in terms of the Mosaic Law. The central declaration of the law is the Shema: "Hear, O Israel: The LORD our God, the LORD is one."[21] Jesus actually says to the young man that none is good except "One, the God," *eis ho theos*, recalling that in the Greek Shema, for example, God, *theos*, is "One," *eis*.

Since the Shema stands as a summary of the first three of the Ten Commandments, concerning devotion to Yahweh as the one true God, by alluding to the Shema Jesus evokes those commandments along with it. Next, Jesus asks the young noble about his keeping of the commandments about treatment of fellow humans, such as those prohibiting murder, adultery and theft. The man claims that he has kept all these "from my youth."

One thing is yet lacking, Jesus tells him. "Go, sell everything you have and give to the poor, and you will have treasure in heaven. Then come, follow me." At this, the young man turns away in distress "because he had great wealth."[22] God had foretold that once the Israelites prospered, their possessions would become the object of their affection rather than him.[23]

The oppressive poverty so common in first century Israel must have led those who were wealthy, such as the young noble, to cling all the more tightly to what they owned. The effect of this subtle idolatry was to keep most of them from following Jesus, who alone could supply their need. The man knew that he was missing something necessary for life, otherwise he would not have asked Jesus what it was. Apart from Jesus all the law-keeping efforts of the young man, like those of Israel itself, proved fruitless.

The young noble's goal of eternal life is one shared by Jesus' followers. Jesus promises them that through him they will possess life, though not without first undertaking suffering in the present world as part of the cost of discipleship. "A woman giving birth to a child has pain be-

---

21 Deut 6:4.
22 Mark 10:17-22.
23 Deut 31:20.

cause her time has come," Jesus says, "but when her baby is born she forgets the anguish because of her joy . . . So with you: Now is your time of grief, but I will see you again and you will rejoice, and no one will take away your joy."[24] The disciples would see Jesus with eyes of flesh after his own resurrection, and eventually see him "as he is" in glory.[25]

With the comparison of everlasting life to the birth of a child, we are brought back again to the predicament of Naomi and Ruth. The male relative of Elimelech and Mahlon is unable to marry Ruth and bring about the longed-for birth of an heir.

The male relative is deliberately left unidentified in the narrative. Boaz is quoted as calling out to him, but where the man's name would appear the writer has substituted the Hebrew term *peloni almoni*, "such a one" or "so and so." The Greek here says *kruphe*, "secret one." In a stroke of rhetorical justice the writer has expunged the identity of the man who would not preserve the name of his dead kinsman.

Elimelech, who seemed destined to be forgotten, is memorialized while the name of the relative who was so concerned about his property is lost to history. The punishment is even harsher than it first appears in that it represents the supreme curse of the law, visited upon willful idolaters by Yahweh himself. "All the curses written in this book will fall upon [the one guilty of idolatry], and the LORD will blot out his name from under heaven."[26]

To the weakness, sterility and death that stalk Elimelech's family may be added namelessness, although the crushing weight of judgment was mitigated insofar as Elimelech's own name was allowed to remain. Israel as well was spared the full measure of God's wrath only by his gracious mercy. "You have punished us less than our sins have deserved and have given us a remnant like this," Ezra confesses.[27] God placed limits on what Israel's enemies could do because, at his own pleasure, "the LORD had not said he would blot out the name of Israel from under heaven."[28]

---

24 John 16:21-22.
25 1 John 3:2.
26 Deut 29:20.
27 Ezra 9:13.
28 2 Kgs 14:27; cf. 1 Sam 12:22.

The male relative must remove one of his sandals in front of the elders of Bethlehem to signify legally that he cannot or will not act as the *gaal*, the repurchaser or redeemer, of Ruth and Naomi. In this he resembles Moses and Joshua. At the burning bush, where he receives the command to lead Israel out of Egypt, Moses is told to remove his sandals because the ground on which he stands is holy.[29] Sandals inevitably are soiled, and unclean articles of any kind are not to come into contact with that which is sanctified.

Removing the sandals is an acknowledgment that the wearer has unclean garments, a symbol of sin.[30] If Moses himself is a sinner, the further implication is that he cannot free the people from bondage to sin. At the end of his career, far from being able to redeem Israel, Moses is unable even to enter the Promised Land but must die east of the Jordan.

With the passing of Moses, the task of shepherding Israel falls to Joshua. When Joshua is about to lead Israel in its conquest of the land, he is given the same instruction about removing his sandals by the Prince of Yahweh's heavenly army.[31] As Moses' successor, Joshua does what Moses cannot do by settling Israel in its inheritance. Joshua achieves only a temporary and prophetic victory, however, not a final one. "For if Joshua had given them rest," the book of Hebrews says, "God would not have spoken later about another day."[32] The reference is to the passage at Psalm 95:3-11, where God warns his people not to rebel against him and suffer the fate of those who came out of Egypt. That generation, like Moses, had not been permitted to enter Canaan, the "resting place."[33]

As the author of Hebrews points out, the warning in the Psalms was given on a "day" hundreds of years after the Exodus, to Israelites who had long been living in the land of Canaan. Obviously Canaan, as a geographical location like any other, is not the resting place other than representatively. Joshua was a sinner like Moses, and no more able than Moses was to usher the people into the kingdom of God.

---

29 Exod 3:5.
30 Isa 64:6; cf. Mal 3:2-3, where purification from sin is represented as laundering.
31 Josh 5:15.
32 Heb 4:8.
33 Deut 12:9.

The comparison of Moses and Joshua to Elimelech's relative is no as-
persion. It has to do strictly with the incapacity of the Mosaic Covenant.
Paul makes a similar comparison by likening the old covenant to Hagar,
Abraham's slave girl and concubine, in contrast with Sarah, Abraham's
wife. We know little about Hagar's character other than that she held
Sarah in contempt.[34] The correspondence Paul sees is between the status of Hagar as a slave and the slavery to sin that Israel continued to
suffer from under the law.[35]

Sarah is an appropriate symbol of the new covenant in Jesus' blood,
according to Paul, because she is a free woman and conceives an heir
through more-than-fleshly means by God's sovereign grace. Sarah,
when we meet her in the Biblical narrative, is old while Ruth is young,
but the odds against either of them having a child are vanishingly slim
by human reckoning. God nevertheless gives each of them a son who
becomes an ancestor of Jesus.

Greater Israel

When Boaz takes Ruth as his wife, the people of Bethlehem are quick
to wish them offspring. "May the LORD make the woman who is coming into your home like Rachel and Leah, who together built up the
house of Israel." The birth of their child is an occasion of rejoicing.
Naomi's friends congratulate her on having a daughter-in-law who is
"better to you than seven sons" and whose newborn baby is called
Naomi's as well as Ruth's.[36]

The language here leads us to two other texts. One is part of the
prayer of Hannah in 1 Samuel, concerning the way God can reverse the
circumstances of humans to suit his will: "She who was barren has
borne seven children, but she who has had many sons pines away."[37]
The other, from Isaiah, concerns the restoration of Israel, and is found
immediately after the depiction of the Suffering Servant: " 'Sing, O barren woman, you who never bore a child; burst into song . . . because

---

34 Gen 16:4.
35 Gal 4:24-26.
36 Ruth 4:13-15.
37 1 Sam 2:5.

more are the children of the desolate woman than of her who has a husband,' says the LORD."[38]

The text from Isaiah about the barren woman might have been written about Ruth, who arrived in the land of Judah without husband, child or home and unexpectedly became not only wife and mother, but ancestress to King David. David in time would come to have a multitude of offspring, according to a prophecy that can only be fulfilled in terms of the life-giving work of the Messiah, the Son of David.[39] So Ruth does come to have far more children than, for example, the woman who lurks unmentioned behind the narrative, the wife of the nameless relative of Elimelech.

In the same passage in which Paul likens the heavenly Jerusalem to Sarah as contrasted with Hagar, he also compares this new "city" or covenant people to the once-barren woman of Isaiah 54.[40] Even though we take different paths from different starting points within the book of Ruth, we arrive time and again at the same place or, to be more accurate, at the same development: a change in relationship between God and man made possible by the coming of Jesus.

Two thousand years removed from the birth of Christianity, it is hard to appreciate how unique the religion of the Jews was at the time and how shocking it was to suggest that the Hebrew God would accept worship from people outside the confines of the Jewish nation. The task of carrying forward this revolution fell to Paul, formerly the Pharisee Saul of Tarsus. As Paul saw it, an earthquake had altered the spiritual landscape. No simple model could capture the transformation.

Looked at one way, God had augmented Israel, "enlarging its borders" to take in people of the nations;[41] considered another way, God had entirely replaced Israel with something new. Scriptures such as John 10:16, where Jesus says that he has other sheep to bring and join to the flock, emphasize the idea of expansion. The rebuke of Jewish leaders in Matthew in which Jesus says that the kingdom will be taken from them and given to another nation stresses the idea of replacement.[42]

---

38 Isa 54:1.
39 Jer 33:22.
40 Gal 4:26-27.
41 Isa 26:15.
42 Matt 21:43.

In Romans 11:1, Paul asks whether God rejected his people Israel and then answers emphatically that he did not. Just a few lines later, in verse 13, he seems to contradict himself by referring to the "rejection" of the Jews by God. A close reading shows that Paul is balancing the notion of Israel's expansion with that of Israel's replacement. The Israel of old has been preserved in that a "remnant" of Jews, including Paul himself, has responded to the gospel (v. 5). These Jewish Christians carry on the ancient line of faithful Israelites that corresponds to Naomi in the book of Ruth.

Ruth had accompanied Naomi, saying that Naomi's God would be hers. The Gentiles who first gave a hearing to the good news about Jesus were the "God-fearers," *hoi phoboumenoi ton theon*, who stood at the back of the synagogue in order to learn more about the God of Israel. From among these came the first Gentile convert to Christianity, the Roman centurion Cornelius, as well as the crowd of Gentiles at Pisidian Antioch who received the word preached by Paul and Barnabas.[43] The status of these sympathetic Gentiles, who had been providing both moral and financial support to the Jews, matches that of Ruth in her relationship with Naomi.[44] The Jewish remnant and the crowds coming in from the Gentile nations would now share a common hope of salvation, as Ruth and Naomi both became mother to their family's newborn son.

In an important sense, then, Israel was preserved and enlarged. At the same time, the majority of Jews, including those who controlled Jewish political and religious institutions, refused to accept Jesus and so placed themselves outside of God's economy. "They did not submit to God's righteousness," Paul says, but instead "sought to establish their own" by recourse to the law apart from the revelation through Jesus.[45]

Also, the religious system with which the Jews were identified, consisting of sacrifices at the temple and maintenance of ritual purity, was giving way to one based on faith in God's provision of Christ. "The ministry Jesus has received is as superior to theirs as the covenant of which he is mediator is superior to the old one," says the author of Hebrews.[46] The new ministry swept aside physical ancestry as a qualifi-

---

43 Acts 10:22; 13:26, 43-48.
44 Luke 7:2-5; Acts 10:2.
45 Rom 10:3.
46 Heb 8:6.

cation for God's acceptance. Peter comes to realize that "God does not show favoritism but accepts men from every nation who fear him and do what is right."[47] "A man is a Jew if he is one inwardly," Paul argues, "and circumcision is circumcision of the heart, by the Spirit, not by the written code."[48]

Gideon's Sign

We turn now briefly to three typological sketches that complement the detailed treatment found in Ruth. The first of these is part of the story of Gideon as told in the book of Judges.[49] Gideon, whom we touched on briefly in Chapter 8, lived perhaps a generation or two before Ruth, in the archaic tribal period of Israel. The narrative about him is set at a time when Israel has been overrun by Midianite marauders. God's angel appears to Gideon and tells him that God will deliver Israel from its enemies by Gideon's hand. Gideon is nervous about battling hordes of desert tribesmen—justifiably, it turns out, since the Midianites will later manifest their brutality by slaughtering Gideon's brothers.

Gideon asks Yahweh to confirm the angel's message by a sign of Gideon's own devising. Gideon will spread out a wool fleece on the local threshing floor and leave it overnight. He requests that the fleece be wetted with dew while the area all around the fleece remains dry. When Gideon checks the next morning, the floor is indeed dry and the fleece is drenched. Gideon asks to be indulged with a second sign so that he can be doubly certain God will be with him. This time, in a reversal of the first sign, he asks for the floor to become wet with dew while the fleece stays dry. Again his prayer is answered, and Gideon goes on to rout the Midianites.

The typological coding of Gideon's sign, expounded by Irenaeus in the second century, is straightforward.[50] The obvious association of the wool fleece or sheepskin is with sheep. In the Hebrew Bible, sheep are the most common metaphor for the people of Israel. An early usage is

---

47 Acts 10:34-35.
48 Rom 2:28-29.
49 Judg 6:11–8:32.
50 Irenaeus, *Adversus haereses* 3.17.3.

in Numbers, where Moses asks God to give the Israelites a new leader "so the LORD's people will not be like sheep without a shepherd."[51] The same figure occurs in book after book of the Old Testament, rarely referring to anyone but Israelites. "Why have you rejected us forever, O God? Why does your anger smolder against the sheep of your pasture?," pleads the Psalmist as he contemplates the disasters that have befallen the Hebrew nation.[52]

"I will surely bring together the remnant of Israel," God answers in the book of Micah. "I will bring them together like sheep in a pen."[53] As we saw in Chapter 7, the illustration of sheep began to be more broadly applied from Jesus' ministry onward. If Gideon's fleece is a symbol pertaining to events that date to before the coming of Jesus, then it likely stands for Israel rather than for mankind at large.

The threshing floor connotes judgment, the process of separating truth from falsehood and guilt from innocence.[54] Threshing floors consisted either of smooth stone or hard-packed earth. We know that the threshing floor Gideon uses is earthen because when he prays for the sign, he actually asks that "all the earth," *kol erets*, around the fleece remain dry in the first instance and become wet in the second. The Hebrew *erets* can mean "ground," "land" or "earth" in the sense of "world." The expression *kol erets* sometimes refers to the realm of mankind outside of Israel. When the Syrian army officer Naaman is healed of leprosy by the prophet Elisha, he declares, "Now I know that there is no God in all the world [*kol erets*] except in Israel."[55] The term *kol erets* appears in the Gideon narrative three times to describe the area around the fleece.

Like rainwater, dew was precious in the semi-arid climate of ancient Canaan and therefore is closely associated with God's favor. When Isaac confers a special blessing upon his younger son Jacob, the forefather of

---

51 Num 27:17.

52 Ps 74:1.

53 Mic 2:12.

54 Mic 4:12; Luke 3:17. The most famous such slab is the threshing floor of Ornan, which became the floor of the Jerusalem temple and is now enshrined within the Dome of the Rock (2 Sam 24:18-25).

55 2 Kgs 5:15; cf. 1 Chron 14:17; Isa 25:8.

the Israelite people, he says in part, "May God give you of heaven's dew and of earth's richness."[56] Isaac withholds the same invocation from Jacob's older brother Esau and instead says of him, "Your dwelling will be away from the earth's richness, away from the dew of heaven above."[57]

Generations later, Moses blesses the tribes of Joseph by wishing them "the precious dew from heaven above" shortly before he declares that Israel as a whole will reside "in a land of grain and new wine, where the heavens drop dew." Moses then concludes, "Blessed are you, O Israel! Who is like you, a people saved by the LORD?"[58]

The sign of Gideon aligns closely with what the New Testament says about the change in Israel's status wrought by the cross of Christ. In his sovereign capacity as Judge of the world, God had extended mercy toward Jacob's descendants by bringing them into a covenant with him.[59] For generations the dew of his kindness fell upon the Israelites in the form of exhortation, guidance and protection.[60] Even when Israel put itself in the path of destruction, God preserved alive a remnant.[61] Consequently, for centuries the knowledge of God's purposes was limited almost exclusively to the Hebrews, while the Gentile nations suffered from a spiritual drought.[62] The dew fell on the fleece but not on the surrounding earth.

When the long-awaited Messiah appeared, however, only a small minority of Jews put faith in him. With the provision of the holy Spirit and the beginning of universal evangelism, Gentiles responded in numbers that surpassed and ultimately dwarfed the Jewish segment of the church. A reversal had occurred. The greater part of those receiving the inspired word of God now were non-Jews of the nations, whereas most Jews remained blind to the outworking of God's plan.

"You [Gentiles] who were at one time disobedient to God have now

---

56 Gen 27:28.
57 Gen 27:39
58 Deut 33:13, 28-29.
59 Exod 33:16-17; Rom 3:1-2; 9:3-5.
60 Deut 32:2; Acts 7:38.
61 Ezra 9:13; Rom 9:29.
62 Deut 4:33-34; Eph 2:11-12.

received mercy as a result of their [the Jews'] disobedience," Paul says.[63] The dew ceased falling on the fleece and instead dampened the earth all around it. The alienation of the Jews and the expansion of the covenant to include Gentiles were foreshadowed by events that took place more than a thousand years before Jesus, and the record of those events in the book of Judges predates their fulfillment by a minimum of several centuries.

The Weak-Eyed Wife and Blind Israel

Paul carefully qualifies his statements about the status of Jews as opposed to Christian Gentiles so that nothing he says can be construed as anti-Semitic. He lays to rest any idea that the Gentiles enjoy God's favor unconditionally. His illustration in this regard is an olive tree representing the Abrahamic covenant. He compares the Jewish people to branches that were broken off the tree so that foreign or "wild" branches, representing the Gentiles, could be grafted in.

"Do not be arrogant, but be afraid," he advises Gentile believers. "For if God did not spare the natural branches, he will not spare you either." He says that the Jews are still loved by God and that in keeping with his ancient covenant he is determined to recover as many of them as possible. "If they do not persist in unbelief, they will be grafted in, for God is able to graft them in again." He predicts that before the Lord's coming the church will benefit from a large influx of Jews and that in this way "all Israel will be saved."[64]

"Inasmuch as I am the apostle to the Gentiles," Paul says, "I make much of my ministry in the hope that I may somehow arouse my own people to envy and save some of them."[65] Paul wants Jews to realize that Gentile Christians possess something valuable—a recognition of Jesus as the Messiah—that they themselves lack. He employs the word "envy" or "jealousy" in a positive rather than a negative sense, based on God's warning that if the Israelites sinned, God would make them "envious" by "those who are not a people."[66] Paul's language leads us to a

---

63 Rom 11:30.
64 Rom 11:17-28.
65 Rom 11:14.
66 Deut 32:21.

story of jealousy or envy, the narrative about Jacob and his wives found in Genesis.

In earlier chapters I described the awkward domestic situation Jacob is saddled with by his uncle Laban. Jacob falls in love with Laban's younger daughter Rachel and agrees to work for Laban seven years in order to acquire her. On his wedding night Jacob receives his bride, who would be heavily veiled according to custom, only to discover in the morning that the woman is not Rachel but her older sister Leah. Jacob is disappointed, understandably, since "Leah had weak eyes, but Rachel was lovely in form, and beautiful."[67] Despite his feelings, Jacob is forced to keep Leah and spend a week-long honeymoon with her before also receiving Rachel.

Leah immediately begins having children, but Rachel is barren for years. The rivalry between the women is so strong that each of them gives her handmaid to be Jacob's concubine, Leah so that she can increase the total of children on her side of the family and Rachel so that she will not remain childless. The women's mutual jealousy, while fraught with heartache, results in the birth of many sons, who in turn father the tribes of Israel.

The experience of Jacob parallels that of God himself as told in the books of Exodus through Deuteronomy. At Sinai Yahweh takes the Israelites into a covenant as his "bride" on the understanding that they are prepared to obey him from their hearts. "We will do everything the LORD has said," is the unanimous response of the people when the law is presented to them.[68] But God does not get the spiritually beautiful wife he has bargained for. Even before the people depart from Mt. Sinai, large numbers of them revert to idolatry. "They have been quick to turn away from what I commanded them," God tells Moses.

Like Jacob, who sees in the light of day who his wife really is, God says that "I have seen these people and they are a stiff-necked people."[69] Centuries later God makes the same bitter assessment of the people's attitude: "Did you bring me sacrifices and offerings forty years in the desert, O house of Israel? You have lifted up the shrine of your king, the pedestal of your idols . . . which you made for yourselves."[70]

---

67 Gen 29:17
68 Exod 19:8.
69 Exod 32:8-9.
70 Amos 5:25-26.

The desert sojourn of Israel is called time of the nation's "espousals" or "bridehood," *keluvlah*, that is, God's honeymoon with his people.[71] It turns out to be a honeymoon spent with the wrong woman, one without the ability to see who God is and what kind of relationship he desires. Shortly before his death Moses laments, "To this day the LORD has not given you a mind that understands or eyes that see or ears that hear."[72]

When Genesis says that Leah has weak eyes it means that her face is not as pretty as Rachel's, but the language equally can describe poor eyesight. The Hebrew here is *rak*, meaning "tender," "weak" or "delicate." Although *rak* is less emphatic than *hala*, the term that underlies the name of Ruth's late husband Mahlon, the sense is similar; in describing Leah's eyes the Septuagint uses *astheneo*, the Greek word Paul uses for the weakness of the Mosaic Law in chapter eight of Romans.

Just three chapters later Paul mentions the spiritual near-sightedness of Israel in the same context in which he discusses jealousy between Jews and Gentile Christians. "God gave them a spirit of stupor," Paul writes, quoting from Isaiah, "eyes so that they could not see and ears so that they could not hear, to this very day."[73] The metaphor of weak spiritual vision was later commented on by Justin Martyr, who understood that the story of Jacob's wives has a typological dimension.[74]

Plainly, Leah, the less loved wife of Jacob, pictures fleshly Israel, leaving the favorite wife Rachel to represent the Gentiles. Is it true that while the old covenant was in effect God loved some Gentiles—those who were righteous—more than his people Israel? By the early sixth century BC the northern kingdom of Israel had been decimated by Assyria, its prominent citizens exiled far to the east, and the southern kingdom of Judah was nearing the limit of God's patience. It is at this juncture that God through the prophet Jeremiah unfavorably compares the corruption of Judah to the virtue of the Rechabites, a clan of law-keeping Midianite Gentiles who allied themselves with Israel.[75]

Later, Jesus cites other Old Testament episodes to make the same

---

71 Jer 2:2.
72 Deut 29:4.
73 Rom 11:8.
74 Justin Martyr, *Dialogue with Trypho* 134.
75 Jer 35:12-19.

point. He reminds the people of his hometown of Nazareth that when God had punished the Israelites with a drought, Elijah was sent to provide miraculous relief, not to any of the poor of Israel, "but to a [Gentile] widow in Zarephath in the region of Sidon." In the same way, Elisha's dramatic cure of leprosy was performed not for one of the many Israelite lepers but for "Naaman the Syrian."[76] The comparison of Rachel with righteously inclined Gentiles turns out to be appropriate.

Leah, Jacob's first wife chronologically, is also the first to receive gifts from God in the form of children. Her leading son, Judah, becomes the fleshly ancestor of Jesus, in keeping with Leah's personification of the nation as defined by genaeology. However, as I noted in Chapter 10 Judah does not prove to be the son who typifies the Messiah. The messianic archetype, Joseph, is born when God finally opens the womb of the "barren" woman Rachel. Rachel bears only two sons, since she dies in childbirth with Joseph's younger brother Benjamin. Joseph eventually saves the lives of his brothers and of the people of Egypt, becoming a kind of father or life-giver to untold thousands. The children of the beautiful but once infertile Rachel come to outnumber those of the initially fertile wife, Leah.

The ancestral relationship between Joseph and Jesus is one of resemblance rather than heredity. By the same standard, who collectively proved to be the offspring or "seed" of men of faith such as Abraham and Joseph? Though at first represented only by Jews, the "offspring" quickly came to consist largely of Gentiles. "If you were Abraham's children," Jesus had told his enemies among the Jewish leadership, "then you would do the things Abraham did."[77] Further, John the Baptist had predicted that "out of these stones God can raise up children for Abraham."[78]

By accepting the gospel, the Gentiles, whom the Jews considered as spiritually lifeless as the stones under foot and as empty of promise as the once barren wombs of Rachel and Ruth, found themselves elevated to the status of God's children.

---

76 Luke 4:25-27.
77 John 8:39.
78 Matt 3:9.

Variations on a Theme

The last sketch we will consider comes from the Old Testament book of Esther. It might be developed into a full-length study all its own, but the key elements are quickly grasped. Esther, an orphaned Jewess of the fifth century BC, is being raised by her uncle Mordecai among the community of Jewish exiles in the Persian city of Susa. Meanwhile, the Persian king, Ahasuerus, finds himself forced to put away his arrogant wife, Queen Vashti, when she refuses to honor the king's summons for her to appear at a state banquet.

A search is begun for a new queen, and Esther, who like Rachel is "beautiful in form," ultimately is selected. Just after she is chosen to be the king's bride, Esther must risk her own life to save her people. Anti-Jewish elements led by a murderous official, Haman, have conspired to deprive Jews throughout the Persian empire of legal protection so that they can be plundered and murdered by anti-Jewish mobs.

To foil the plot Esther must enter the king's presence unbidden, an act punishable by death. Her only hope is that the king will offer her grace by extending his scepter when she approaches his throne. The king in fact spares Esther and listens to her plea on behalf of her people. The Jews are allowed to arm and defend themselves, which they do successfully, and the anti-Jewish plotters are executed.

In the fulfillment of the story of Esther, the king is Jesus, whose spiritual summons is rejected by the institutional nation of Israel, which corresponds to Queen Vashti. The faithful Jewish remnant portrayed by Naomi in the book of Ruth is here represented by Mordecai, Esther's guardian and tutor, who prepares her for her destiny and whose wise counsel enables her to save her people.

Esther herself is the young church in its predominantly Gentile identity, called upon to act as the replacement for institutional Israel (in the Jewish view the Gentiles, not having descended from Abraham, were spiritually fatherless like Esther). This new congregation, its numbers swelled by Gentile converts, took its guidance from the Jewish sacred Scriptures and from Jewish Christian apostles and missionaries. In the Esther narrative, Mordecai is saved along with Esther by means of the grace she receives from the king, just as Naomi is rescued along with Ruth by Boaz's gracious decision to redeem Ruth in levirate marriage. A long list of texts documenting specific fulfillments helps to establish the prophetic coding of Esther.[79]

The books of Ruth and Esther were probably written in the first few decades after the end of the Babylonian exile. Ruth contains language markers dating it to that period even though the events it portrays took place centuries before. Ruth's story is just the kind of oral history that would be preserved as family tradition and later recorded as important ancestral information about David. Ruth solves an otherwise puzzling detail of David's biography by explaining why David, when his life was threatened by King Saul, sent his parents to the king of Moab for protection; David's extended family had ties of blood and friendship in Moab dating back to Elimelech's sojourn east of the Jordan.[80]

Some scholars think that the book of Ruth with its Moabite heroine was written as a counterweight to the exclusionary policies of Ezra and Nehemiah. It would have had a moderating influence whether or not such a motive lay behind it. A subtle association between overzealous enforcers of cultural purity and the unhelpful male relative in the book of Ruth, though improbable, is possible.

What is not possible is that Ruth's author consciously intended to portray the incapacity of the law as an instrument of salvation and the need for a new covenant, much less the role of the Messiah as repurchaser. I have already remarked on how alien such ideas would have been to the thinking of pre-Christian Jews and how momentous they were in the view of Paul. Their significance is evident from the fact that at least four separate typological narratives are devoted to them, from the books of Genesis, Judges, Ruth and Esther. To appreciate how unlikely it would be for such an alignment to have occurred by accident, try to think of even one of Shakespeare's plays with a plot equally suited to the purpose.

---

79 Cf. Esth 1:10-11 with Ezek 16:10-14; cf. Esth 1:12, 15 with Jer 35:17b; Dan 9:10; Matt 22:2-5; cf. Esth 1:19 with Ps 95:11; Jer 23:39; Matt 21:43; cf. Esth 2:7a with Isa 51:2; 63:16; cf. Esth 2:7, 20 with Gal 3:23-24; cf. Esth 4:16 with Exod 19:21, 24; Isa 58:6-9; Jer 30:21b; cf. Esth 5:1 with Hos 6:2; Luke 21:36; cf. Esth 5:2 with Ps 5:11-12; Heb 4:16; cf. Esth 6:10-13 with Isa 49:22-23; 2 Cor 2:14-16; cf. Esth 8:5-13 with Isa 49:25; Col 2:14; cf. Esth 9:24-25 with 2 Thess 1:6-8.

80 1 Sam 22:3-4.

It took two millennia, during which God occupied himself primarily with the family of Abraham, for the doors of divine grace to swing open for the Gentiles. The plan of salvation had been foreshadowed generations before Abraham, however, as we will consider next.

13

Between Two Worlds

In 1996 two geologists from Columbia University's Lamont-Doherty Earth Observatory found themselves in a media spotlight when they claimed to have evidence for the deluge described in Genesis. Walter Pittman and Bill Ryan made their case in the book *Noah's Flood*, explaining that several thousand years ago, at the end of the last ice age, what is now the Black Sea was a much smaller lake.[1] Up until about 4500 BC, sea levels around the world were rising by an average of several feet per century for many centuries, creating conditions for flooding that have not been seen since nor are likely in the foreseeable future.

At a critical point, according to Pittman and Ryan, the land bridge separating the Mediterranean from the lake gave way, allowing a cataclysmic torrent of seawater to inundate a vast area. Despite the attention garnered by the "Black Sea Flood" hypothesis, it is not without scientific problems nor is it entirely consistent with what the Bible says. For one thing, the Biblical floodwaters are said to have subsided from at least part of the land they covered.

The Bible provides only vague hints about where and when the flood occurred, and presents it as a partly miraculous event. Since it represents a departure from the natural order, we cannot expect to explain the deluge in purely natural terms.

---

1   Walter Pitman and William Ryan, *Noah's Flood: The New Scientific Discoveries About the Event That Changed History* (New York: Touchstone, 2000).

For the same reason, we cannot assume that it was intended to leave behind unambiguous evidence in the geological record. The flood story teaches spiritual lessons about God's sovereignty and the inevitability of judgment, and proof of its occurrence is more likely to be found in divine revelation than in natural history.

The Earth of Old

Some Christians believe that the Biblical deluge must have been global and that it created all the earth's geological strata, although most of them do not condemn believers who hold a different view. The physics of continental drift or "plate tectonics" and the constitution of the world's mountain ranges are not easily reconciled with the global interpretation, nor is the world's distribution of plants and animals.[2] The extent of the earth's geological layers raises the question of where, apart from long eras of erosion, such immense volumes of finely grained sediment came from, let alone how they were almost immediately lithified into blocks so strong that they could be tilted into mountains thousands of feet high.

Genesis says that the Euphrates and Tigris (Hiddekel) rivers were already flowing long before the flood,[3] yet the courses of these rivers are dependent on landforms that according to the global flood interpretation did not exist until the floodwaters created them. The mountains that form the drainage system for these rivers consist of fossil-bearing strata. Geological surveys for oil and gas drilling in the Tigris and Euphrates delta in southern Iraq reveal that under the landscape there, too, are sedimentary layers like those found elsewhere around the world.

We might speculate that the names Genesis uses for rivers were later recycled, but only by abandoning the "plain sense" interpretation that is insisted upon by those who argue for a global flood. Genesis describes the courses of these rivers in terms of countries and regions with the same names and general characteristics that they had after the flood, which makes no sense if the earth's surface features had been reshaped.[4]

---

2   A global flood makes it difficult to explain why both kangaroos and kangaroo fossils are found only in Australia and both kiwis and kiwi fossils are found only in New Zealand, to cite just two examples.

3   Gen 2:10-14.

4   Cf. Gen 2:10-14; 25:18.

Admittedly, proving or disproving what happened thousands of years ago is not easy. Anyone who investigates all sides of the question is free to believe that the evidence points to a global deluge. But that is not the only view that accords with the Scriptures, seeing that none of the terminology used in the Bible concerning the deluge proves that it was global.

In Chapter 10 we saw that Joseph's brothers traveled to Egypt to find food because "there was famine in all the other lands."[5] "The famine was spread over all the face of the earth," Genesis continues, and repeats a third time that "the famine was severe in all the earth."[6] It hardly seems reasonable to insist from these verses that the famine afflicted faraway Scandinavia, China or Indonesia, or extended beyond the area of the Middle East relevant to the narrative.

Another example is found in Deuteronomy, where God reassures Israel of success in conquering the Canaanites by telling them that "all the peoples of the earth" would hear of Israel and be afraid.[7] In their original application these words cannot be taken globally, as if they included the tribesmen that even then inhabited Central Africa, North America and Australia.

Neither can the apostle Paul be understood literally when he writes well before the close of the first century that the gospel about Jesus already had already been "proclaimed to every creature under heaven."[8] These expressions are used to designate a sphere of divine activity that for the purpose of the narrative or argument is treated as universal, and they are the same ones Genesis uses of the deluge. The "earth" or "land" is overwhelmed with water, the high "mountains" or "hills" are covered and every breathing creature on the "face of the earth" that is "under heaven" perishes. Noah's life-preserving ark finally comes to rest on the mountains (or, hills) of Ararat, meaning the uplands extending northward from Mesopotamia.

Biblical language may not demand that Noah's flood or Joseph's famine be taken as global events, but they were intended to make statements about global realities, and to make those statements in particular

---

5   Gen 41:54.

6   Gen 41:56-57, NASB.

7   Deut 28:10; cf. the use of *eretz*, "earth," at Josh 6:27; 2 Chron 9:23.

8   Col 1:23.

ways. It seems odd that God would put Joseph, Jacob and Rachel through a harrowing, years-long ordeal for the sole purpose of saving their family from a famine. It would have been simple enough for God to prevent the famine from ever occurring or provide food miraculously for Jacob's household when the need arose. But lessons were being taught through the events God allowed to transpire in the life of Joseph, and clues were being left about the plan of salvation through Jesus.

In Noah's case, too, God could have acted more directly and efficiently if his only objectives were the destruction of an evil society and the preservation of Noah. The New Testament treats the flood as a model of God's judgment of humanity and of the salvation he extends through Jesus.

Jesus says that the Second Coming will resemble the deluge. The people of Noah's society pursued their own desires untroubled by the evil around them, uncaring of God's judgment, until the day Noah entered the ark. "They knew nothing about what would happen until the flood came and took them all away," Jesus warns. "That is how it will be at the coming of the Son of Man."[9] 2 Peter makes the same comparison, saying that by water an ancient world was destroyed and that "by the same word the present heavens and earth are reserved for fire, being kept for the day of judgment and destruction of ungodly men."[10]

Just as the flood made a fresh start possible for Noah, his family and the earth itself, Peter says, "We are looking forward to a new heaven and a new earth, the home of righteousness."[11] We are justified, at least according to the New Testament, in seeing the deluge account as a comment on God's larger purpose.

The Arks of Noah and Moses

Noah builds an ark to carry human and animal life through the waters of death. The ark was not a navigable ship with a bow and stern but a barge that amounted to little more than a floating box. Two other smaller arks or wooden chests should be compared, the first of these being the basket Moses was placed in as a baby. Moses' miniature ark,

---

9   Matt 24:37-39.
10 2 Pet 3:6-7.
11 2 Pet 3:13.

like that of Noah, was coated with pitch and set afloat on the water in the hope of preserving life.[12] The second small ark was the Ark of the Covenant housed in the Most Holy recess of the temple and seen by no one but the High Priest on Yom Kippur.

The Ark of the Covenant held two tablets containing the Ten Commandments, the core of the Mosaic Law. It also held a jar containing some of the manna that had sustained the Israelites in their desert wanderings. Finally, the on top of the chest, or perhaps leaning against it, was the staff that had belonged to Aaron, Israel's first High Priest.[13] Aaron was Moses' older brother and had accompanied Moses during his confrontations with Pharaoh. Aaron's staff was used to perform signs and functioned as the equivalent of Moses' staff.[14] Each article in this group—the Tablets of the Testimony, the manna or "heavenly bread," and the rod—represents the Mosaic Law.[15]

The "arks" of Noah, of baby Moses and of the Covenant are designated in various passages either by the Hebrew *teba* or the Greek *kibotos*, or by both. The second and third arks are similar to one another in that both contain and preserve "Moses" for the sake of the Israelite nation, bodily when Moses is a baby and later in the sense of preserving the law delivered through him. In some verses of the New Testament, the Law of Moses is referred to simply as "Moses."[16]

Noah's ark, like the Mosaic Law associated with the Ark of the Covenant, is a temporary protective instrument. Noah, his family and the creatures of the earth could not survive in the ark indefinitely. The great wooden box that at first offers a refuge from the floodwaters quickly becomes a prison from which its occupants need to be rescued. The same is true of the Mosaic Law, as we saw in the last chapter.

By reminding Israel that God expects righteousness from his people the law kept them from drowning in a sea of idolatrous superstition. The law did not regenerate Israel, however, and by leaving its people struggling in a sea of spiritual death it put the prospect of universal renewal far off. Previously I noted Isaiah's lament that Israel had not

---

12 Exod 2:3.
13 Num 17:10; Heb 9:4.
14 Exod 7:19-20; cf. Exod 17:5.
15 Exod 34:28; Deut 8:1-3; Ezek 20:37.
16 E.g., Acts 15:21.

"given birth to the people of the world."[17] With Israel lay the hope of
recovering the glorious potential of mankind and of the entire created
order, which had been placed under human authority by God and then
lost as a consequence of man's rebellion. As the period of the prophets
drew to a close in the fifth century BC with Israel's destiny still unreal-
ized, the Jewish nation found itself adrift.

Israel's situation duplicates that of Noah and his family as they bob
precariously on the flood tide. Even when the ark grounds, only the
tops of the hills can be seen like barren islands in the distance, offering
no hint of a habitable environment. What Noah and Israel seek is an assurance that, having left behind a world consumed by moral corruption,
they can yet expect a renewed creation flourishing with life.

Noah eventually removes the hatch on the ark and releases two birds,
a raven and a dove, to see what their behavior may tell him. In the Law
of Moses the raven is designated an "unclean" bird, unfit to be eaten or
sacrificed, while the dove is designated as clean for those purposes. At
first, neither bird finds a home away from the ark or gives any sign that
life is returning to the flood-ravaged landscape. Noah, like Israel, must
wait on God.

A Pledge of New Life

I have been speaking about a parallel between Noah and Israel in its
hope for a better world of God's making. Servants of God in the pre-
Christian era endured the same longing as individuals. Our foremost example is Job, an Edomite but a worshiper of Yahweh. As portrayed in
the book of the same name, Job struggles frankly with doubt as he suffers the loss of his children and the intense pain of an apparently
terminal illness. Although at points he questions God's care for his creatures, Job manages to cling to his faith and in the end is pronounced
virtuous by God. Along the way Job must confront the seeming invinci-
bility of death. Is it really possible that what the grave relentlessly
devours can be reclaimed by a God whom Job can neither see nor hear?

Like Noah straining his eyes at the oceanic blankness around him,
Job surveys the horizon of human existence and sees nothing but the
void. "As water disappears from the sea or a riverbed becomes parched

---

17 Isa 26:18.

and dry," Job observes, "so man lies down and does not rise; till the heavens are no more, men will not awake." The insensible plants seem better off by comparison. If a tree is cut down, it may revive. "Its roots may grow old in the ground and its stump die in the soil," says Job, "yet at the scent of water it will bud and put forth shoots."[18]

In spite of the empty appearance of the world, Job reaffirms that even after death God will remember him in the resurrection. "You will call and I will answer you; you will long for the creature your hands have made."[19] Through God's power, a human being can live again just as a dry tree stump may be given life by water. Not only is the illustration of the tree stump a vivid one, we have run across it before. In earlier chapters I referred to a text from Isaiah that says concerning the Messiah, "A shoot will come up from the stump of [David's father] Jesse; from his roots a Branch will bear fruit" and another that calls the messianic Servant "a shoot" out of "dry ground."[20]

The stump of Isaiah 11 is the dynasty of David, which came to an end with the destruction of Jerusalem by the armies of Babylon. Post-exilic Judah would continue to have rulers, some of whom were called kings, but no sovereign monarchs who sat on Yahweh's throne in fulfillment of God's promise to David. The Davidic dynasty appeared to be as dead as an old tree stump, and with it the nation's aspirations.

Once again, the imagery can be broadened to include the human family as a whole. Man was intended to be the benevolent ruler over all creation but was dethroned and subjected to a state of death, cut off from the "water" of God's life-sustaining Spirit. The prospects of Israel and of every human individual for life beyond the present sin-burdened world appeared to recede as long as the pledge of a Davidic heir remained unfulfilled.

The promise, however, was kept at last. In Matthew's Gospel, a Jewish man of David's lineage is told in a dream that Mary, his betrothed, has become pregnant by the holy Spirit and that the son she is carrying will be the savior of Israel. According to Luke's Gospel, an

---

18 Job 14:7-12.
19 Job 14:15.
20 Isa 11:1; 53:2.

angel tells Mary that her child, Jesus, will inherit "the throne of David his father."[21] The "water" of the Spirit touched the "stump" or dormant family of David and caused it to sprout. Jesus fulfills not only the prophecy from Isaiah about the shoot from the stump of Jesse, but other passages that call the coming king a "branch" or "twig."[22]

What kind of tree do the prophecies refer to? In Ezekiel it is a cedar, a stately emblem of Solomonic magnificence.[23] An almond tree is suggested by the rod of Aaron that was placed upon the Ark of the Covenant, since God had designated Aaron to be priest by causing the dead wood of the rod miraculously to sprout a fresh almond branch.[24] The figure of the almond blossom was prominent in the decoration of sacred temple articles, and the episode of the Aaron's rod sprouting hints that the coming Messiah will be a priest as well as king.[25]

The dominant image here is the sprout from the "stump" of David's dynasty as described in Isaiah 11 and alluded to in Isaiah 53. The type of tree is not named in Isaiah, but we find it indicated in a psalm attributed to David in which the writer says of himself, "I am like an olive tree flourishing in the house of God."[26] The olive and cedar are combined in a passage of Hosea where God promises concerning Israel that "his splendor will be like an olive tree, his fragrance like a cedar of Lebanon."[27]

The figure of the new sprout from the stump of the Davidic olive tree brings us back at last to the story of Noah, who sends out birds to find land but without success. The dove he releases at first finds "no resting place [*manowach*] for the sole of her foot."[28] There is a play on words here related to the word for rest. Noah himself is named "rest," *nuwach*, in the hope that he will bring rest to his family.[29] As the waters abate the ark comes "to rest" on the hills of Ararat, but the dove still cannot find a "resting place," showing that the ordeal is not over. With

---

21 Luke 1:32.
22 Jer 23:5; Ezek 17:22-23; Zech 3:8.
23 Ezek 17:22-23; cf. 1 Kgs 7:1-3.
24 Num 17:8.
25 Ps 110:4; Zech 6:12-13.
26 Ps 52:8.
27 Hos 14:6.
28 Gen 8:9.
29 Gen 5:29.

the passing of another week, Noah again sends out the dove. In the evening, apparently after dark, the dove returns and "in its beak was a freshly plucked olive leaf! Then Noah knew that the water had receded from the earth."[30]

The theme of rest, which centers on the dove, associates this part of the story with God's holy Spirit. It is God's Spirit that "gives rest" to Israel after the exodus from Egypt.[31] God's Spirit "finds rest" in the land of the north according to one of the visions of Zechariah.[32] Most importantly, the Spirit comes to rest on the Messiah:

> A shoot will come up from the stump of Jesse;
>> from his roots a Branch will bear fruit.
> The Spirit of the LORD will rest [*nuwach*] on him—
>> the Spirit of wisdom and of understanding,
>> the Spirit of counsel and of power,
>> the Spirit of knowledge and of the fear of the LORD.
>> —Isaiah 11:1-2

The dove when first sent out does not find rest, just as the ark is not a real resting place for its passengers and just as Joshua in leading the people of Mosaic Covenant into the promised land does not give them genuine rest from sin and its effects.[33] On its second flight, the dove does find a resting place—on a newly growing olive tree. The dove then carries a "leaf" or "leafy branch," *aleh*, back to Noah.[34] From comparing the Genesis narrative with Isaiah 11:1-2, we see that the dove encodes God's Spirit coming to rest on the metaphorical olive branch, the Messiah.

In the Gospels, a graphic fulfillment occurs when Jesus is baptized and "the Holy Spirit descended on him in bodily form like a dove."[35] The work of introducing the Messiah is performed in stages, however. First, God's Spirit brings the Son of God into the world of mankind though the miraculous conception of Jesus in the womb of Mary. Then

---

30 Gen 8:11.
31 Isa 63:14.
32 Zech 6:8.
33 Heb 4:8.
34 Cf. Neh 8:15.
35 Luke 3:22.

the Spirit introduces Jesus to Israel at his baptism. Finally, the Spirit raises Jesus from the dead and brings him to his disciples. "He was put to death in the body but made alive by the Spirit."[36] "Through the Spirit of holiness Jesus was declared with power to be the Son of God by his resurrection from the dead."[37]

When Noah receives the olive branch, he finds rest himself because he now has unmistakable evidence that somewhere out of sight a living world is emerging. Likewise, to those who receive him as messianic Savior Jesus promises, "You will find rest for your souls."[38]

The writer of Hebrews says that those who respond in faith to the good news about Jesus enter into God's "rest."[39] The book of Acts quotes Paul as telling the disbelieving philosophers of Athens that the resurrection of Jesus is evidence that God's purpose for the future is certain to be realized. "For [God] has set a day when he will judge the world with justice by the man he has appointed. He has given proof of this to all men by raising him from the dead."[40] Jesus, the "man whose name is the Branch," is for Paul the guarantee of a new created order just beyond human sight, the way the sprig of olive delivered by the dove acts as a guarantee of a new world after the deluge.[41]

1 Corinthians 15 contains an essay by Paul on the doctrine of the resurrection. In the view of Paul, the general resurrection is a key event of Christ's parousia or "second coming," part of a universal regeneration. He invokes the resurrection of Jesus to rebut those who have been sowing doubts about the resurrection of all the dead. "For if the dead are not raised, then Christ has not been raised either." Without the resurrection, he says, "our preaching is useless and so is your faith" and Christians who have died, "those who have fallen asleep in Christ," are lost.

"But," Paul insists, "Christ has indeed been raised from the dead."[42] The re-making of the universe has already begun with Jesus' own tri-

---

36 1 Pet 3:18; cf. Rom 8:11.
37 Rom 1:4.
38 Matt 11:29.
39 Heb 4:1-8.
40 Acts 17:31.
41 Zech 6:12.
42 1 Cor 15:12-20.

umph over death and decay. The Gospel Age is a necessary lull in the transformation of a dying world into what Paul calls a liberated creation and 2 Peter calls a "new heavens and new earth."[43] Jesus is "the first fruits of those who have fallen asleep." A token of Jesus' status as "first fruits," *aparche*, of the new creation is that he was resurrected on the first day of the week after Passover, which the Law of Moses designates as the day for offering to God the first fruits from the earliest grain harvest of the Jewish sacred year, the barley harvest.[44]

Finding Rest in Jesus

With Jesus, therefore, the faithful Jewish remnant see what they have waited for generation after generation. This remnant is well pictured as a man of great age, the way Genesis depicts Noah. And it is not Noah alone who represents the aged remnant of Israel, since he is accompanied on the ark by his wife and family. In the New Testament we find a man and woman who, although not husband and wife, jointly represent the patient remnant so eager for a sign that Israel's destiny will be fulfilled. These are the prophet Simeon and the prophetess Anna, who jointly encounter Jesus when he is taken to Jerusalem after circumcision.[45]

According to Luke, Simeon has been "waiting for the consolation of Israel." He must be advanced in years, because the Spirit has revealed to him that he will not die before he looks upon the Messiah. Moved by God's Spirit to go to the courts of the temple, he sees a baby. The infant Jesus is there in the company of his parents, who apparently are also carrying a pair of doves, *peristera*, the same type of bird that delivers the olive sprig to Noah. The narrative notes that doves or pigeons had to be brought as an offering after the birth of a child.[46]

---

43 Rom 8:21; 2 Pet 3:13.
44 1 Cor 15:20; Lev 23:10-11, 15, LXX. The Pharisaic tradition, which came to dominate Judaism by the close of the first century, was to offer the first fruits of barley on Nisan 16, the day after the eating of the Passover. But the Sadduccees had adhered to the actual words of Leviticus, which state that the offering was to be made "the day after the Sabbath," that is, the first day of the week.
45 Luke 2:22-38.
46 Luke 2:24; Gen 8:8, LXX.

Appropriately, the last three letters of the name "Simeon" when reversed spell Noe, the Greek form of "Noah." And Simeon finds rest when he looks upon the baby in Mary's arms, just as Noah does when he sees the olive branch in the beak of the dove:

> Sovereign LORD, as you have promised,
>> you now dismiss your servant in peace.
> For my eyes have seen your salvation,
>> which you have prepared in the sight of all people.
>> —Luke 2:29-31

As Simeon finishes speaking, the aged prophetess Anna approaches. "She gave thanks to God and spoke about the child to all who were looking forward to the redemption of Jerusalem."[47]

In the Genesis story, the day comes when Noah, his wife and family set foot again on dry land. Noah then offers sacrifices of ceremonially clean animals. The dove that brought the olive branch is not sacrificed, since as it has flown into the sky and is not seen again until its descent at Jesus' baptism.[48] But one or more doves must be among the offerings, as they were at Jesus' presentation, since additional specimens of domestic animals and birds are present.[49] As the smoke of the sacrifice ascends, God smells a "restful" aroma, niychowach (from nuwach) in keeping with the theme of rest or peace being restored to creation. God gives Noah basic commands for living and then offers the appearance of a rainbow as a sign that never again will he bring a great deluge upon the earth.

The narrative need not mean that rain and rainbows had never before occurred, but that the refracted light of the sun as it pierces the clouds now will become a covenant pledge. The overarching rainbow, the outermost color of which is always red, will serve as a model for a sign of divine grace yet to come.

As the Israelites of later history prepare to make their exodus from Egypt, God tells them to take the blood of the Passover lamb and splash it "on on the top and on both sides of the door frame" of each

---

47 Luke 2:38.
48 Gen 8:12; Matt 3:16.
49 Gen 7:2-3; 8:20.

Israelite house.[50] The crimson-stained arch formed by the doorway will deter the avenging angel so that the peace of the residents may remain undisturbed. We have only to compare the language of Genesis and Exodus to see how the idea is repeated:

> I have set my rainbow in the clouds, and it will be the sign [*oth*] of the covenant between me and the earth . . . Whenever the rainbow appears in the clouds, I will see [*raah*] it and remember the everlasting covenant between God and all living creatures of every kind on the earth. —Genesis 9:13-16

> The blood will be a sign [*oth*] for you on the houses where you are; and when I see [*raah*] the blood, I will pass over you. No destructive plague will touch you when I strike Egypt.
> —Exodus 12:13

The Passover lamb typifies Jesus, the "lamb of God" whose blood shields believing mankind from the deadly judgment upon sin.[51] The blood of Jesus is prefigured in the iridescent red of the rainbow as surely as it is in the blood-splashed doorway at Passover.

The evidence is strong that the deluge of Genesis is a systematic portrayal of man's plight and of Jesus as God's means of salvation. The emphasis of the story is on universality—the universally corrupting consequences of sin and the universal nature of the restoration God is accomplishing. Like Noah's family huddled in the ark as the implacable waters swirl around, human beings even with all the advancements of science find themselves confined to a tiny bubble swirling through the uncaring depths of space. Only the metaphors of divine revelation give us a glimpse of a new creative order emerging through the mystery of God's work in Christ. We will turn our attention next to two other portrayals of this divine project.

---

50 Exod 12:22.
51 Isa 53:7; Jer 11:19; John 1:29.

14

Wonderworkers of the North

The prophets of Israel were not, as a rule, known for mighty works of a supernatural character. Their authority came from the weight of their divine messages, with miracles serving as rare punctuation marks. The exceptions are Moses, Joshua, Elijah and Elisha. The last two were prophets to the northern kingdom of Israel, which may explain why miracle-working was an such an important feature of their ministries. The northern kings discouraged their subjects from visiting the temple in Jerusalem. The authentication of powerful deeds would have been more important to prophets in the north than in Judah, which possessed genuine priests of Yahweh and and a rich written tradition.

Typological meaning is to be found in two miracles, one performed by Elijah and one by Elisha. We will consider the narrative about Elisha first, even though it is the second chronologically, because I have already laid the groundwork for understanding it. One of its symbols is the staff or rod, which I demonstrated from Chapter 1 onward to represent primarily the Mosaic Law. Closely connected to the rod is an idea reflected in the book of Ruth, that of the insufficiency of the law as an instrument of salvation. I will begin by reviewing certain sayings of Jesus from the Gospel of Luke.

Luke had a special interest in the people of Samaria and their history, a fact that we will explore in detail in a later chapter. The beloved parable of the Good Samaritan, for example, is recorded only in Luke. Jesus seems to have created the parable by reworking a story from the long historical record of the northern kingdom that occupies the last half of the book of 1 Kings and the first half of 2 Kings.

The story behind the Good Samaritan is one we touched on in Chapter 11, concerning a prophet who is sent from Judah northward to Israel to pronounce judgment against King Jeroboam I. After delivering the message, the prophet disobeys God's instruction to return southward immediately and so is killed by a lion. Passersby leave his corpse lying in the road unattended until another prophet, a Samaritan, carries the man's body away on a donkey and gives him an honorable burial.[1]

In Jesus' parable, the prophet from Judah becomes an ordinary Judean who, rather than being killed by a lion, is attacked by robbers and left "half-dead" on the roadside. A priest and a Levite temple-keeper both pass by the injured man without offering aid. Finally, a sympathetic Samaritan sees the man and takes pity on him. He pours oil and wine on the man's wounds, puts him on his own donkey and takes him to an inn where he can be nursed back to health.[2]

The Good Samaritan story advocates compassion, but it does so by means of a plot that is coded. The symbolism was recognized by a long succession of church fathers beginning with Irenaeus.[3] The stricken man in the road is a good picture of humanity dying in its state of alienation from God. The priest and Levite represent the Mosaic Law, of which they were custodians. It is not callousness alone that prevents them from helping the injured man, but the law. The man looks as if he might already be dead, and the ceremonial uncleanness caused by touching a dead body would bar them from religious duties for at least a week.[4] The inability of the law to save is here graphically depicted just as

---

1   1 Kgs 13:1-32; 2 Kgs 23:17-18. The compassionate action of the northern Israelites during another episode (2 Chron. 28:8-15) also appears to have been a model for the parable recorded in Luke. See J. D. M. Derrett, "Law in the New Testament: Fresh Light on the Parable of the Good Samaritan," *New Testament Studies* 10 (1964): 22-37.

2   Luke 10:30-37.

3   Irenaeus, *Adv. Her.* 3.17.3.

4   Lev 21:10-12; Num 19:22.

it is in the book of Ruth by the unwillingness of Elimelech's unnamed relative to become the repurchaser of Ruth and Naomi.

The actions of the Samaritan of the parable are closely aligned with those of Jesus.[5] Jesus is the one who for the salvation of humanity administers the sanctifying Spirit and his own sacrificial blood as symbolized by the oil and wine.[6] The Spirit is pictured also by the money left with innkeeper as a down payment for treatment of the injured man, judging from other texts that call the Spirit a "down payment" to initiate the transformation of believers.[7]

The Samaritan promises the innkeeper that he will settle the man's bill in full when he returns, using a verb form that occurs nowhere else except in a passage about Jesus' own return at the *parousia*.[8] To help those in need as the Samaritan does is to imitate the love of Christ, who restores life where the Mosaic Law cannot.

The Quickening Touch of the Master

The subtext of the Good Samaritan is the same as that of the resurrection performed by Elisha, as we will see shortly. Other connections between Elisha and Luke's Gospel also are noteworthy. Luke is the only book of the New Testament to refer to Elisha by name.[9] More subtly, Luke alone records a command given by Jesus to his followers that duplicates one given by Elisha to his servant. Matthew, Mark and Luke all have Jesus advising his disciples not to take extra money or garments when they go on a preaching tour but instead to have faith that hospitality will be extended to them. Only Luke adds the instruction, ". . . and do not greet anyone on the road."[10] The urgency of their mission demanded that they travel quickly to the villages where they were being sent and not become distracted with socializing along the way.

---

5   In John, when Jesus is accused of being "a Samaritan and demon-possessed," he replies, "I am not possessed by a demon" (John 8:48-49). Though ethnically Jewish, he leaves open the possibility that in some sense he can indeed be thought of as "a Samaritan."

6   1 Pet 1:2.

7   2 Cor 1:22.

8   Greek, *epanerchomai* in Luke 10:35; 19:15.

9   Luke 4:27.

10 Luke 10:4.

Elisha, also, had commanded his servant to undertake a mission without stopping to exchange formal greetings with those whom he passed on the road. The full narrative, at 2 Kings 4:8-37, begins when Elisha travels through Shunem, the village from which Solomon's bride Abishag had come. He and his servant receive hospitality at the home of a woman there, and the woman even suggests to her husband that they furnish a room exclusively for Elisha to use when he is in the area.

The woman could be one of the many sympathetic Canaanites who live in Israel, because when Elisha gratefully offers to obtain a favor for her from the Israelite king she demurs, saying, "I have a home among my own people." Determined to do something for the woman, when Elisha learns that she has no son he promises her that within a year's time she will be holding a baby boy. The woman asks the prophet not to give her false hope, but within a few months she becomes pregnant and bears a son.

To this point the story reminds us of the birth stories involving Sarah and Ruth. We have already seen that such accounts have an underlying theme, namely, that what cannot be accomplished through fleshly means—the formation of a divinely blessed people—can only be done by God's grace in Christ. Failure to obtain the blessing is symbolized in those episodes by the woman's barrenness. Another way to illustrate that failure could be by the birth of a child who dies without reaching maturity.

A son who died before passing on the family name was, in a certain sense, equivalent to one who had never lived. We know this because of what next happens in the story. When the Shunammite's son is still a young boy, just reaching the age when he can help his father in the fields, he develops an agonizing headache, perhaps due to fever, and dies. The woman immediately gets on her donkey and goes to Elisha at Mount Carmel. "Did I ask you for a son, my lord?," she asks plaintively when she sees him. "Didn't I tell you, 'Don't raise my hopes'?"[11] To be given a son who dies in his youth is in the woman's eyes equivalent to being promised a son who is never born.

It is now that Elisha hands his staff to his servant Gehazi and tells him to run ahead to the Shunammite's house without stopping to greet those he passes on the road. When Gehazi reaches the house he is to lay

_____
11   2 Kgs 4:28.

Elisha's staff on the face of the dead boy. In the meantime, Elisha and the woman follow at a slower pace.

Gehazi does as he is told, but the application of the staff has no effect. Assuming that the staff pictures the law, what is being portrayed is the failure of the Mosaic Law to bring to life the promises of God regarding Israel. The staff cannot revive the boy, just as in the story of Ruth Elimelech's sons cannot produce an heir. The wording of the Hebrew narrative confirms this interpretation. The staff is "laid" or "set," *siym*, upon the boy's "face," *paneh*. God similarly had set his law before Israel, the word "before" being an idiom that literally means "to the face." Three times the giving of the law is referred to that way:

> So Moses went back and summoned the elders of the people and set [*siym*] before [*le-paneh*] them all the words the LORD had commanded him to speak. The people all responded together, "We will do everything the LORD has said." —Exodus 19:7-8

> These are the laws you are to set [*siym*] before [*le-paneh*] them.
> —Exodus 21:1

> This is the law Moses set [*siym*] before [*le-paneh*] the Israelites.
> —Deuteronomy 4:44

The law had been delivered by Moses, the servant of Yahweh, just as the staff was carried and applied by the servant of Elisha.[12] But the law did not raise Israel to the glorious destiny promised them any more than the staff raises the young boy's corpse.

Gehazi must go out to meet Elisha and the child's mother with the dispiriting news, "The boy has not awakened." When the prophet gets to the house, he goes alone into the room where the boy is lying face up. He then lies on top of the child, "mouth to mouth, eyes to eyes, hands to hands." As Elisha "stretches himself out" upon the body, circulation returns and the boy's flesh grows warm. The boy is still unconscious, though, so Elisha gets up, leaves the room and paces back and forth in the house. Finally, he goes back into the room and stretches himself out on the body again. The boy sneezes several times

---

12 The title "the servant of the LORD" is applied to Moses 16 times in the Old Testament: e.g.g., Deut 34:5; Josh 1:1; 2 Kgs 18:12.

and opens his eyes. Elisha presents the boy alive and well to his mother, who bows before the prophet in gratitude.

The "man coming after" the prophet Elijah was in a ceremonial sense the anointed king of Israel, Ahab, and in a chronological sense a prophet who would perform works greater than Elijah's, that is, Elisha. On a larger scale, both the anointed king and the greater prophet function as types for the ultimate successor of Elijah, Jesus. With that identification in mind, it is easy to understand Elisha's action as representative of the coming of God's Son.

"The Word became flesh," John says, "and made his dwelling among us." The Mosaic Law having proved ineffective, the Son of God who shares the Father's glory put himself into direct contact with humanity. John continues, "For the law was given through Moses; grace and truth came through Jesus Christ."[13]

The book of Exodus says that God spoke to Moses "face to face, as a man speaks with his friend," to indicate the extraordinary closeness of their communication.[14] A similar statement is found at Numbers 12:8, but the common translation "face to face" there is a paraphrase of the Hebrew, which says literally "mouth to mouth." From the language about Moses we can decipher the act performed by Elisha as a symbol of close personal communication, but the fulfillment brought a closeness to God that even Moses did not enjoy.

With the coming of Jesus, men and women were brought face to face with the divine. "We saw his glory, glory as of the only begotten from the Father, full of grace and truth."[15] "Anyone who has seen me has seen the Father," Jesus says.[16] The letter of 1 John overflows with the wonder of God having drawn near in Christ:

> That which was from the beginning, which we have heard, which we have seen with our eyes, which we have looked at and our hands have touched—this we proclaim...we proclaim to you the eternal life, which was with the Father and has appeared to us.
>
> —1 John 1:1-2

---

13 John 1:17.
14 Exod 33:11.
15 John 1:14.
16 John 14:9.

The words of the Elisha narrative, "mouth to mouth, eyes to eyes, hands to hands," encode the mystery of the incarnation. That mystery in turn leads to another, a resurrection, but it does so in two stages. Elisha has to leave the boy and return before life is fully restored. Here we need to turn back to the parable of the Good Samaritan and note again the process by which the dying man is healed. The Samaritan starts the man on his way back to health by making arrangements for his care, leaving a deposit for the costs incurred. He promises to come back and pay whatever else is owing, indicating that in time the man's recovery will be complete. The real "Good Samaritan," Jesus, garnered the full price of man's restoration at Calvary, but he applies that price in stages.

The New Testament maintains a dynamic tension between statements about the present and future state of faithful Christians. Believers are saved, yet they await salvation.[17] They are redeemed, yet they await redemption.[18] They have righteousness credited to them, yet they await righteousness.[19] As we have already seen, Jesus earned the right to pour out God's Spirit as a "down payment" or "deposit" on the universal regeneration yet to come. In the first phase of Elisha's resurrection miracle, the boy's flesh becomes warm, indicating that the heart has been restarted.

The Bible says that the "deposit" of the Spirit is an infusion of divine life into the figurative heart, the seat of motivation.[20] During the Gospel Age, the Spirit works in the hearts of believers, not bringing instant perfection, but gradually weeding out vice and nurturing its place the fruitage of "love, joy, peace, patience, kindness, goodness, faithfulness, gentleness and self-control."[21] Paul reminds the Christians in Philippi that "he who began a good work in you will carry it on to completion until the day of Christ Jesus."[22]

"Now we see but a poor reflection as in a mirror; then we shall see

---

17 Eph 2:5; 1 Pet 1:5.
18 Gal 3:13; Luke 21:28.
19 Rom 5:1; Gal 5:5.
20 2 Cor 1:22; Gal 4:6.
21 Gal 5:22.
22 Phil 1:6.

face to face," Paul writes to Christians at Corinth.[23] He is referring to the return of Jesus, when all human dead will be resurrected, beginning with the faithful. He tells the Thessalonians that the Lord will descend from heaven and "the dead in Christ will rise first."[24] Jesus will transform believers into his own glorious image.[25] Here the raising of the boy by Elisha corresponds to the literal resurrection of Christ's disciples.

Elisha comes back into the room where the boy lies alive but unconscious, just as Jesus re-enters the world at the end of the Gospel Age. The boy awakens at Elisha's second touch, fully revived, as believers do when the returning Jesus gives the supernatural command for them to rise "on the last day."[26] The two-stage awakening is evident from Jesus' statement in John that "a time is coming [at the *parousia*] and has now come [with Jesus' ministry] when the dead will hear the voice of the Son of God and those who hear will live [first by spiritual awakening, later by bodily resurrection]."[27]

The account of Elisha's resurrection miracle combines a spare but gripping narrative with straightforward symbolism. The subject of the portrayal makes it all the more enthralling. What from a naturalistic point of view looks like one legend among thousands, just another undistinguished relic of pre-scientific ignorance, we can now see as a revelation of cosmic proportions.

Jesus' work of redeeming not just the world as we know it but all of reality extends beyond the ambitions—even beyond the imaginings—of human beings. It makes sense that God would confirm such a revelation by metaphor because in no other way can truths beyond the reach of our senses be communicated. The diagram of an atom as an orbital system, the description of electricity as a "current" and the measurement of radiation by "wavelength" demonstrate the indispensability of metaphors even in the sciences. Illustrations, like wax paper windows, are transparent enough to reveal the shape of objects viewed through them yet opaque enough to be distinguished from those objects.

---

23 1 Cor 13:12; cf. 1 John 3:2.
24 1 Thess 4:16.
25 Phil 3:21.
26 John 6:40.
27 John 5:25.

Glorification on Mt. Carmel

Elijah, the forerunner of Elisha, also had performed a resurrection of a young boy, though that brief incident takes place immediately after the boy's death.[28] The greatest miracle of Elijah, however, is the "Fire Test" on Mt. Carmel.[29] The test is a showdown between Elijah and four hundred priests of Baal near the end of Elijah's ministry. The patroness of the Canaanite deity is King Ahab's Phoenician wife Jezebel, who has made a place for the Baal priests by systematically murdering the prophets of Yahweh. Elijah challenges the priests to prepare an ox as a sacrifice and then induce Baal send fire upon it. The priests lay out the offering and call upon their god, but no answer comes in response to hours of chanting and ecstatic dancing.

Elijah then prepares his own sacrifice. With the help of Israelite onlookers he repairs the neglected altar of Yahweh, which consists of twelve stones corresponding to Israel's tribes. He places the pieces of the slaughtered ox on the altar atop a pile of wood. He has the people dig a trench around the altar and pour water over the sacrifice. Three times the people douse the offering, until the water draining off the altar fills the trench.

Finally, Elijah begins to pray. "Answer me, O LORD, answer me, so these people will know that you, O LORD, are God, and that you are turning their hearts back again." The awe-inspiring answer comes instantly: "Then the fire of the LORD fell and burned up the sacrifice, the wood, the stones and the soil, and also licked up the water in the trench." In a spasm of contrition the people praise the God of Israel, then seize the priests of Baal and put them to death.

It seems that Elijah pours water over the offering to heighten the miracle. With the sacrifice and altar thoroughly drenched there can be no question of the prophet surreptitiously setting fire to the wood, or of anything else igniting it other than heat like that of a blast furnace. Why, then, is the trench dug? Simply pouring the water over the sacrifice should be sufficient.

The water must serve an additional purpose, one that becomes apparent by looking at the altar-shrine as a whole. The trench having been

28 1 Kgs 17:17-24.
29 1 Kgs 18:20-40

filled by runoff, the earth under the altar becomes an island in a miniature ocean. The Septuagint Bible refers to the trench by the Greek word
thalassa, "sea." Such a combination of earth and water could function as
a model of the earthly creation, corresponding to the Biblical picture of
the habitable world as an expanse of land surrounded by the oceanic
deep.[30] "I worship the LORD, the God of heaven, who made the sea
and the land," says Jonah as a way of calling Yahweh the creator of everything.[31] In the Psalms, as well, the combination of land and sea
encompasses the world:

> The earth is the LORD's, and everything in it,
>   the world, and all who live in it;
>   for he founded it upon the seas
>   and established it upon the waters.
>   —Psalm 24:1-2; cf. 104:5-9.

The dry ground at the center of the Mount Carmel microcosm supports the twelve foundation stones of the altar. The image suggests the
New Jerusalem and spiritual temple, figurative structures that stand for
the faithful church. The church, as we have considered in previous
chapters, is "built on the foundation of the apostles and prophets."[32]
"The wall of the city had twelve foundation stones," says Revelation,
"and on them were the twelve names of the twelve apostles of the
Lamb."[33] The "living stones" of the congregation "are being built into a
spiritual house," says 1 Peter, for the purpose of "offering spiritual sacrifices."[34]

Elijah's altar-shrine, too, acts as a rudimentary temple, the minimum
structure necessary for presenting sacrifices to God. The association of
stones with the founding ancestors of a nation, and the repair of a structure as a figure for the regathering of God's people can be documented
from the Old Testament as well as the New.[35]

---

30 Ps 104:5-9; Prov 8:29. This simple model of the earth and sea made possible
    the vision of a mountain that "filled the whole earth" in Dan 2:35.
31 Cf. Acts 14:15.
32 Eph 2:20.
33 Rev 21:14, NASB; cf. Isa 54:11-13.
34 1 Pet 2:5.
35 Exod 24:4-5; Amos 9:11; Acts 15:14-17.

On top of the altar is the sacrificial ox or bull laid upon the wood. Jesus is the sacrifice of which most animal offerings under the Old Covenant are shadows. His blood, Hebrews says, atones in a way that the "blood of goats and bulls" cannot.[36] In Genesis we see how Isaac, as a type of Jesus, is designated as a sacrifice to God. Following the instructions of his father, Abraham, Isaac carries the firewood for the offering up a lonely hill near the village that will one day be Jerusalem, just as Jesus will later carry the horizontal beam of the cross to Golgotha. At the top of the hill, Abraham arranges the wood on an altar and then lays Isaac "upon the wood," *epano ton zulon* in the Greek of the Septuagint.[37]

Near the top of Carmel, Elijah likewise takes the slaughtered bull and lays it "upon the kindling," *epi tas skidakas*. Referring to Jesus' death on a wooden cross, 1 Peter 2:24 says that he bore our sins in his own body "upon the tree" or "upon the wood," *epi to zulon*. We therefore have good reason to see the sacrificial ox on the altar as representing Jesus.

So far we see that Elijah's altar complex could signify Jesus as the offering upon the wood, the church as the stones of the altar and the patch of ground surrounded by water as the whole of earthly creation. It is these items order from top to bottom that are triply baptized with water and then consumed by the heavenly fire.

"Consumed" is an appropriate term because a "holocaust" or whole burnt offering was not destroyed for destruction's sake, but to symbolize its transference from man's sphere to God's. That which was touched by divine fire became holy.[38] The antitype of whole burnt offerings under the law is Jesus, whose sacrificial death culminated in his resurrection to a glorious estate and his ascension into the presence of God.[39]

Christians, too, are spoken of as "living sacrifices" in the sense that they are devoted to God and destined to be received into his presence.[40] Their glorification occurs after that of Jesus, of course, just as the altar stones are consumed by the heavenly fire only after the ox and wood.

---

36 Heb 9:13-14.
37 Gen 22:9, LXX.
38 Num 16:35-37; Isa 6:6-7.
39 Exod 29:14; cf. Heb 13:11-12.
40 Rom 12:1.

"All will be made alive," Paul says, "but each in his own turn: Christ, the first fruits; then, when he comes, those who belong to him."[41]

In keeping with the events at Carmel, the living stones of the church are baptized with water in the three-fold name of Father, Son and Spirit.[42] The baptism of water is followed by one of fire.[43] A graphic token of fire baptism accompanied the inauguration of the spiritual temple at Pentecost, when as reported in the book of Acts tongues of fire miraculously appeared over the heads of the gathered disciples.[44] Baptism in water and in the fire of the Spirit comes to fruition only through the process of death and resurrection.

"All of us who were baptized into Christ Jesus were baptized into his death," Paul tells Roman believers. "If we have been united with [Jesus] like this in his death, we will certainly also be united with him in his resurrection."[45] In the resurrection, Christ "will transform our lowly bodies so that they will be like his glorious body."[46] The resurrection and glorification of the church are represented by the fiery disappearance of the stones of Elijah's altar. Moreover, the fire that descends on the altar has still further effects.

Chapter 9 discussed the reward promised David for killing Goliath, which included the release of David's family estate from taxation. We learned that this release corresponded to the liberation of the physical universe from the effects of sin as described by Paul in the book of Romans. After reminding believers that God's Spirit can enliven them as it did Jesus at his resurrection, Paul goes on to say that "the creation itself will be liberated from its bondage to decay and brought into the glorious freedom of the children of God."[47]

Other passages place the same promise of a regeneration or "restoration of all things" alongside the promise of eternal life for believers. Ephesians 1:5-11, for example, speaks of the redemption of the elect as taking place in connection with God's purpose "to bring all things in heaven and on earth together" under Christ. According to 1 Corinthians

---

41 1 Cor 15:22-23.
42 Matt 28:19.
43 Matt 3:11; Luke 3:16; John 3:5.
44 Acts 2:3.
45 Rom 6:3-5; cf. Mark 10:39.
46 Phil 3:21.
47 Rom 8:11, 21.

15, cited above, the raising of Jesus to glorious life is to be followed by the raising of the church and the placing of "everything under Christ's feet" until death is banished forever.[48] The allusion in 1 Corinthians is to Psalm 8, where "everything" placed "under the feet" of man embraces "the beasts of the field, the birds of the air, and the fish of the sea" along with all the "work of God's hands."

The concluding portion of the book of Revelation similarly introduces "a new heaven and a new earth" just after portraying the resurrection of the church and the resurrection of mankind in general. God himself unveils the beautified universe by proclaiming, "I am making everything new!"[49]

The doctrine of the recreation allows us to decipher the last detail of the Mount Carmel miracle. As with the amount of water poured over the sacrifice, the astral heat of the fire seems exaggerated insofar as it vaporizes not just the offering and wood but the stones, the earth beneath the altar and the water in the trench. We now are able to see the real reason for what occurs. Recall that the island of earth surrounded by water is a model of the creation. In order to depict the assumption of the created order into divine glory, the fire must consume those parts of the shrine just as it does the bull and the altar stones.

The foremost miracle of Elijah, like that of Elisha, typologically declares the sovereign purpose of God in Christ. The two stories summarize different aspects of salvation history stretching from the fall of man and the giving of the law through the incarnation, the sacrifice of Jesus, the second coming and the redemption of man and the universe.

In their day, the northern prophets by their powerful works demonstrated the existence of the God of Israel; long after their death, the record of those works continues to do so. The only known writing of either prophet consists of a single, brief letter from Elijah to Jehoram, king of Judah.[50] Even without leaving behind written prophecy, Elijah and Elisha, like the other prophets, bore witness to "the sufferings of Christ and the glories that would follow."[51]

---

48 1 Cor 15:25-26; cf. Heb 2:6-9.
49 Rev 20:4-21:5; cf. 2 Pet 3:13.
50 2 Chron 21:12-15.
51 1 Pet 1:11.

We have so far examined many ways in which the Hebrew prophets announced the coming of Jesus, but the prophets were not the only messengers to do so. In the Psalms we are told that the sun, moon and stars also prophesy. This heavenly chorus is the subject of our next study.

15

What the Heavens Declare

"When I consider your heavens," the Psalmist tells God, "the work of your fingers, the moon and the stars, which you have set in place, what is man that you are mindful of him, the son of man that you care for him?"[1] There is no reason to think that the writer had anything like a scientific view of the stars and planets or, given his circumstances and calling, that he needed it. The educational gulf between his understanding of the heavens and ours is difficult to overestimate. Easily, though, shared emotion bridges the intervening centuries.

The Psalmist gazes up into the immensity of the night sky and feels at once a flush of admiration and a pang of insignificance. Can anyone claim that our accumulated knowledge about the cosmos, plotted on scales of time and distance that tax the human imagination, fails to arouse in us the same response as that of the Psalmist? Who is unmoved contemplating the billions of galaxies that scatter through the void like noiseless fireworks, each of them unfathomably huge and yet as ornate as a pinwheel of spun glass?

Today the infinitesimal size of man's home when weighed against the vastness of the universe is usually thought to be inconsistent with the Biblical notion of a Creator. If God envisaged man as the apex of his creation, the argument goes, then why would he consign him to a puny spec of a planet orbiting a run-of-the-mill star dangling at the edge of a monotonously average galaxy? Why should we find ourselves confined to the tiniest grain of sand on the cosmic beach?

---

1   Ps 8:3-4.

That way of thinking is childish—literally—because the mistake of confusing size or location with moral significance is one a child is likely to make. The Psalmist commits no such error, but instead praises God for a world where moral and spiritual dimensions exist independently of physical size, and where creatures immeasurably dwarfed by the stars can be destined for "glory and honor."[2]

We find it written in Psalm 19 that "the heavens declare the glory of God, and the work of his hands the expanse is telling." What in human terms appears needlessly large, the Psalm reminds us, is appropriate as the product of a transcendent Creator-God. We might as well reproach Michelangelo for having made his "David" a towering giant instead of a palm-sized miniature. How, exactly, was God supposed to engender in us the awe we rightly feel when we behold the extent of the universe other than by making it as large as it is? Assuming there is a Supreme Being, he need not scrimp on space as if it were a limited commodity.

To the Psalmist, the heavenly architecture is one way in which the majesty of the invisible God is made perceptible. "Day after day [the heavens] pour forth speech," he writes, and "night after night they display knowledge."[3] With wordless eloquence the skies testify to man about their Maker.

A Great Light to Rule the Day

"Heavens" in the nineteenth Psalm means the upper regions with their constellations. The poet quickly narrows his focus, however. "In the heavens [God] has pitched a tent for the sun," he continues, "which is like a bridegroom coming forth from his pavilion, like a champion rejoicing to run his course." We also encounter the imagery of the bridegroom in the Song of Solomon. Solomon, son of David and type of the Messiah, takes as his wife the Shulammite, representing the church as ideal Israel.

The New Testament contains many references to Jesus as husband and all four Gospels describe him as the bridegroom.[4] It also associates

---

2   Ps 8:5.
3   Ps 19:4.
4   Matt 25:1; Mark 2:19; Luke 5:34; John 3:29.

him with the sun. When Matthew relates the beginning of Jesus' ministry in Galilee, he paraphrases the Hebrew Bible:

> "Land of Zebulun and land of Naphtali,
> the way to the sea, along the Jordan,
> Galilee of the Gentiles—
> the people living in darkness
> have seen a great light;
> on those living in the land of the shadow of death
> a light has dawned." —Matthew 4:15-16

When we turn to the source of the quote, at Isaiah 9:1-2, we find that it introduces the promise of child who will reign from David's throne to establish justice, righteousness and peace forever (vv. 6-7). The comparison of the Messiah's coming to the rising of the sun also occurs in Luke, in a prophecy about John the Baptist. The prophecy attributes the preparatory ministry of John to "the tender mercy of our God, by which the rising sun [the Messiah, Jesus] will come to us from heaven to shine on those living in darkness and in the shadow of death."[5]

During the episode called the Transfiguration, three of the disciples accompany Jesus up a mountain at night and see him transformed so that his face shines "like the sun."[6] In the opening vision of Revelation, likewise, Jesus' face has the brilliance of the sun.[7]

A preliminary identification of Jesus with the sun of Psalm 19 draws our attention to the parallel descriptions of verses five and six. In verse five the sun is a bridegroom coming out of his pavilion who joyfully runs a course or path as does the winning contestant in a footrace. Verse six says more prosaically that the sun's "circuit" is from one end of heaven to the other and that nothing on earth escapes its penetrating heat. We seem to be looking at a typical Hebrew parallelism in which a theme is developed by restatement. Here, however, the repetitive descriptions happen to align with the first and second comings of Jesus.

In Hebrew society a newlywed couple commonly lived for a time in

---

5   Luke 1:78-79.
6   Matt 17:2.
7   Rev 1:16.

the groom's father's house or tent, the "patrilocal residence."[8] Customarily, the groom was provided a room or even a nearby tent that he could prepare as a "honeymoon cottage." In 2 Samuel the rebel Absalom mocks this custom by having his partisans pitch a nuptial tent for him on the roof of his father's palace.[9] Genesis provides a positive example when Isaac takes his bride Rebecca to a tent that must have been made available to him by his father, Abraham.[10]

It is from such a nuptial pavilion, set up by God in the heavens, that the "sun" comes forth as a bridegroom according to the Nineteenth Psalm. At the incarnation, the divine Son follows the pattern of the Psalm by coming forth from God's dwelling or "tent."[11] Heaven, not as the physical location of the stars but as the supernatural abode of God, is both the place the Son came from and the place designated as the figurative nuptial chamber for his bride, the church. In John's Gospel he tells his apostles that he will prepare a place for them to be received at the time of his return. "I will come back and take you to be with me that you also may be where I am."[12] "When he appears, we shall be like him, for we shall see him as he is."[13]

Paul agrees, writing that "the Lord himself will come down from heaven" at the Second Coming, or *parousia*, and "the dead in Christ will rise first." The resurrection of the faithful dead is accompanied by the rapture of living believers. "After that, we who are still alive and are left will be caught up together with them in the clouds to meet the Lord in the air [that is, the supernatural heavens]. And so we will be with the Lord forever."[14] The gathering of the united congregation to be "with the Lord forever" is the spiritual honeymoon or wedding feast at which Jesus drinks anew the cup of joy with his followers.[15] The resurrected disciples must go to Jesus so that they can be revealed in company with him when he manifests himself to the world.[16]

---

8   Raphael Patai, *Sex and Family in the Bible and the Middle East* (Garden City, NY: Doubleday, 1959), 29, 63.

9   2 Sam 16:22.

10 Gen 24:67.

11 Ps 15:1, NASB; John 1:18; 16:28.

12 John 14:3.

13 1 John 3:2; cf. John 17:24.

14 1 Thess 4:17-18; cf. 2 Cor 4:14.

15 Matt 25:1-13; 26:29.

16 Col 3:4.

Immediately after coming forth from his heavenly abode, the sun of Psalm 19 sprints to his destination like a "champion" or "mighty one," *gibbor*. In Chapter 9 we noted the equivalence of the Hebrew term for "mighty one" and the Greek terms *ischuros*, *dunatos* and *gigantes* meaning respectively "strong one," "powerful one" and "giant." Although *gibbor* is used of David's satanic opponent, Goliath, it is also used of the Greater David, the Messiah, at Isaiah 9:6. In the parable of the "strong man" Jesus declares himself to be a "stronger (one)," *ischuroteros*, compared with his adversary, the devil.[17]

When we turn to the Septuagint text of Psalm 19:5, the sun is a "giant" who rejoices to run his "course" or "way," *hodos*. Jesus also had a course laid out for him, as is clear from the Gospels. "Prepare the way [*hodos*] for the Lord, make straight paths for him," are words from Isaiah that anticipate the coming of Jesus, according to Mark's Gospel.[18] "The Son of Man will go as it has been decreed," Jesus says, just as a racer must follow the course as it is mapped out.[19]

"Running" can refer to carrying out a mission from God as the Hebrew prophets did. The Psalmist says to God, "I run in the path of your commands," presaging Jesus' claim that he came into the world to fulfill the law and to carry out the commands of the Father.[20] The New Testament specifically compares a life of godly devotion to a footrace. "Let us throw off everything that hinders and the sin that so easily entangles," advises the book of Hebrews, "and let us run with perseverance the race marked out for us. Let us fix our eyes on Jesus, the author and perfecter of our faith, who for the joy set before him endured the cross."[21]

By saying that Christian runners in the race for life are to have Jesus as their model, the writer of Hebrews implies that Jesus ran such a race to its finish line at the cross. The word here for the "perseverance" of believers, *hupomone*, is derived from the word for the "endurance" of Jesus, *hupomeno*, setting up the parallel. The *NIV Study Bible*, in a note to

17 Luke 11:22.
18 Mark 1:3; cf. Isa 40:3.
19 Luke 22:22.
20 Ps 119:32; Matt 5:17; John 15:10.
21 Heb 12:1-2; cf. 1 Cor 9:24.

Hebrews 12:2, interprets the verse as saying that Jesus has run the race and won the prize in advance of believers.

Hebrews indicates that Jesus ran his race "for the joy set before him." The word translated "joy" in that verse is different than the word for the rejoicing of the sun in the Septuagint, but the thought is similar in either instance. To "run" in expectation of a joyful reward, as Jesus did, is to experience foretastes of that joy even while the race is underway. "Consider it pure joy, my brothers, whenever you face trials of many kinds," James exhorts believers. "Blessed is the man who perseveres [*hupomeno*] under trial, because when he has stood the test, he will receive the crown of life" as did Jesus.[22] The Gospels speak of the joy Jesus experienced in doing his Father's work and of the imparting of that joy, in turn, to Jesus' followers.[23] The roots of this "joy" theme involving the Messiah lie in Old Testament passages such as Psalm 21:1-6 and Psalm 45:7.

The Eye in the Sky

The harmony we have documented thus far between Psalm 19:5 and the sending of God's Son into the world consists of seven elements: (1) the "sun" or enlightener and (2) spiritual bridegroom (3) comes forth from heaven, the place where he intends one day to bring his beloved, and (4) like an athletic champion he (5) joyfully (6) runs (7) a path that leads him to the agony of the cross. To these elements from the fifth verse we will add two more. "It rises at one end of the heavens," verse six says of the sun, "and makes its circuit to the other; nothing is hidden from its heat."

The expression, "from one end of heaven to the other," indicates universality. Moses invites the people of Israel to inquire "from one end of the heavens to the other" to see if anything has been witnessed to compare with the miracles God performed in the course of delivering them from Egypt. Jesus promises that at his Second Coming his sovereignty will allow him to gather his people "from one end of the heavens to the other."[24]

---

22 Jas 1:2, 12.
23 Luke 10:21; John 17:13.
24 Matt 24:31.

What is left unstated but understood in Psalm 19 is the direction of the sun's movement. The "end of heaven" it starts from is the east, while the western horizon is where it finishes. With the sun's motion in mind, we turn to two of Jesus' statements about the Second Coming. "For the Son of Man in his day will be like the lightning," he says in Luke, "which flashes and lights up the sky [*ouranos*, heaven] from one end to the other."[25]

By supernatural means Jesus will make himself known to all, "as lightning that comes from the east is visible even in the west," according to Matthew.[26] A more literal translation of the verse from Matthew reads, "For just as lightning comes from the east and flashes even to the west, so will the coming of the Son of Man be."[27] The simile of lightning rather than sunlight is necessary in this context to convey the suddenness of Jesus' appearing, but the lightning follows the sun's path from east to west. Looking closely at the accounts of the transfiguration, we find that the luminescence emanating from Jesus combines the brilliance of sunlight and lightning.[28]

The last clause of Psalm 19:5-6 says about the sun that "nothing is hidden from its heat." The sun's light as such may not find its way into the earth's caves and crannies, but its energy warms the entire landscape. If we consider both the visible and invisible parts of the sun's spectrum, nothing on earth is untouched by its radiance. The same verse in the Septuagint reads, "No one shall be hidden [*apokruphos*] from his heat." We don't have to look far to find a correspondence with the coming of Jesus. Paul, in defending himself against aspersions cast on his motives, tells Corinthian Christians to "judge nothing before the appointed time; wait till the Lord comes. He will bring to light what is hidden [*kruptos*] in darkness and will expose the motives of men's hearts."[29]

The Hebrew Bible uses light and darkness to illustrate the sifting of a man's innermost being by God. "O LORD, you have searched me and you know me," the Psalmist says. "If I say, 'Surely the darkness will hide

---

25 Luke 17:24.
26 Matt 24:27.
27 Matt 24:27, NASB.
28 Matt 17:2; Lk. 9:29.
29 1 Cor 4:5.

me'. . . even the darkness will not be dark to you; the night will shine like the day."[30] "Everything is uncovered and laid bare before the eyes of him to whom we must give account."[31] The Messiah will not have to rely on outward appearances in order to render judgment.[32]

"There is nothing concealed that will not be disclosed," Jesus tells the disciples, "or hidden [*kruptos*] that will not be made known."[33] Paul says that persons who lived in ignorance of divine revelation had the testimony of conscience, so that their inmost deliberations can be made to give testimony for or against them. He concludes, "This will take place on the day when God will judge men's secrets [*kruptos*, hidden things] through Jesus Christ, as my gospel declares."[34]

The same light that exposes all works to judgment also enlightens and gives life. Recall from the last chapter that during the Gospel Age a start is made on the restorative work to be completed at Christ's return; an inner "resurrection" occurs in the minds and hearts of believers, anticipating the bodily resurrection yet to come. The New Testament describes this process as an enlightening of those who were once in spiritual darkness.

"Everything exposed by the light becomes visible," the book of Ephesians says, "for it is light that makes everything visible. This is why it is said: 'Wake up, O sleeper, rise from the dead, and Christ will shine on you.' "[35] The image here is that of a sleeping person who is awakened by light on their face from the newly risen sun. The book of 2 Peter, using a similar figure, reminds Christians to be guided by the illumination of the prophetic Scriptures "until the day dawns and the morning star rises in your hearts" at Jesus' coming.[36] The symbolism of these passages assumes that darkness as profound as that of the unregenerate human heart, like that of the grave, can be dispelled only by a light of divine intensity.

---

30 Ps 139:1, 11-12.
31 Heb 4:13.
32 Isa 11:3-4.
33 Luke 12:2.
34 Rom 2:15-16.
35 Eph 5:13-14.
36 2 Pet 1:19; cf. Hos 6:2-3.

Astronomy and Revelation

The description of the sun in Psalm 19 is remarkable for what it is, a coded prophecy, as well as for what it is not, namely, a scientific description of the sun. We take for granted that the Psalm is concerned only with the perceived motion of the sun and does not teach that the sun in literal fact travels a circuit around the earth, but such was not necessarily apparent to people living five centuries or more ago.

The Italian astronomer Galileo collided spectacularly with papal authorities by publicly arguing that the earth revolves around the sun, not vice versa. The heliocentric model of the earth, sun and planets championed by Galileo had earlier been proposed by the Polish astronomer Copernicus, who was prudent enough to delay publication of the theory until he was on his deathbed. Galileo, by contrast, was confident that he could persuade a papal commission not only that the case for the revolution of the earth around the sun was incontestable, but that by reinterpretation the Bible could be harmonized with heliocentrism.

Galileo underestimated his task. Powerful institutions, whether religious or political, look with suspicion upon ideas that have the potential to undermine bureaucratic authority. We have considered in previous chapters how jealousy for power and esteem led to the crucifixion of Jesus. To make matters worse for Galileo, his treatise on the earth and sun seemed to poke fun at the pope personally. Galileo escaped the type of crucifixion popular at the time—burning at the stake—by bowing to church authorities and recanting his assertions. The tormentors of Galileo may be excused for clinging to obsolete ideas of astronomy, but as shepherds they could hardly have found in the examples of Peter and Paul any justification for threatening their religious opponents with imprisonment, torture and murder.

Setting aside the issue of Galileo's treatment, it is difficult to fault the Biblical argument for geocentrism as opposed to heliocentrism. The Psalm that we have been studying is one of several passages that describe the sun as traveling across the heavens, while others say that the earth is stable and unmoving.[37] It was pointed out to Galileo that when God miraculously extended the hours of daylight to give Joshua victory

---

37 Ps 104:19; Eccl 1:5; cf. 1 Chron 16:30; Ps 93:1; 96:10; 104:5.

over the Canaanites, the sun and moon reportedly stood still, not the earth.[38]

In the Genesis creation story, God places the sun above the earth, which hardly sounds as if it is saying that the sun was formed and then the earth was moved into an orbit around it. All the pertinent Biblical statements are more consistent with geocentrism, and no one by reading them would be led in any other direction. By any honest appraisal, the fundamentalist plea to accept the plain sense of the Bible's words would put us on the side of the churchmen rather than Galileo.

Can the Bible be reconciled with our modern knowledge of the solar system? Yes, but not if we uniformly insist on the natural sense of its words. Aside from the question of the relative movement of earth and sun, there is an even simpler problem in the Biblical account of the cosmos. According to Genesis 1:6-7, in the early stages of creation God separated the "waters below," consisting of the seas or ocean, from the waters "above." The passage unmistakably locates the "firmament" or "expanse" of the sky, Hebrew *raqia*, "in the midst of" or "between," *tawech*, these upper and lower waters. Verses 14 through 17 just as straightforwardly locate the sun, moon and stars in this same "expanse." The heavenly waters therefore must be above the the stars.[39]

No "plain sense" reading can find more than one expanse in the first chapter of Genesis, or find that it is located anywhere but below the upper waters, or find that the sun, moon and stars are located anywhere but within this expanse. Those who persuade themselves otherwise are either unable or unwilling to see that they are forcing the passage, against all indications of the words themselves, to conform to knowledge derived from astronomical science.

Martin Luther noted that Moses speaks of a "firmament" containing the sun and planets, all of them orbiting, as Luther understood it, around the earth. He went on to say that above and below this firmament were waters. He flatly rejected any attempt to bend the language of Scripture to fit astronomical observations by saying that if some of the statements of Genesis are difficult to understand, "like those before us concerning the waters above the heavens," nevertheless "we must be-

---

38 Josh 10:13.
39 Cf. Ps 148:4.

lieve them rather than wickedly deny them or presumptuously interpret them in conformity with our understanding."[40]

Those who find Luther's opinion less than reasonable must conclude that these verses of Genesis are not offering us a scientific account, nor would that kind of narrative have been intelligible to its original audience. There are indeed "waters" high above the earth in the form of clouds.[41] To observers on the ground, clouds appear to extend up so far that the sun, moon and stars can be enveloped by them, not merely obscured.[42] Clouds serve to mark the upper boundary of the sky dome, in which the heavenly bodies have been placed in the sense of being projected as visual images.

God caused the sun to move across the sky by causing the sun to appear to move across the sky, the physical mechanics of the process being at odds with the appearance. Likewise, when the stars physically originated is not the same question as when and how they first appeared in the visible vault of the sky.

What is clear from Genesis is that creation occurred in stages under God's conscious direction, proceeding from darkness to light, from indistinction to clarity, from formlessness to form. The image of God's Spirit brooding over the dark ocean suggests the watery darkness in which an embryo gestates. Job 38:8 refers to the primeval seas "bursting forth from the womb" the way a woman's uterine waters burst out of the embryonic sack to initiate birth.

It would not be surprising if God coalesced physical objects out of fluid energy, just as the taming of the watery deep causes sky, ocean and land to appear in Genesis. Water is an ideal medium to communicate this process. As we noted in the last chapter, even today we resort to water metaphors when we talk about electrical "currents" and electromagnetic "waves." In the Psalms we find that the power on display in the parting of the Red Sea is also the power by which God overcame

---

40 Martin Luther, "Lectures on Genesis," Vol. 1, *Luther's Works* (St. Louis: Concordia, 1958), 25, 30. Luther confesses more than once that he does not understand the description of waters as being "above" the expanse and that correct interpretation may be impossible until the "Last Day." Ibid., 25-31.

41 Ps 104:3; Prov 8:28.

42 "Covered" at Ezek 32:7 can mean "enveloped" or "wrapped"; cf. Job 9:7.

primal chaos to establish an orderly world.[43] In Job 38, too, imposing
order on the initially chaotic state of creation is compared to the
damming of floodwaters.[44]

Unavoidably, God expects us to interpret the Scriptures in the light
of honest scientific observation. From the trials of Galileo, if from
nothing else, we learn that blind insistence on the "plain words" of the
Bible without fair-minded consideration of evidence from God's creation cannot be the way God intends us to approach his Word. The
opposite error is to subscribe to every fashionable speculation offered
up as science and pretend that biases whether religious, political or
philosophical never influence scientists in their opinions.

There is not space here to wade into the time-worn controversies
over whether or to what extent animals have "evolved," whether the
earth is "old" or "young" and related questions. It is enough to acknowledge that God's written word is both confirmed and illuminated
by the declarations of the heavens and all creation. As we will consider
in another chapter, the very success of scientific reasoning such as that
employed by Galileo speaks convincingly for a Sovereign Creator of everything around us.

When we return to Psalm 19, we need not be embarrassed that it fails
to depict the earth's astronomical movement. Its poetic tribute to the
sun's daily passage, equally understandable to ancient and modern readers, contains a total of nine descriptive elements typologically related to
Jesus. And the order of these elements aligns chronologically with Jesus'
incarnation, his ministry and his return at the *parousia*.

Some of the identifiers I have cited, such as the passages at Matthew
24 and Hebrews 12, are from the New Testament and in theory could
have been manufactured. However, not only are those references scattered between books distant from one another in style and probable
authorship, they are so thoroughly grounded in their separate contexts
that it is unreasonable to argue that they were "salted" into the text.
Besides, all of the New Testament identifiers reflect imagery from the
Hebrew Bible and merely sharpen that imagery in the course of applying
it to Jesus.

---

43 Ps 74:13-14.
44 Job 38: 9-11.

Taking Stock

We have now completed more than a dozen typological studies, enough to reach a judgment about divine inspiration of the Bible based on the criteria listed in Chapter 6:

1) General resemblance between sketches and fulfillments
2) Presence in the tradition of key symbol identifiers
3) Economy of distribution of typological material
4) Integration (interconnectedness) of coded sketches
5) Purposefulness of type coding within the tradition

Items 1 and 2 are matters for each reader to decide based on the individual studies. Number 3 depends on the length of the Bible as a whole when weighed against the combined lengths of the prophetic narratives, the passages that function as symbol identifiers and those that comprise the fulfillments. That ratio must then be evaluated in relative terms. How many pages would have to be sifted to produce a similar body of typological material from non-Biblical literature such as Greek mythology, Japanese folk tales or Shakespeare's plays, assuming it could be produced at all?

In considering item 4, recall how often we have referred back to previous scriptural passages as we have progressed from one study to the next. If such back-referencing has been frequent—and I believe most readers will agree it has—then we have established the integration of the various sketches. We have discovered that Biblical symbols and themes are the interlocked filaments of a single cord.

The collective purposefulness of typological prophecies is a function of their role in confirming central New Testament themes about Jesus. It is beyond argument that our various studies share that focus, but is typology sensible as a means God might use? If so, then the fifth condition is satisfied.

Far from seeing the hand of God at work, a skeptic who reviewed some of the studies in this book chalked them up to the human mind's "amazing ability to make connections." He was implying, of course, that my own imagination had worked overtime to draw connections that had no basis in reality, after which I had organized Biblical references cleverly enough to mislead my readers. I expect many others to respond the same way once they determine that my quotations and statements of fact are reliable. Even so, I doubt that critics harbor the impression that a system of such connections is easily conjured. Common sense tells us we are looking at something extraordinary, and the limitations of common sense do not justify brushing off the verdict it renders so loudly in this case.

I can say little more to those who without explanation remain unconvinced except that their devotion of further thought to the subject is the wisest of investments. On the other hand, those who allege that manipulation of references can consistently create the appearance of typological alignment must show us exactly how.

As far back as Chapter 1, we noted that a large reservoir of religious and folk literature exists outside the Bible. Assuming a naturalistic origin of what we have discovered, there is no reason why a prominent historical figure other than Jesus cannot be made the focus of a contrived typology no less convincing than that contained in the Scriptures. Of course, any alternative scheme must meet the five criteria listed above to the same extent as does the Biblical model. An entire book of counterexamples is not required, but evidence must be produced sufficient to demonstrate that such a book could be written. Secular critics ought to back their speculations with the hard currency of fact rather than offering us poker table IOUs that they have no intention of redeeming.

In his book, *How We Believe: The Search for God in an Age of Science*, Michael Shermer, past director of the Skeptic's Society, says that the evolutionary struggle for survival has made humans so sensitive to patterns in their surroundings that they tend to see patterns even where there are none.[45] He speculates that this obsessiveness may lie behind our belief in God, leading us to see his hand at work when blind chance and the mindless operation of physical laws alone are responsible.

It is difficult to understand, though, how the habit of perceiving patterns where none exist would be an aid to survival; it seems transparently obvious that survival is promoted by the identification specifically of genuine patterns. Shermer's assertion man is a "pattern-

---

45 Michael Shermer, *How We Believe: The Search for God in an Age of Science* (New York: W. H. Freeman, 2000), 61ff.

seeking animal" is itself based on the perception of a pattern in human behavior—a pattern that may well be imaginary according to Shermer's own reasoning.

To be fair to Shermer's argument, we must admit that human beings can fool themselves in various ways. It is easy to see how—and why—a gambler deludes himself that his odds of winning at the craps table are improved by blowing on the dice. The gambler chooses to remember vividly the times that the ritual has accompanied winning rolls and minimizes the many times he performed the ritual and lost. The gambler's superstition gives him the illusion of control over uncontrollable events. A subtler danger is that of scientists reporting skewed results of a study or experiment, which is why such results are considered to be reliable only after others have carefully reviewed them, or better, independently verified them.

Recognizing the limits of our knowledge and the insidious nature of our biases, we do well to withhold judgment on any number of questions for which neither common sense nor science can give us solid answers. When it comes to judgments that bear urgently on our ethics and therefore on the decisions we have to make each day, we cannot afford the luxury of fence-sitting. If Jean-Paul Sartre was right about little else, he spoke the truth when he said that we are condemned to choose.[46]

Whether God exists and whether he has in Christ reached out to reclaim fallen humanity are questions we must decide based on what we know now, since the putting them off is itself a decision. Nevertheless, the reasons others give for their own belief might not inspire us with confidence. People whose religious profession depends on family ties or social convenience predictably have few justifications to offer for it, but even thoughtful believers are not always able to defend their hope eloquently and may resort to weak arguments.

If Christians sometimes struggle to justify their convictions, it is because the case for Christ is not easily boiled down to a few terse statements, nor does it consist of historical claims that we can appraise in isolation. As I said in the Introduction, faith results from weighing the whole of our experience and then feeling our way forward.[47] Acquir-

---

46 Cf. Josh 24:15.
47 Acts 17:27.

ing faith does not mean solving an equation but arriving at a judgment based in part on moral introspection.

Paul said that he could observe in himself an inability to carry out, consistently and fully, what he knew to be right. "I see another law at work in the members of my body," he writes, "waging war against the law of my mind and making me a prisoner of the law of sin."[48] Those who have had an experience like Paul's must ask themselves whether it betrays the reality of sin, for which the redemptive act at the cross is the remedy, or instead is a mirage that we can dispel with psychotherapy. Which of those explanations rings true and which gives off the cloying aroma of self-delusion?

It is true of the Bible as well that the reasons for accepting it are not easily distilled into a formula. I believe that the typological prophecies we have surveyed demonstrate the inspired character of the Scriptures, but few Christians are familiar with this material. There are explicit prophecies in the Bible too, although precisely what a given prophecy predicts, when it was written and how thoroughly it was fulfilled are usually settled points only for someone who already believes.

Whatever it is that first opens a person's mind to the gospel, it is the impact of the array of its features, of form as well as content, that surmounts innumerable unanswered questions and results in conviction.

Christians think that ultimately it the Spirit of God speaking through the Biblical message about Jesus and working in an individual's heart that tips the scales. A rough comparison can be made to the tug of intuition that leads a scientist on to a breakthrough discovery. The scientist needs a measure of faith in an unproven conjecture in order to give direction to his research and spur him on in spite of setbacks. If he is wrong his determination may prove to be nothing more than stubbornness, but if vindicated he will be admired for his prescience and tenacity.

It seems that under some circumstances having a lower threshold of belief than others can be a mark not of credulity but of insight. Without this mysterious inner sense, intelligence is of limited value. The person who has the most in the way of sheer intelligence does not always become the visionary artist, the courageous dissenter, the compassionate healer or the wise counselor.

Among the clues we must weigh when evaluating the Bible is the ef-

---

48 Rom 7:23.

fect of its message on human behavior. History provides us with a catalog of injustice, murder and mayhem perpetrated in the names of God and of Christ, as it does of atrocities committed in the service of such noble abstracts as "liberty, equality, fraternity" and "land, bread, peace." However, no one can credibly claim that the words of Jesus and the apostles condone wanton violence, nor can they deny that those same words advocate a standard of charity and peaceableness so high that it has inspired a long list of selfless acts.

To his credit, Michael Shermer in *How We Believe* admits that religious organizations are more likely than secular ones to offer disaster relief and humanitarian aid.[49] No one has a monopoly on compassion, but people who emigrate far from their homes at material sacrifice to themselves solely for the purpose of helping the needy are primarily missionaries and aid workers with a strong belief in God, not secular activists. Moreover, those who reach out to minister across barriers of culture, language and socio-economic status are more likely to come from the Christian spiritual tradition than from any other.

Fitting the body of evidence we have compiled into the larger picture of human experience is a task we will return to. In the meantime, exhibits still remain to be added to that evidence. Chapters 3 and 4 were devoted to an incident from the life of Israel's great lawgiver, Moses, but we can learn something as well by considering the pattern formed by various other episodes from his biography, which we will do next.

---

49 Shermer, *op. cit.*, 141.

16

Mosaic Miniatures

A young woman holds a baby boy in her arms. Owing to a divine miracle the baby is hers even though she is a virgin. The child is appointed to deliver his people from the power of the enemy, mediate a covenant between them and God and usher them into a place of joy and peace. The woman is not Mary but the daughter of an Egyptian Pharaoh, and the baby is not Jesus but Moses. In a moment we will take a closer look at this narrative of virginal motherhood from the book of Exodus, but notice first that it does not involve actual conception in the womb of a virgin.

The Old Testament contains no "virgin birth" tales, while ancient non-Hebrew traditions are strewn with them. The Christian apologist Justin Martyr in his *Dialogue with Trypho* is chided by his Jewish opponent with the charge that mythology is behind the nativity stories in the Gospels. "In the fables of those who are called Greeks," Trypho says, "it is written that Perseus was begotten of Danae, who was a virgin, he who was called among them Zeus having descended on her in the form of a golden shower. And you ought to feel ashamed when you make assertions similar to theirs."[1]

Some of the better known virgin birth myths, like the one cited by Trypho, are sexual fantasies about the seduction of mortal women by the gods and therefore have a different tenor than the accounts of Jesus' nativity. In other cases, the seemingly superhuman exploits of leaders like Alexander the Great suggested to the minds of admirers the likelihood of superhuman paternity.

---

1   Justin Martyr, *Dialogue with Trypho*, 67.

Insofar as the legends do bear a resemblance to the birth story of Jesus, they give a backhanded testimony to the logic of the incarnation. What better means could God use to cut through the shroud of human mortality than the appearance of new life, a process that already has about it an air of the miraculous?

Compare another kind of story, the Greek myth of Daedalus and his son Icarus, who used artificial wings to ascend into the sky from the coast of Crete. Two other male relatives, the Wright brothers, actually did make artificial wings in the form of an airplane and soared into the air at Kitty Hawk on the North Carolina coast in 1903. Coincidence is evident in the comparison, particularly since the names "Daedalus" and "Wright" both mean "craftsman," but the coincidence is not pure: the longing for flight, like the longing to see God plant the seed of salvation in a dying world, wells up from the deepest reservoirs of the human heart.

If Trypho errs in alleging that the nativity is recycled myth, he seems safer in implying that it is simply unjewish. In connection with the birth of Jesus to Mary, Matthew's Gospel quotes a prophecy, from Isaiah 7:14, that "the virgin will be with child and will give birth to a son." Critics never tire of pointing out that the Hebrew word *alma* does not uniformly mean "virgin" (no single word in the Hebrew Bible does). Also, the subsequent verses of Isaiah chapter seven say that the sign would occur before the nations of Israel and Syria were overthrown by Assyria, which happened within a few years of the prophecy.

Like many prophecies, however, Isaiah 7:14 can have more than one fulfillment. Matthew points out that the most astonishing reading of verse 14 would be that a young woman would conceive while still in a state of virginity, an event confirming God's promise in verse eleven that he could provide any sign that might be contemplated, "whether in the deepest depths or in the highest heights." Not surprisingly, since the extent of the prophecy's fulfillment could be appreciated only in retrospect, it defied Jewish expectations.

The birth story of Moses, like that of Jesus, is often chalked up to legend. Exodus relates how in order to save her baby from death during an Egyptian pogrom Moses' mother sets him adrift on the Nile in a waterproof basket, which is found by the daughter of Pharaoh. The account is similar to an ancient inscription about King Sargon I of

Akkad (c. 2300 BC), which claims that his mother, a priestess, conceived him by an unknown father and set him adrift on a river in a basket, after which he was found and raised by a boatman.

The Exodus story need not have been plagiarized. In the ancient world, abandonment or "exposure" of infants was common, either as a form of passive infanticide or an act of desperation akin to leaving a baby on a doorstep. Newborns could be left where strangers might take pity on them. The choice of a river is not surprising, since in the minds of pre-scientific people the currents of a river behave mysteriously and could serve as a medium through which God or the gods might rescue an otherwise doomed child.

The Drawing Up of the Blessed Son

The tale of Moses' birth is a coded "vignette," that is, a sketch done with a few suggestive lines. While vignettes contain fewer identifiable symbols than do the prophecies we have studied up to this point, they still provide secondary evidence of interconnectedness among Biblical themes. The birth story is one of several prophetic miniatures to be found among incidents from Moses' life.

The second chapter of Exodus says that Moses' mother is especially anxious to save her baby when she sees that he is a "fine child." In place of the Hebrew word "fine" or "good" the Septuagint has the Greek *asteios*, meaning "pretty" or "graceful" according to Liddell & Scott's *Greek-English Lexicon*.[2] The book of Acts expands the language of Exodus to read *asteios to theo*, "beautiful to God" ("no ordinary child," in the NIV's rendering of Acts 7:20). The obvious parallel is to what John 1:14 says about Jesus: "The Word became flesh and made his dwelling among us. We have seen his glory, the glory of the One and Only, who came from the Father, full of grace and truth."

The baby Moses is set adrift on the Nile River, which here has two contrasting associations. As we have seen repeatedly, God's Spirit can be represented by water, including water in the form of a river.[3] In Exodus the river is what conveys the basket and child, yet at the same

---

2 Henry George Liddell and Robert Scott, *A Greek-English Lexicon* (NY: Oxford University Press, 1992), 260.

3 Isa 30:28; 33:21; 44:3.

time the story leaves no doubt that God's power delivers the baby to the maiden daughter of Pharaoh. The river and the miracle-generating Spirit become indistinguishable in their effects. From the holy Spirit a baby is voluntarily received into the arms of a woman who, given the narrative's identification of her solely with reference to her father, must be a virgin.

In the outworking of the typological pattern, the Israelitess Mary of Nazareth, a virgin daughter of the Sovereign of the universe, voluntarily receives her firstborn son from the Spirit.[4] "Do not be afraid to take Mary home as your wife," Mary's husband-to-be, Joseph, is told by an angel, "because what is conceived in her is from the Holy Spirit."[5]

Besides connoting the Spirit, water is symbolic of death, especially death at the hands of evildoers. 2 Samuel equates "violent men" and "enemies" with "waves of death" and "torrents of destruction," imagery that recalls what Exodus says about Egyptian soldiers killing Israelite babies by throwing them into the Nile River.[6] By passing safely through the deadly waters that had become the grave of other Hebrew infants, the baby Moses serves as a portent of how Israel as a nation with Moses at its head will later pass miraculously through the waters of the Red Sea and out of the clutches of the Egyptian army.

The same kind of foreshadowing is on display in Genesis, when Abraham journeys to Egypt to escape the ravages of a famine. Abraham's wife Sarah becomes the prisoner of Pharaoh, whom God afflicts with plagues until Sarah is freed to accompany the patriarch back to Canaan.[7] The pharaoh encountered by Abraham and Sarah is not malicious like those described in Exodus, but the couple's stay in Egypt anticipates the enslavement of Israel so closely that its prophetic function cannot be doubted. Like the captivity and liberation of Sarah, the saving of the infant Moses through the waters of the Nile is prophetic of Israel's deliverance from Egyptian bondage.

It may seem contrived to say that the waters of the Nile simultaneously prefigure both God's Spirit and the depths of the grave until we remember that this double meaning is present in Christian baptism. "I

---

4   Luke 1:38.
5   Matt 1:20.
6   2 Sam 22:3-5.
7   Gen 12:10-20.

baptize you with water," John the baptist tells his followers, "but he [the Messiah] will baptize you with the Holy Spirit."[8] Later Jesus asks two of the apostles, "Can you drink the cup I drink or be baptized with the baptism I am baptized with?"[9] The medium of immersion in the second passage is not the purifying Spirit but the grave, which Jesus descended into and ascended out of just as a baptismal candidate is plunged into and out of water. It is the second sense that Paul has in mind when he asks Roman Christians, "Don't you know that all of us who were baptized into Christ Jesus were baptized into his death?"[10]

Pharaoh's daughter recognizes that the baby she has found in the Nile is an Israelite. Eventually she gives him a royal Egyptian name, but she does so because of what the name means in Hebrew rather than in Egyptian. To draw an analogy, it would be as if a Japanese couple adopted an English baby and decided to give the child the Japanese name "Hiro" because that name corresponds phonetically to the English word "hero." The name "Moses," translated "drawn out" in Hebrew, not only commemorates the baby's miraculous rescue from the Nile but also anticipates Moses' coming up out of the Red Sea with the nation of Israel following behind him.

David used identical language when speaking with a messianic voice, as can be seen by comparing passages:

> She named him Moses [*Mosheh*], saying, "I drew [*mashah*] him out of the water [*mayim*]." —Exodus 2:10

> He [Yahweh] reached down from on high and took hold of me;
>   he drew [*mashah*] me out of deep waters [*mayim*].
> He rescued me from my powerful enemy. —2 Samuel 22:17-18

The Sea Baptism

The "drawing up" symbolism appears in the New Testament when Paul quotes from the Mosaic Law and applies it to Jesus. God reminds Israel at Deuteronomy 30:11-14 that the law he has given them is not

---

8   Mark 1:8; cf. 1 Cor. 12:13.

9   Mark 10:38.

10 Rom 6:3.

difficult to understand, as if by their own devices they had to ascend to heaven or travel across the sea to grasp his intent. Instead, God says, he has put his word on their tongues and in their hearts.

Seeing Jesus as the embodiment of the law, Paul adds parenthetical glosses to the language of Deuteronomy: " 'Do not say in your heart, "Who will ascend into heaven?" ' (that is, to bring Christ down) 'or "Who will descend into the deep?" ' (that is, to bring Christ up from the dead)."[11] Paul uses the verse to illustrate that God has done what was humanly impossible, sending his Son down from heaven and resurrecting him from the dead, and then placed the accomplished work of redemption before mankind as his gift. The "word of Christ," or message about God's work of grace, is no less accessible than the law, whose requirements Jesus perfectly satisfied.

When citing Deuteronomy, Paul makes an alteration from the original Hebrew. By changing the words "cross the sea" to "descend into the deep" he can more easily evoke Jesus' descent into and out of the abyss of death. Paul still retains the sense latent in the Old Testament text. The words about ascending to heaven and crossing the ocean recall what God did through Moses in order to bring Israel into the Law Covenant. Moses in a sense "ascended into heaven" when Yahweh brought the thunderous clouds of heaven down on the peak of Sinai and Moses climbed up the mountain.[12]

Moses went where the trembling masses of Israel were unable to go so that he could receive the law on their behalf. In order to get to Mount Sinai in the first place, Moses had conducted Israel "across the sea," a leg of the journey they never could have completed under their own power. The traversing of the Red Sea, whose towering waters God held on either side by supernaturally driven winds, required Moses and the nation to descend all the way down to the sea bed and then ascend again on the far shore. In the context of the exodus, therefore, crossing the sea and coming up out of it are different ways of describing the same event.

Isaiah 63:11 recalls the Red Sea crossing under the leadership of Moses by asking, "Where is he [Yahweh] who brought them through

---

11 Rom 10:6.
12 Exod 19:9-20; 20:22; see Isa 14:13 for another example of a mountaintop symbolizing heaven.

the sea, with [Moses] the shepherd of his flock?" The Septuagint text of this verse reads slightly differently: "Where is he that brought up from the sea the shepherd of the sheep?" The New Testament book of Hebrews paraphrases this passage when it refers to "the God of peace, who brought up from the dead the great Shepherd of the sheep . . . Jesus our Lord."[13] The allusion is unmistakable because of the expression "shepherd of the sheep," which occurs nowhere else in the Bible but in these two places, and because of the obvious symbolism linking the "sea" or oceanic "deep" with the grave. The word for "brought up" in Hebrews, a synonym of the word at Isaiah 63:11 in the Septuagint, is the same word, *anago*, used by Paul in Romans 10 to speak about God "bringing Christ up" from the abyss of death.

To summarize, the scene of Moses being drawn up from the Nile by Pharaoh's daughter, portraying the virgin birth, points to yet another vignette, that of Moses leading Israel up out of the Red Sea as a figure of Jesus' resurrection. Colossians says that Christ is the "the head of the body, the church; he is the beginning and the firstborn from among the dead."[14] To Paul, whatever length of time might separate the resurrection of Jesus from that of his congregation is an insignificant interruption in the regenerative process. "In Christ all will be made alive. But each in his own turn: Christ, the first fruits; then, when he comes, those who belong to him." Moses' ascent out of the sea symbolizes the ascent of the greater Moses, Jesus, out of the grave with the church following just behind.

The idea of a reprise of the exodus drama is not foreign to the Hebrew Bible. "I will bring them back from Egypt and gather them from Assyria," God says of his people in Zechariah. God here contemplates the final defeat of his enemies in every quarter, represented by the Egyptian empire that first enslaved his people and the Mesopotamian powers of Assyria and Babylon that together destroyed the royal houses of Israel and Judah. The passage continues by saying of the Israelites, "They will pass through the sea of trouble; the surging sea will be subdued and all the depths of the Nile will dry up. Assyria's pride will be brought down and Egypt's scepter will pass away."[15]

---

13 Heb 13:20.
14 Col 1:18.
15 Zech 10:11.

Because of its nationalistic association with Egypt the Nile here is imaginatively blended with the Red Sea, but the distinction is trivial in that both bodies of water jointly stand for death in the narratives about Moses. Zechariah's prophecy is eschatological, looking toward the end of the world age, and can be fulfilled by nothing less than the regathering of God's elect people in the resurrection.

One more scriptural thread binds the miraculous sea crossing of Moses to the resurrection pioneered by Jesus. The passage, which we first examined back in Chapter 2, is a comment of Paul's about the meaning of the exodus: "For I do not want you to be ignorant of the fact, brothers, that our forefathers were all under the cloud and that they all passed through the sea. They were all baptized into Moses in the cloud and in the sea."[16] Cloud and sea here correspond to the Spirit and water associated with baptism in other New Testament texts.[17] The Red Sea crossing becomes for Paul a type of Christian baptism, which in turn is a rehearsal of the journey down into and up out of the grave after the pattern of Jesus.[18]

A Prince Among Slaves

We will now add a third account from Moses' life to the two we have just examined, this one concerning his decision to identify with the enslaved people of Israel. Exodus provides no details of Moses' youth, saying simply that he becomes the son of Pharaoh's daughter, but it invites us to picture him growing up amid the pomp and privilege of the Egyptian royal court. The book of Acts says, "Moses was educated in all the wisdom of the Egyptians and was powerful in speech and action."[19] Upon reaching manhood, he takes a fateful step. "He went out to where his own people were and watched them at their hard labor."[20]

More than just watching his people, for their sakes Moses risks everything he has, including his life. When he sees an Egyptian taskmaster beating a Hebrew slave, he saves the Hebrew by killing the Egyptian and

---

16 1 Cor 10:1-2.
17 John 3:5; Acts 1:5.
18 Rom 6:3-5; 1 Thess 4:14.
19 Acts 7:22.
20 Exod 2:11.

burying his body. The book of Hebrews comments about this incident, "By faith Moses, when he had grown up, refused to be known as the son of Pharaoh's daughter." Later, when Moses tries to stop a fight between two Hebrews, he is spurned. "Who made you ruler and judge over us?," one of them demands to know. "Are you thinking of killing me as you killed the Egyptian?" The very people whom Moses is trying to help now imperil his life, implicitly threatening to betray him to the Egyptians. Moses is forced to flee eastward into the desert, where he will pass many years before returning to lead Israel to freedom.

We saw in Chapter 8 that the Son's relinquishing of supernatural glory to enter the world of mankind is represented by young David removing the armor of the king of Israel, leaving the presence of the king and descending from the army's high encampment to the valley below. It is not difficult to see the incarnation similarly portrayed by Moses' leaving behind the luxury of Pharaoh's palace for the sweltering brickyard's and dusty slave quarters where the Israelites suffer.

The book of Hebrews says that the Son of God was "not ashamed" to call human beings his brothers, since he and they have the same Father. He was moved, as was Moses, to look upon the plight of his afflicted brethren up close by "partaking" of their "flesh and blood" existence. By enduring the penalty of sin, as Moses unjustly came under the wrath of Pharaoh, Jesus has become a sympathetic high priest who can "bring many sons to glory."[21] The author of Hebrews goes on to note the superiority of Jesus' ministry to that of Moses, but he gives no hint of having noticed specific parallels between the actions of the two figures.

Moses subdues the enemy in the form of the taskmaster just as Jesus during his ministry restrains Satan and releases his victims from demonic possession and disease.[22] The reception accorded the deliverer in either case betokens resentment rather than gratitude, and culminates in his being betrayed into the hands of an otherwise hated foreign government. The sarcastic question, "Who made you ruler and judge over us?" is wryly alluded to by Jesus when someone asks him to intervene in an inheritance dispute. Jesus replies, "Man, who appointed me a judge or an arbiter between you?," dismissing the self-serving request while

---

21 Heb 2:10-18.
22 Mark 3:22-27; Luke 13:16.

suggesting that he, Jesus, will fare no better than young Moses in the eyes of the people.[23]

Unlike Jesus, Moses is not actually executed, but his flight into the desert under a capital sentence effectively leaves him dead to his people. For decades Moses remains hidden from the view of Egypt's inhabitants with a single exception. As Moses is on his way back to the land of the Nile endowed with divine authority, God brings his brother Aaron to meet him on Mt. Horeb.[24] These events correspond to the physical absence of Jesus during the Gospel Age and then the rapture of believers, Christ's "brothers," to Jesus' side at the Second Coming.[25]

In the course of these studies Moses as a type for Jesus has come up repeatedly, beginning in Chapter 3. The prophecy in Deuteronomy that foretells the coming of a great prophet "like Moses" was applied to Jesus by the early church.[26] The New Testament repeatedly associates the two figures.[27] By describing Moses as "powerful in speech and action," *dunatos en logois kai ergois*, Acts repeats almost verbatim the statement in Luke's Gospel that Jesus was "mighty in deed and word," *dunatos en ergo kai logo*.[28] When Paul says that ancient Israel as a nation was "baptized into Moses," his source is the expression that members of the church are "baptized into Christ."[29]

The misery of Israel during the Egyptian bondage illustrates the torturous enslavement of all mankind to corruption. The original sentence upon Adam for sin reads like a description of slave labor: "By the sweat of your brow you will eat your food until you return to the ground, since from it you were taken."[30] On the border of the promised land, the Israelites are advised of the penalties they will suffer if they give themselves over to evil. "Because you did not serve the LORD your God joyfully and gladly in the time of prosperity," Moses warns them, "therefore in hunger and thirst, in nakedness and dire poverty, you will

23 Luke 12:13.
24 Exod 4:27; 7:1.
25 Rom 8:29; 1 Thess 4:15-17; Col 3:4.
26 Deut 18:15; Acts 3:22.
27 John 1:17; 5:46; 6:32-33; 9:28-29; Heb 3:2-6; Rev 15:3.
28 Acts 7:22; Luke 24:19, NASB.
29 1 Cor 10:2; Gal 3:27.
30 Gen 3:19.

serve the enemies the LORD sends against you. He will put an iron yoke on your neck until he has destroyed you."[31]

After the return from Babylonian captivity, the people confess in prayer that their continued domination by Gentile empires is a penalty for sin: "But see, we are slaves today, slaves in the land you gave our forefathers . . . Because of our sins, its abundant harvest goes to the kings you have placed over us. They rule over our bodies and our cattle as they please."[32]

The oppression of Israel by the Gentiles continued down to the time of Jesus and beyond. According to Paul, the "kings you have placed over us" ultimately are greater than any human rulers. Sin and mortality have dominated man since his original rebellion, with liberation possible only through Jesus.[33] "Just as sin reigned in death," Paul declares, "so also grace might reign through righteousness to bring eternal life through Jesus Christ our Lord."[34] We find language about sin's subjugation of man in John's Gospel as well. In answer to the Pharisees' claim that "We are Abraham's descendants and have never been slaves of anyone," Jesus answers them, "I tell you the truth, everyone who sins is a slave to sin."[35]

Moses and Jesus both assume the role of liberator of God's people, but since Moses himself is a sinner he can offer only temporary, limited relief to the Israelites. "Moses was faithful as a servant in all God's house," writes the author of Hebrews, "But Christ is faithful as a son over God's house."[36] "Now a slave has no permanent place in the family, but a son belongs to it forever. So if the Son sets you free, you will be free indeed," Jesus tells his listeners.[37] "God sent the Spirit of his Son into our hearts," Paul says, "So you are no longer a slave, but a son."[38]

---

31 Deut 28:48.
32 Neh 9:36-37.
33 Rom 5:14-21.
34 Rom 5:21.
35 John 8:33-34.
36 Heb 3:5-6.
37 John 8:35-36.
38 Gal 4:6-7.

It is not merely identifiers that link incidents in the life of Moses to the New Testament portrayal of Jesus, but the order in which the incidents take place. Those that symbolize the virgin birth and incarnation necessarily fail to occur in the same sequence as their fulfillments because Moses, as an ordinarily human, could not choose to identify with enslaved Israel prior to his birth. From that point onward the lives of the two figures correspond well chronologically.

Moses reaches out to his people only to be rejected and then is forced to make what amounts to his own "exodus" from Egypt into the desert, where he meets with God on Mount Sinai. The book of Revelation says that in a figurative sense the place of Jesus' crucifixion is "called Sodom and Egypt," while the Gospel of Luke uses the Greek word *exodus* for the process of death, resurrection and ascension by which Jesus leaves the world to rejoin God the Father.[39]

When Moses returns to Egypt after a long absence, he is armed with invincible power in order to break Egypt's hold on Israel once and for all. Jesus is predicted to do the same thing at his Second Coming, when he will vanquish all opposition to his kingdom and release his people from the bonds of corruption.[40]

The departure of Israel from Egypt reaches its climax on the eastern shore of the Red Sea as the Israelites celebrate their deliverance by God. "In Your loving kindness You have led the people whom You have redeemed," they sing. "In Your strength You have guided them to your holy habitation."[41] The same exultation awaits God's people on the far prophetic horizon according to both the Old and New Testaments: "They will enter Zion with singing; everlasting joy will crown their heads."[42] "Then the righteous will shine like the sun in the kingdom of their Father."[43]

After the natural dividing point of the Red Sea deliverance, Israel begins its long desert trek. A new typological scheme unfolds, keyed to a different period. The sojourn of Israel corresponds to the journey of the church through the world from Jesus' first advent to his *parousia*.

---

39 Rev 11:8; *exodus* at Luke 9:31 is usually rendered in English as "departure."
40 Matt 24:30-31; Luke 21:27-28.
41 Exod 15:13, NASB.
42 Isa 35:10.
43 Matt 13:43.

Symbolic prophecy regarding later church history is outside the scope of this book, but it makes a fascinating study in its own right. A brief example is what happens when Moses ascends Mount Sinai to receive God's words. The climbing of the mountain by Moses invites comparison with the ascension of Jesus into the heavenly presence of the Father. The faith of the nation is tested when Moses fails to return as quickly as expected. Some of the Israelites forge an idol in the shape of a golden calf, a figure associated with Egyptian sun worship, and engage in idolatrous festivities. The faithless behavior of Israel foreshadows the despotism and self-indulgence that Jesus predicts will emerge within the church over time. Setting Old and New Testament texts alongside each other makes the comparison vivid:

> When the people saw that Moses was so long in coming down from the mountain, they gathered around Aaron and said, "Come, make us gods who will go before us. As for this fellow Moses who brought us up out of Egypt, we don't know what has happened to him . . ." So the next day the people rose early and sacrificed burnt offerings and presented fellowship offerings [before their calf idol]. Afterward they sat down to eat and drink and got up to indulge in revelry.
> —Exodus 31:1, 6

> But suppose that servant is wicked and says to himself, `My master is staying away a long time,' and he then begins to beat his fellow servants and to eat and drink with drunkards.
> —Matthew 24:48-49

> First of all, you must understand that in the last days scoffers will come, scoffing and following their own evil desires. They will say, "Where is this 'coming' he promised? Ever since our fathers died, everything goes on as it has since the beginning of creation."
> —2 Peter 3:2-3

At a minimum, then, we have shown that items from Moses' biography can be assembled into a compelling symbolic portrait of Jesus—a "mosaic" in every sense of the word. Forming a composite by sorting scenes from a larger story is more subjective than analyzing a single narrative sequence. That still doesn't explain the close correlation between the careers of Moses and Jesus, especially when the correspondence is confirmed by identifiers. We have seen that the waters of Egypt represent God's Spirit in one respect and death in another, and that the enslavement of Israel in Egypt can be equated to that of mankind to sin.

While we have not documented a figurative meaning for everything recorded about Moses, those incidents that do foreshadow Jesus are pivotal events in the first half of Moses' life.

Moses and the "Law of Death"

Before we leave the subject of Moses, we must address the issue of the grisly brutality with which the Israelites under the leadership of Moses and Joshua made war on their Canaanite enemies. In the minds of many readers, the portrayal of what seems like genocide against the nations of Canaan disproves any claim that the first several books of the Bible were inspired by a loving God.

Admittedly, reading the command to wipe out Canaanite populations brings us face to face with a hideous reality, but the claim of the New Testament is that it is a reality about the nature of sin, not about cruelty in God's character. When Paul claims that "the letter [of the Law of Moses] kills" and that the revelation through Moses was a "ministry that brought death" he is stating a principle that is on display in the war for Canaan.[44]

Occasionally people express longing for a world in which justice operated as dependably as the law of gravity, not realizing what the results would look like. The backdrop of the campaign against the Canaanites is that they had manifested exceptional depravity for generation after generation, foregoing every opportunity for reform.[45] They were, according to the Scriptures, practiced murderers of their own children, burning babies in return for fruitful harvests or other favors from their gods.[46]

Archeology has been unable confirm or deny the prevalence of child

---

44 2 Cor 3:6-7.
45 Gen 15:16.
46 Deut 12:31.

sacrifice in Canaan, but the Moabite stone, a period inscription that boasts of the wholesale slaughter of captured men, women and children in honor of the god Chemosh, indicates that savagery was routine for the region. What would the result be if the violence perpetrated by the Canaanites returned back upon them like the swinging of a pendulum? It would look like the warfare carried on against them by Israel.

"Life for life, eye for eye, tooth for tooth, hand for hand, foot for foot, burn for burn, wound for wound, bruise for bruise," the Mosaic Law intones, a principle as terrifyingly relentless as the Newtonian dictum, "For every action there is an equal and opposite reaction."[47] When the Israelites capture a Canaanite leader, the sheik of Bezek, they cut off his thumbs and big toes. "Seventy kings with their thumbs and big toes cut off have picked up scraps under my table," he laments. "Now God has paid me back for what I did to them."[48] Retribution descends just as inexorably upon the Canaanites as a whole. The unyielding application of a formula can be fearful, but formulaic justice is the essence of law.

We find another clue about the conquest of Canaan in what Jesus says about divorce under the Mosaic Law. "Moses permitted you to divorce your wives," he says, "because your hearts were hard."[49] The law's relatively lax statute on divorce was cruel because it allowed a man in middle age to discard his first wife for a younger woman, leaving the older woman destitute.[50] Nevertheless, Israelites in their early history were capable of no higher standard.

Jesus, associating the law closely with Moses, notes that it was geared to the people's cultural circumstances and sinful limitations, a principle that applies to their stance toward the native inhabitants of Canaan. To the question, "Were the Israelites capable of resisting Canaanite decadence without being commanded to wage total war on the Canaanites?," the answer is horrific, and dictated the horrific campaign Israel was to undertake.[51] The barbarity of the conflict is therefore an index of the depravity of the human heart.

---

47 Exod 21:23-25.
48 Judg 1:6-7.
49 Matt 19:8.
50 Mal 2:14.
51 Deut 20:17-18.

"Make no treaty with them, and show them no mercy," God commands Israel concerning the Hittites, Hivites, Jebusites and other
Canaanite peoples. Then, where we might expect a repetition of the
command for bloodshed, instead we read instructions about the symbols of Canaanite religion. "This is what you are to do to them: Break
down their altars, smash their sacred stones, cut down their Asherah
poles and burn their idols in the fire."[52]

What God wants eradicated is a debased culture, and Canaanites who
relinquish that culture live alongside the Hebrews with Yahweh's evident blessing. God brings disaster on David's house when David
conspires against Uriah, a Hittite officer in his army, in order to steal
Uriah's beautiful wife Bathsheba. Later, God sends a famine on Israel itself over the violation of a treaty with a peaceful Canaanite tribe, the
Hivites of Gibeon.[53] Although Yahweh has deeded the whole land to
Israel, David obtains the most sacred portion, the tract for Yahweh's
temple, by buying it at full market value from its Canaanite owner,
Araunah the Jebusite.[54] People of Canaanite ancestry prove to be a
threat to Israel only insofar as they practice idolatry, sacred prostitution,
sexual perversion, human sacrifice and spiritism.

After the conquest of Canaan, the Israelites are forbidden from ever
again carrying out massacres of their enemies.[55] Moses also warns them
in vain that if they indulge in evil, they will become the victims of the
same type of warfare they have waged.[56] Israel must decimate and in
turn be decimated before it is psychologically capable of learning certain
lessons.

When Yahweh says to his people, "As the heavens are higher than
the earth, so are my ways higher than your ways and my thoughts than
your thoughts," he is talking about his unfathomable patience with evildoers in the hope of their recovery.[57] "As surely as I live," God declares
with an oath, "I take no pleasure in the death of the wicked, but rather

---

52 Deut 7:5.
53 2 Sam 12:9-10; 21:1-2.
54 2 Sam 24:18-24.
55 Deut 20:10-16.
56 Lev 18:26-28.
57 Isa 55:9.

that they turn from their ways and live."[58] Israel begins to understand that unless God's mercy finds a way to triumph over the implacable judgment on sin, none can hope to survive.[59]

The Law of Moses proved to be as stern a "schoolmaster," to use Paul's term, as was necessary for a human heart that is "deceitful above all things and beyond cure."[60] The bloody trail of Israel's history led to that instrument of unyielding justice, the cross, and to the Son of God who while hanging upon it assumed the full curse of the law, including the curse on the Canaanites.[61]

We have now examined typological portrayals from a number of Bible stories and from the poetry of the Psalms. We have discovered as well that a combination of successive episodes from the life of Moses aligns symbolically with what the New Testament tells us about Jesus. Our last example will be drawn from yet another genre of Biblical literature, ecstatic visions.

---

58 Ezek 33:11.
59 Isa 1:9.
60 Gal 3:24; Jer 17:9.
61 Gal 3:13.

17

What Ezekiel Saw

Why are there four Gospels in the New Testament? That question has confronted Christians since the second century as it has scholars and historians. Why is there not a single narrative of Jesus' life comparable with, say, the story of Moses in the Pentateuch? Christians tend to view the differences among the Gospels as reconcilable. They argue that a single, longer biography would somehow lack the richness provided by our four-sided portrait of Jesus.

From a non-Christian perspective, touting the superiority of four Gospels amounts to forging virtue from necessity. Even the earliest Christian apologists were challenged to account for the variances if not outright contradictions between the books of Matthew, Mark, Luke and John. Tatian, a Christian writing in the second century, attempted to solve the problem by blending the four Gospels into one narrative, the *Diatesseron* (meaning, "through the four").

Not only is the number of Gospels an oddity, the process that gave us four official stories of Jesus looks haphazard. The Synoptic (meaning "seen together") Gospels of Matthew, Mark and Luke contain passages that are so nearly identical that borrowing seems the only reasonable explanation. In spite of these duplications, each Gospel has its own narrative style. Each contains its own particular assortment of events and its own chronology. The Gospel of John stands so far apart from the Synoptics that some critics claim it presents a different Jesus.

None of the Gospels straightforwardly identifies its writer or records the time and place of writing. Nor does any Gospel offer more than vague comments about how or from whom its information was gathered; all we know in that regard comes from later, historically fuzzy church tradition. The author of Luke mentions other written accounts, which he nevertheless fails to identify and which he implicitly finds inadequate.

Few people have heard of the Gospels of Thomas, of Peter, of Philip, of the Hebrews or of the Egyptians, but those works and two dozen or so others from the first two centuries prove that the urge to produce a report of Jesus' life or teachings struck more than four ancient writers. If the canonical Gospels are the oldest surviving examples of the genre, as most (though not all) New Testament scholars believe, they may owe that distinction to the reading preferences of early Christians. Any older gospels that might have been written never achieved wide enough circulation to leave behind recognizable traces let alone win formal acceptance by the bishops of subsequent centuries.

To put it bluntly, even if the Gospels are correctly attributed to Matthew, Mark, Luke and John they seem to have been cobbled together from memories, anecdotes, oral tradition and in some cases earlier writings, then chosen through a kind of popularity contest. No serious historian, whether secular or Christian, believes that a person or persons in the early church planned the creation of the four as a coordinated project. For one thing, it is hard to imagine that collaborators would have failed to harmonize more closely their narratives so that, to cite just one example among dozens, the order of Jesus' three wilderness temptations would be the same in Luke as in Matthew.[1]

Then there is the question of how anyone could have engineered

---

1   Matt 4:1-11; Luke 4:1-13.

popular acceptance of four different Gospels to such an extent that none of them could later be rejected by church authorities. Critics seize on the chance nature of Gospel selection as if it undercuts any claim of divine inspiration for these books, when in reality it affords an opportunity to verify that claim. If a central plan or blueprint is found to underlie the Gospels, it could have been executed only by someone capable of controlling the inscrutable twists and turns of history.

The Four Gospels in Ezekiel?

A Christian bishop of the second century, Irenaeus of Lyons, implies that such a blueprint is contained in the Old Testament book of Ezekiel.[2] Ezekiel was an Israelite exile in Babylon who was called to be a prophet early in the sixth century BC. In the opening scene of his book, Ezekiel falls into a vision and sees Yahweh clothed in supernatural light, riding a heavenly chariot with an escort of angels or cherubim. Each of the angels has four wings and four faces, the first face being "the face of a man, and on the right side each had the face of a lion, and on the left the face of an ox; each also had the face of an eagle."[3] Ezekiel's depiction of the cherubim is closely paralleled in the New Testament book of Revelation, although in that book the man, lion, ox and eagle appear as a group of separate beings.[4]

In his work *Against Heresies*, Irenaeus symbolically relates each of the four faces of Ezekiel's cherubim to one of the Gospels.[5] He sees Matthew's Gospel as corresponding to the man's face because it opens with a human genealogy of Jesus and because, in the opinion of Irenaeus, Jesus' humanity is emphasized throughout the book. Luke begins with a narrative involving priestly duties, therefore Irenaeus associates it with the only sacrificial animal in the foursome, the ox. He links the early mention of the holy Spirit in Mark with the winged crea-

---

2 Irenaeus does not name the Biblical books he is referencing, but his descriptions correspond to those contained in Ezekiel and Revelation. See T. C. Skeat, "Irenaeus and the Four-Gospel Canon," *Novum Testamentum* 34 (1992): 194-199.

3 Ezek 1:10.

4 Rev 4:7.

5 Irenaeus, *Adv. Her.* 3.11.8.

ture, the eagle, while proposing that John's prologue concerning Jesus' divinely "royal" parentage associates that book with the regal animal, the lion.

Irenaeus writes about the alignment of the faces with the Gospels as if he is expressing a belief common among Christians of his time. It may have seemed natural that God would incorporate a symbolic prophecy about the gospel message into the visible form of the angels, since angels frequently function as messengers.[6] Wherever the idea originated, it continued to fascinate Christian scholars even as their tendency to reshuffle the face-to-Gospel assignments cast doubt on it. Augustine (lived 354-430) like Irenaeus assigned the ox to Luke but gave the lion to Matthew, the man to Mark and the eagle to John.[7] In agreement with Augustine, Jerome (347-419) linked the Fourth Gospel with the eagle, because when he read its prologue he felt as if he were winging his way to heaven. For Matthew and Luke Jerome stuck with Irenaeus' assignments of man and ox, respectively, while giving the lion to Mark.[8]

Jerome's scheme has proven to be the most popular, but commentators have periodically revisited the subject and suggested yet other combinations.[9] What all these theories have in common is a reliance on subjective judgments such as Jerome's impression that the opening verses of Mark have the boldness of a lion's roar. Interpretations of that kind can be produced to match any of the faces with any of the Gospels, making the enterprise appear futile if not comical. Moreover, there are other, less sensational reasons for the occurrence of these four-faced angels in the book of Ezekiel.

Anyone who has seen representations of gods from Egypt and Mesopotamia knows that they frequently combine parts of different animals as well as parts of animals and humans. Likewise, attending spirits or genii are portrayed as griffins, sphinxes and winged bulls.

The cherub was a composite figure placed as a spirit guardian on the

---

6   The Hebrew and Greek words for angel literally mean "messenger." Although the creatures of Ezekiel are simply called cherubs, several texts classify all spirit attendants of God as angels (Ps 103:20; 148:2; Heb 12:22; 1 Pet 3:22).

7   Augustine, *The Harmony of the Gospels* 4.10.

8   Jerome, *Commentary on Ezekiel* 1.1.

9   E.g., Matthew/lion, Mark/ox, Luke/man and John/eagle; see Chuck Missler, *Cosmic Codes* (Coeur d'Alene, ID: Koinonia, 1999), 208.

side panels of thrones and in other locations of sacred or strategic significance. The oldest example may be a 3,200-year-old bronze cult stand from Cyprus, which portrays a creature with the head of a man, the wings of an eagle, the forelegs of a lion and the hindquarters of a bull.[10] The combination is not as odd as it sounds in that each of these creatures was seen as dominating some sphere of the natural world: the lion over wild animals, the bull or ox over domestic animals, the eagle over birds and man over creation in general.

The cherubim of Ezekiel therefore are easier to understand in an ancient context than in a modern one. What better way to depict the otherworldly power of the angelic beings attending God's throne than by attributing to them ferocity, strength and swiftness using stock symbols of the time?

It is tempting to stop with a cultural explanation of Ezekiel's vision and conclude that relating the cherubim to the Gospels is a misguided though understandable attempt to rationalize the presence of four biographies of Jesus in Scripture. But a systematic approach to typological coding has served us well till now. When we suppress our skepticism long enough to examine objective differences among the Gospels and then relate those differences to symbol identifiers, we find to our surprise that the church fathers were partly right. A relationship between the cherubim and the Gospels does exist, although it is more complex than those who first wrote about it imagined.

Faces, Gospels and New Testament Categories

To appreciate what it is that links the Gospels to the vision of Ezekiel, we must review some information from previous chapters. Beginning in Chapter 7 we learned that the New Testament divides mankind into ethnic categories based on Israel's historical status under the Mosaic Covenant. The broadest division is simply into Israelite and non-Israelite—Jew and Gentile. "The gospel is the power of God for the salvation of everyone who believes," says Paul, "first for the Jew,

---

10 Elie Borowski, "Cherubim: God's Throne?," *Biblical Archeology Review* 21, No. 4 (1995): 39.

then for the Gentile."[11] Paul also refers to these two groups as the "circumcised" and the "uncircumcised."[12] To these we can add a nation of circumcised law-keepers that nevertheless fell outside of Judaism, the Samaritans.

Technically, therefore, mankind can be divided into Jew, Samaritan and Gentile in keeping with Jesus' early mission instructions: "Do not go among the Gentiles or enter any town of the Samaritans. Go rather to the lost sheep of Israel."[13] With the emergence of the Christian church, members of all these classes were admitted into a covenant relationship with God as witnesses of his purpose in Christ. The ability to view the Christian congregation as either a two-fold body of Jews and Gentiles or as a three-fold union of Jews, Samaritans and Gentiles happens to fulfill the Mosaic principle that "a matter must be established by the testimony of two or three witnesses."[14]

Recognizing the ethnic-spiritual classes of Jew, Samaritan and Gentile turns out to be indispensable to understanding the plan of the Gospels. Each of the Synoptic Gospels (Matthew, Mark and Luke) has an ethnic subtext or coloration that corresponds to one of these groups. Each group in turn is associated in the Scriptures with one of the animals whose faces appear on the cherubim. Finally, the Gospel of John with its emphasis on the person of Jesus belongs with the remaining face, that of the man. This interpretation is supported by evidence rather than subjective feelings.

Matthew and the Lion of Judah

The first Gospel in canonical order, Matthew, has long been recognized as characteristically Jewish in its point of view. At the outset it documents Jesus' Hebrew ancestry from Abraham through David and his successors in the dynasty of Judah. Matthew contains 26 occurrences of the names "Judah," "David" and "Solomon," nearly as many as the total of 28 for the other three Gospels combined. Only in Matthew does Jesus presuppose ongoing worship at the Jerusalem temple, the

---

11 Rom 1:16; Paul here uses the word "Greek" to connote Gentile.
12 Rom 3:30.
13 Matt 10:5-6; cf. Acts 1:8.
14 Deut 19:15; cf. 2 Cor 13:1.

center of Jewish religious life, by saying that it is imperative to reconcile with an estranged brother before offering a sacrifice at the altar.[15]

In keeping with Jewish reverence for the Hebrew Scriptures and for the Law of Moses in particular, Matthew speaks more highly of the law than do the writers of Mark, Luke and John.[16] Matthew also refers repeatedly to Jesus' fulfillment of Hebrew prophecy.

A standard reference work supplies totals for quotations of Old Testament Scripture in the four Gospels.[17] This allows us to compare the figures for each:

Matthew	66
Mark	34
Luke	43
John	21

In addition to quoting prolifically from the Hebrew Bible, Matthew lays greater stress than the other Gospels on the priority of the Jewish people. Matthew alone contains Jesus' command, cited above, that the disciples are to preach to Israel, meaning Jews, rather than to Samaritans or Gentiles.[18] Unlike Mark's account of the Syro-Phoenician woman, Matthew's version has Jesus pointedly say to her, "I was sent only to the lost sheep of Israel."[19]

When, in Matthew, Jesus advises that any Christian who lapses into unrepentant sin should be shunned, he tells the disciples to treat the wrongdoer "as a Gentile and a tax collector" in keeping with peculiarly Jewish social attitudes.[20] These verses are a small part of the evidence of Matthew's Jewish orientation, as can be verified by anyone willing to consult annotated study Bibles, commentaries and scholarly literature.

Although scholars generally agree that Matthew lacks the earmarks of a translated work, the statements of church fathers that Matthew was

---

15 Matt 5:23-24.
16 Matt 5:17-19; 23:2-3.
17 Robert Bratcher, *Old Testament Quotations in the New Testament* (NY: United Bible Societies, 1987), 1-27.
18 Matt 10:5-6.
19 Matt 15:24; cf. Mk. 15:27.
20 Matt 18:17.

originally written in Hebrew confirm its close association with Jewish Christians, as do Hebrew language versions of the Gospel dating back at least to the Middle Ages. The "Jewishness" of Matthew is so well attested as to be a settled issue except for remarks made in recent years by a few scholars to the effect that the book of John is the most "Jewish" of the Gospels. Those comments must be seen as a reaction against the once commonplace assumption that John's Gospel was heavily influenced by Greek thought.

Due especially to Dead Sea Scrolls research, scholars now acknowledge that John's expressions are as likely derived from first century Judaism as from Greek sources. That is not to say that John actually is more Jewish in its outlook than Matthew. John's routine description of Jesus' audience as "the Jews," in contrast to a single such usage in Matthew, places the reader of John at a relatively greater distance from Jewish culture. John 2:6, which notes that "nearby stood six stone water jars, the kind used by the Jews for ceremonial washing," stands as one example. When all factors are considered, Matthew's status as the "Jewish" Gospel is beyond dispute.

With the ethnic identification of Matthew, we are able to make our first assignment of one of the faces from Ezekiel's cherubim. Jews or Judeans are primarily members of the dominant tribe of the southern kingdom, Judah, from which the northern tribes eventually withdrew, as we saw in Chapter 10.[21] The animal symbol for Judah is the lion, as is plain from passages in both Old and New Testaments. "You are a lion's cub, O Judah," says Genesis, and, "Like a lion he crouches and lies down."[22] Revelation famously describes Jesus as "the Lion of the tribe of Judah."[23]

Mark and the Roman Gentile Eagle

We now turn to Mark's Gospel. Because Mark's author goes out of his way to explain Jewish customs and Aramaic terms, scholars generally recognize that he has a Gentile readership in mind. Commentaries often cite verses three and four of chapter seven describing the concern of

21 Josh 18:5.
22 Gen 49:9.
23 Rev 5:5.

"the Pharisees and all the Jews" with ritual purity, but the entire chapter in which the passage occurs reinforces the same point. The comment at the end of verse nineteen, saying that Jesus effectively "declared all foods clean," implies that Jesus authorized in advance the admission of Gentiles into the church.[24] A similar pronouncement that formerly forbidden foods are now "clean" occurs in the book of Acts as part of the story of the first Gentile convert to Christianity, the Roman centurion Cornelius.[25]

The indirect connection between Mark's Gospel and the first Gentile Christian convert is not the only link between Mark and the Roman people. Mark contains more Latin loan words than any of the other Gospels, and while these words are part of the vernacular of some other Jewish literature, their presence still leaves Mark relatively more latinized than Matthew, Luke or John.

The tradition dating back as early as the second century that Mark was written in Rome is revealing as well, since factual or not there must be a reason for it, just as there is for the idea that Matthew was composed in Hebrew.[26] As far as we know, symbolic interpretations of the book of Ezekiel had nothing to do with early Christian claims that Mark's Gospel was written at Rome; surmises about where the book originated likely were prompted either by its documentary history or by its contents.

In the opening words of Mark, "The beginning of the gospel [*evangelion*, "good news"] about Jesus Christ," some scholars hear an echo of tributes to the greatest of the Caesars, Augustus.[27] Augustus had been proclaimed "Son of God" and "Savior" for supposedly bringing peace to the world through the military might of the Roman Empire, and his birth was described as the "beginning of good news [*evangelion*]." Mark's challenge to such Roman pretensions might be read, "Here is the genuine good news, about Jesus, the man who (unlike Augustus) truly is the world's Savior."

All the Synoptic Gospels refer to the Roman officer who presided

---

24 Mark 7:19.

25 Acts 10:10-22.

26 Both traditions date to the late second century; see Irenaeus, *op. cit.*, 3.1.1.

27 Craig A. Evans, "Mark's Incipit and the Priene Calendar Inscription: From Jewish Gospel to Greco-Roman Gospel," *Journal of Greco-Roman Christianity and Judaism* 1 (2000): 67-81.

over Jesus' crucifixion, but Mark does so by spelling out the Latin word "centurion" in Greek letters as *kenturion* instead of translating it into the Greek word *hekatontarchos*, as do Matthew and Luke. Mark has the demons calling Jesus the "Son of God" in defiance, but no one is shown confessing Jesus' divine sonship until the centurion exclaims, "Surely this man was the Son of God."[28] The Roman soldier's testimony serves as the climactic declaration of Jesus' identity in Mark.[29]

The Roman Gentile affinity of Mark is the key to our second face identification. To use it we must sort through a menagerie of snakes, lions, leopards, bears, wolves, goats and other animals to which the Gentile nations are likened in the Hebrew Bible.[30] Rome is not explicitly mentioned, but empires that had a dominant status comparable to Rome's offer a clue. These are Egypt, Assyria, Babylon, Media-Persia and Greece. Two on this list, Assyria and Babylon, fulfilled a prophecy at Deuteronomy 28:49-52 that as punishment for Israel's rebellion, "The LORD will bring a nation against you from far away, from the ends of the earth, like an eagle swooping down . . . They will lay siege to all the cities throughout your land until the high fortified walls in which you trust fall down."

In keeping with the language of Deuteronomy, Assyria and Babylon are later referred to under the figure of a hovering or swooping eagle.[31] Media-Persia is called a "bird of prey."[32] Ezekiel, the book in which the four-faced cherubim appear, portrays the kings of both Babylon, the dominant power of Ezekiel's time, and Egypt, its southern rival, as eagles.[33] Greece is not associated with the eagle in the Bible, but Alexander the Great adopted the eagle owing to its status as the sacred bird of Zeus, the head of the Greek pantheon.

It was not just the ancient Mesopotamian empires that fit the description of the predatory eagle of Deuteronomy 28. In AD 70 Rome responded to the First Jewish Revolt by invading Judea in force. Bearing

---

28 Mark 15:39.

29 See Tae Hun Kim, "The Anarthrous Hyios Theou in Mark 15,39 and the Roman Imperial Cult," *Biblica* 79 (1998): 221-241.

30 Jer 5:6; Dan 7:2-6; 8:3-8.

31 Jer 48:40; 49:22; Hos 8:1.

32 Isa 46:11.

33 Ezek 17:3-15.

standards crowned with Rome's animal ensign, the eagle, Roman legions besieged and overran Jerusalem, razed the temple and killed or enslaved thousands of Jews. The eagle therefore is the appropriate Biblical symbol for Rome just as it is for previous Gentile empires. We are safe in concluding that Mark, the "Gentile Gospel," is represented by the eagle's face.

Luke and the Samaritan Bull

Of our three categories of Jew, Samaritan and Gentile, only "Samaritan" is left, with the Gospels of Luke and John still to be assigned. It is not apparent that either of those books was written for the limited audience represented by first-century Samaritans, but Samaritans are prominently mentioned in both.

Luke contains (1) the refusal of a Samaritan village to allow Jesus to pass through on his way to Jerusalem, (2) Jesus' parable of the "Good Samaritan" and (3) Jesus' healing of ten lepers, one of whom is a Samaritan.[34] John, on the other hand, contains (1) the story of the Samaritan woman Jesus encounters at a well and the favorable reception he receives at the nearby Samaritan town of Sychar, and (2) the accusation by Jesus' enemies, stemming perhaps from his controversial visit to Sychar, that Jesus is himself Samaritan.[35] On casual reading neither Gospel seems to be more "Samaritan" than the other.

If we look more closely we find that the second and third Samaritan-related passages from Luke are unlike anything else in the Gospels, including the Sychar story from John, in that they portray Samaritans as being more righteous than Jews. After Jesus heals ten lepers, only a Samaritan turns back to thank him; the majority if not all of the remaining nine are Jews, as can be understood from Jesus' instructions to them to show themselves to the priests as well as by his concluding reproach.

In the Good Samaritan parable, preserved only by Luke, the title character offers lifesaving aid to an injured man by the side of the road after a Jewish priest and a Levite pass him by. New Testament scholar Ben Witherington observes that the exemplary place accorded in Luke to a Samaritan over and against those who were seen by the Jews as the

---

34 Luke 9:51-56; 10:30-35; 17:11-19.
35 John 4:4-42; 8:48.

official custodians of Mosaic Law is "striking."[36] The extent of the honor Luke's Gospel accords upright Samaritans is further evident from the typology of the story. As discussed in Chapter 14, a parallel is implied between the charitable Samaritan and Jesus himself inasmuch as Jesus furnished salvation for dying humanity when the Mosaic Law, represented by the priest and Levite, could not.

Less obvious than the heroic status that the Good Samaritan story confers upon a member of a nation despised by Jews is its relationship to the history of that nation. Samaria began its national existence as the northern kingdom of Israel following the split with Judah in the tenth century BC. The Old Testament narrative running from 1 Kings chapter twelve through 2 Kings chapter seventeen consists primarily of early Samaritan history, and allusions to this portion of the Hebrew Bible abound in Luke's Gospel.

Chapter 14 showed how Jesus created the Good Samaritan parable by reworking the tale of the Judean and Samaritan prophets, along with that of kindly Samaritans from the book of 2 Chronicles.[37] The mission instruction Jesus borrows from Elisha, also cited in Chapter 14, is one of the many narrative details unique to Luke that correspond to events from Samaritan history.[38] References to Samaritan history that are absent from Luke but present in the other Gospels are far less extensive.[39]

Among the Gospels, only Luke contains the names of both great prophets of Samaria, Elijah and Elisha, and only Luke reports the Elijah- and Elisha-like resurrection of the son of a widow in the village of Nain just a few miles from where Elisha performed a similar miracle.[40] In Luke's genealogy, "Joseph" is the most frequently occurring name, evoking the tribal forefather of the northern Israelites.[41]

Recognizing the Samaritan sympathies of Luke's Gospel allows us to

36 Ben Witherington III, *Jesus the Sage: The Pilgrimage of Wisdom* (Minneapolis: Augsburg Fortress, 1994), 195.

37 1 Kgs 13:1-32; 2 Kgs 23:17-18; 2 Chron 28:5-15.

38 Cf. Luke 9:51 with 4 Kgdms 2:1, 9, LXX (2 Kgs, MT); cf. Luke 9:54; 12:49 with 2 Kgs 1:9-16; cf. Luke 9:61-62 with 1 Kgs 19:19-20; cf. Luke 10:4b with 2 Kgs 4:29b; cf. Luke 12:54 with 1 Kgs 18:43-44; cf. Luke 17:7-8 with 1 Kgs 17:10-13; cf. Luke 24:15-16, 31 with 2 Kgs 6:17-20; cf. Luke 19:41-44 with 2 Kgs 8:11-12.

39 Cf. Matt 3:4; Mark 1:6 with 1 Kgs 1:8; cf. John 16:32 with 1 Kgs 22:17, 36.

40 Luke 4:25-27; 7:11-15; 1 Kgs 17:17-24; 2 Kgs 4:8-37.

41 Luke 3:23, 24, 30; 1 Chron 5:1-2.

solve a long-standing puzzle having to do with the most popular of all of Jesus' parables, that of the Prodigal Son. The story of a son who sinfully squanders his father's money, repents and is accepted back by the father but scorned by his older brother is an illustration of God's patient love for humanity. But the plot is unusually detailed for a parable. Is it based on the experience of an actual family or instead representative of some aspect of Israel's history?

None of the many theories about the origin of the Prodigal Story has won general acceptance, but the suggestion of some scholars that the Prodigal is based on the northern kingdom of Israel is in keeping with Luke's interest in Samaria.[42] The Jews were descendants of Judah, an older brother of the principal forebear of the Samaritans, Joseph.[43] It was the northern kingdom, the "younger brother," that withdrew from the national family and squandered its spiritual inheritance, becoming ethnically and ritually impure in the process.[44] The various details of the story correspond closely to the experiences and attitudes of the Judean and northern Israelite peoples (see Appendix).

The majority of northern Israelites traced their descent from Joseph's sons, Manasseh and Ephraim, with the second son's tribe being so dominant that the term "Ephraim" became synonymous with the "house of Joseph."[45] Joseph's symbol is the bull or "wild ox,"[46] which is paired with Judah's symbol the lion to symbolize greater Israel from the wilderness wandering through the reign of Solomon.[47]

The association of Joseph/Ephraim with the figure of the bull is inseparably entwined with economic and religious history. From the northern pastures that were Israel's prime cattle-raising territory came

---

42 See John Bowman, *The Samaritan Problem: Studies in the Relationships of Samaritanism, Judaism, and early Christianity* (Pittsburgh: Pickwick Press, 1975), 83; Gottfried Quell in *Theological Dictionary of the New Testament*, ed. G. Friedrich, trans. G. W. Bromiley (Grand Rapids, MI: Eerdmans, 1976), 973; David Ravens, *Luke and the Restoration of Israel* (Sheffield: Sheffield Academic Press, 1995), 102-103.

43 Gen 29:31-30:24; Ezek 37:16.

44 See the Hebrew of Judg 1:3 for an example of entire tribes being referred to as individual brothers.

45 Josh 18:5; Isa. 11:13.

46 Deut 33:16-17.

47 Num 23:22-24; 1 Kgs 7:29.

the "bulls of Bashan," famous for their size and strength.[48] God referred to the ten-tribe federation as an "unruly calf" and a "stubborn heifer" and its women as the "cows of Bashan on Mount Samaria."[49] The miracle-working prophets of Samaria, Elijah and Elisha, made special offerings of bulls and oxen.[50] Idolatry in the north, too, was directed to images of bulls and calves.[51]

In Luke's Prodigal Son story, the compassionate father slaughters a fattened young bull order to hold a feast for his repentant younger son. The symbolism of Christ as the bull that is offered to sustain those who repent in faith was not lost on Irenaeus, who saw it as confirmation of the bull as Luke's symbol. Irenaeus's sole correct guess about a face-to-Gospel assignment owes in part, therefore, to a typological clue. For an even broader hint, compare one of Jesus' sayings in Matthew to the version of it from Luke:

> He said to them, "If any of you has a sheep and it falls into a pit on the Sabbath, will you not take hold of it and lift it out? How much more valuable is a man than a sheep! —Matthew 12:11-12

> Then he asked them, "If one of you has a son or an ox that falls into a well on the Sabbath day, will you not immediately pull him out?"
> —Luke 14:5 (cf. 13:15)

Jesus is teaching a lesson in mercy based on the care of domestic animals. The animal symbol for Judah, the lion, is inappropriate for this purpose, but Jesus has another metaphor to draw upon, that of the "lost [Jewish] sheep of Israel" who are so carefully distinguished from Gentiles and Samaritans in Matthew's Gospel. But while Matthew records the figurative equation between a human and a sheep, Luke instead preserves a comparison of man with the ox (or bull), *bous*. Luke's

---

48 Ps 22:12.
49 Jer 31:18; Hos 4:1, 16; 10:11; Amos 4:1.
50 1 Kgs 18:33; 19:21.
51 1 Kgs 12:28; Hos 8:5-6. See Amihai Mazar, "Bronze Bull found in Israelite 'High Place' from the Time of the Judges," *Biblical Archeology Review*, Sept/Oct (1983): 34.

man-ox symbolism reflects what the Hebrew Bible says about the northern kingdom.

God says through Jeremiah that Ephraim "strayed" and had to be disciplined "like an unruly calf."[52] Having handed Samaria over to Assyrian oppression, God nevertheless is anxious to recover his wayward people. "Is not Ephraim my dear son, the child in whom I delight?," he asks. "Though I often speak against him, I still remember him . . . I have great compassion for him."[53] If Ephraim is a renegade calf in need of recovery, then his rehabilitation might be likened to pulling a young ox out of a well.

The bovine Ephraim (Samaria) of Jeremiah 31 is a "dear son," hearkening forward to Luke 14:5, where son and ox alike are worthy of compassion. We now have a variety of references that combine to identify Luke as the "Samaritan Gospel" under the symbol of the third animal face, that of the bull.

Animal Symbols and Classes of Mankind in Ezekiel

With the three animal symbols tentatively assigned, we turn for corroboration to Ezekiel, the book in which the cherubim are described. Ezekiel is the one of just two books in the Hebrew Bible that provide identifiers for more than one of the animal faces of the cherubim. Deuteronomy connects the bull to Joseph (and therefore to Samaria) and the eagle to Gentile empires, while Ezekiel confirms the symbolism of the eagle and the lion.[54]

The symbol for Samaria, the bull or ox, seems to be missing from Ezekiel until we look closely at instructions the prophet is given for a mock assault upon Israel. He is told to pantomime a siege of the northern kingdom for 390 days, followed by a 40-day siege of Jerusalem and Judah.

During the first siege he must eat coarse bread baked over a fire made with human excrement to illustrate the consumption of unclean food by impoverished Samaritan refugees. When Ezekiel protests that the enactment is too revolting for him to bear, God allows him to cook with

---

52 Jer 31:18-19.
53 Jer 31:20.
54 Deut 33:16-17; 28:49-52; Ezek 17:3-15; 19:1-9.

manure of cattle (*bous*, LXX) in place of human offal.[55] The concession subtly equates the people of Samaria with cattle or oxen, just as Luke's Gospel places "son" in parallel with "ox."

Ezekiel, besides being the only book containing identifiers for all three of the animals represented by the cherubim, is also the only book to predict God's reconciliation to himself of mankind in terms of three ethnic/spiritual classes corresponding to Jew, Samaritan and Gentile. Ezekiel represents these categories as three cities: Jerusalem, Samaria and Sodom.[56] This theme cannot be divorced from Ezekiel's prophecy about the coming messianic king.

References to the Messiah occur at Ezekiel 34:24 and 37:25. Consequently, Ezekiel contains the ingredients of a foursome consisting of the three divisions of humanity and the Messiah. It is also significant, given the association of the Messiah with the temple, that a mysterious "man" who reveals a plan for a new temple stands beside Ezekiel in the inner temple court just as God announces this room to be the resting place for the "soles of my feet."[57]

John's Divine Man

The subject of the Messiah as distinct from sinful men brings us to the Gospel of John, since it alone is left to correspond to the human face of the cherubim. John is noteworthy for its sweeping observations concerning mankind in relation to the messianic Son of God. Of Jesus' coming, John says, "The true light that gives light to every man was coming into the world."[58] "This is the verdict," John intones about humanity, "Light has come into the world, but men loved darkness instead of light because their deeds were evil," while saying of Jesus, "He did not need man's testimony about man, for he knew what was in a man."[59]

John also stresses the importance of faith in the person of Jesus as opposed to faith merely in his message or his work. The idea of "believ-

---

55 Ezek 4:9-15.
56 Ezek 16:45-56.
57 Ezek 43:6-7; cf. Isa 60:13.
58 John 1:9.
59 John 2:25; 3:19.

ing in Jesus" occurs only three times in the Synoptics, whereas in John we find it expressed more than twenty times.[60]

Each of the Gospels is centered on Jesus, of course, but in terms of its emphasis on the divine Man, John is the "Jesus Gospel." To further prove the point, we need only count the number of times the word "man," Greek *anthropos*, designates Jesus in the various Gospels, discounting the many places where "man" is interpolated in translation. The tally is revealing:

Matthew	3
Mark	2
Luke	5
John	15

The occurrences in John begin at 4:29 with the invitation of the woman at the well, "Come, see a man who told me everything I ever did," and culminate in Pilate's declaration at 19:5: "Here is the man!"

It is time to credit Irenaeus and the Christians of the second century for their for their spiritual intuition. The relationship between the four faces of the cherubim and the canonical Gospels is so systematic that it defies coincidence. Irenaeus's failure to assign all the faces correctly is excusable when we consider that any attempt to do so without first determining the ethnic associations of the Gospels is a blind draw with 23-to-1 odds against success.

To account naturalistically for the alignment of Matthew-Jew-lion, Mark-Gentile-eagle, Luke-Samaritan-bull and John-Jesus-man is as daunting a challenge as our studies have so far posed. In the following chapter, we will probe to see how deeply the Gospel pattern is embedded. We will also make some observations about the patterned structure of the universe itself.

---

60 Matt 18:6; 27:42; Mark 9:42; cf John 2:11; 3:15; 4:39; 6:35; 7:31; et al.

18

Everything According to the Pattern

Someone suggested to me that even though it is impossible to believe that the four Gospels were deliberately written with the four-faced cherubim in mind, second-century Christians could have edited early versions of the Gospels after deciphering the symbolism of Ezekiel. The first problem with this theory is the convenient way the faces align with the divisions of mankind, Gospels aside.

We have already seen that the combination of lion, bull, eagle and man as "cherub" dates back well over three thousand years, to before Israel existed as a monarchy, let alone as northern and southern kingdoms. For reasons already discussed, the ancestors of the Samaritan Israelites may have come to see the bull as their emblem even before they constituted a nation, and the Judahites of the south could have distinguished themselves later by adopting the Davidic lion. It would be a mild coincidence that these animals already were components of the cherub figure.

What the chance occurrence of the lion and bull as Israelite symbols fails to explain is why the eagle is so prominent in the iconography of so many ancient Gentile empires.

In theory, Deuteronomy's description of the destroyer of Israelite cities as an "eagle" could have been written after the Assyrian conquest under the influence of Mesopotamian usage. It would still be astonishingly lucky, on a par with being dealt an ace-high straight off the top of a poker deck, that such an imperial symbol would happen to be the one animal left on the cherub composite after subtracting the two that stand for Israel. The straight proved to be a royal flush when when Greece under Alexander the Great made the eagle its emblem of royal majesty and later Rome, the final desolater of Judea, adopted it as well.

Gospel Identities and the Four-Way Pattern

Imposing as the odds are against the accidental coding of Ezekiel's animal faces with the three-fold division of mankind, any gambler would gladly take them over the odds against the Gospels' having been reworked or "redacted" to conform to Ezekiel. What distinguishes each of the Gospels is like the combination of baked-in characteristics that make a loaf of whole wheat bread different from a loaf of rye or sourdough, not like flavors of jam spread on generic slices of toast.

Qualities of Mark and Luke that integrate style and content serve to illustrate this last point. The Roman Gentiles whose perspective Mark reflects were builders and soldiers who valued deeds above words. Mark therefore presents Jesus' teaching in pithy parables, proverbs and admonitions. Mark's narrative has Jesus moving from one dramatic event to the next with the adverb *eutheos*, "immediately," frequently serving as a connector. Jesus according to Mark is not just "the carpenter's son," as in Matthew, but "the carpenter"—a builder who reveals himself also to be a tireless healer, teacher, commander of men and nature and finally, at the cross, the very Son of God.[1]

If Mark is a tale of action, Luke is a work of literature, specifically of Greek literature. Luke's rich vocabulary and articulate phrasing set him apart, not only from Matthew, Mark and John, but from every other New Testament writer except the author of Hebrews. The *Anti-Marcionite Gospel Prologues*, one of the ancient sources that tell us about the

---

1   Mark 6:3; cf. Matt 13:55.

Judean origin of Matthew's Gospel and the Italian origin of Mark, claims that Luke wrote his Gospel in the district of Achaia, the Greek heartland where the ancient cities of Athens and Corinth were located.[2]

Luke's command of Greek letters and Greek culture is related to the Samaritan sympathies evident in both his Gospel and the sequel to it, Acts of the Apostles. More than three hundred years before Jesus, the Samaritans had resisted the Greek forces of Alexander the Great and in return had been brutally suppressed. A Greek colony was established at the town of Samaria, capital of the district of the same name, and in time the Samaritans accommodated themselves not only to Greek rule but, to a considerable extent, to Greek culture. Recurrent bouts of warfare sent Samaria's capital into decline, but King Herod rebuilt it as a Hellenistic (Greek-style) city and renamed it Sebaste in honor of Caesar Augustus, whose name in Greek is "Sebastos." A Greek-inspired Olympic stadium was built at Samaria-Sebaste, where Herod hosted the 192nd Olympiad.

Samaria's history would lead us to expect that in the first century, as in the three centuries prior to it, a larger proportion of fluent Greek-speakers was to be found among inhabitants of Samaria than among those of Judea. From Greek-educated Luke we learn that good news about Jesus was first preached to the Samaritans by one of the ministers of the *hellenistes*, Christian Jews in Jerusalem who were conversant in Greek.[3]

More evidence is available than I can review here, but already we can see that excising from any of the Gospels the features that link it to its corresponding face on the cherubim would render it not just unrecognizable but incoherent. Assuming that we could somehow extract everything from Matthew that makes that book distinctively Jewish, for example, would the denatured residue still have the appeal that gained Matthew its readership? Or, to put the question another way, can the hypothetical process of adding to a source document the "Jewishness" that transformed it into the Gospel of Matthew be described as anything less than composition?

---

2   See Helmut Koester, *Ancient Christian Gospels* (Harrisburg, PA: Trinity Press, 1990), 335.

3   Acts 6:1-5; 8:5; cf. 6:9, where Stephen is portrayed as debating with Greek-speaking Jews.

We might as well propose that the Gospels were custom made to fit the four-sided pattern as claim they were edited to conform to it. Either way, the parties to this alleged hoax were not only brilliant enough to produce four narratives each with a unique style and perspective, but influential enough to get the four resulting documents into circulation among Christians in widely scattered regions of the Roman Empire. And imagine their good fortune that all four of the gerrymandered Gospels established themselves as fixtures in Christian tradition.

We should take a moment here to distinguish between manipulation and ordinary accumulation of textual variations. The latter refers to variant spellings, differences in word order and the presence or absence of details that the average reader would consider minor, along with a comparatively small number of differences affecting whole verses and blocks of text. It has nothing to do with the planned introduction of scores of targeted alterations into circulating documents.

Wholesale alteration of religious literature such as the Gospels might occur if the community that preserved it came to see it as deficient, but neither the early history of Christianity nor the distinguishing characteristics of the Gospels point in that direction. Potentially, a central religious authority such as the Papal See could have introduced changes into texts that fell under its control. But ecclesiastical power has its limits and church leaders run a risk by flagrantly tampering with writings already viewed as sacred.

Even if there was a time when Christian bishops could have promoted sweeping revisions of the Gospels, manuscript copies dating to previous periods still would preserve earlier, undoctored versions. We are able to rule out a church-mandated rewrite of the Gospels because manuscript fragments are available dating back as far as the second century, prior to when any bishop or body of bishops enjoyed such power.

Long before we reach a dead end trying to imagine how the Gospels could have been stretched, enriched and molded to conform to the four-way pattern found in Ezekiel, we have left behind anything that passes for scholarship. Credible professionals in the field of Biblical studies offer no support for the idea of cooperative authorship of the "Holy Four." Conspiracy theories are accorded little attention by the scholarly community and even less respect.

The opinions of experts can be wrong, of course, and one of the conclusions to be drawn from typological study is that to adopt those opinions uncritically would be a mistake. But when scholars across the religious spectrum from conservative evangelicals to hardened skeptics find it more than apparent that the Gospels were written at different times and places by writers with different perspectives and somewhat different purposes, it says something about the evidence.

Critic R. J. Hoffman argued that each of the Gospels is "tendentious" relative to the others, that is, each Gospel implies that its story is uniquely true or complete in contrast to other accounts.[4] We need not adopt Hoffman's skepticism to acknowledge that teamwork would be bound to produce a degree of harmony that the Gospels lack. The inconsistency does not prevent a unified portrait of Jesus from emerging, but it does prove to be part of a phenomenon for which no naturalistic explanation is adequate.

The New Testament book of Hebrews quotes an instruction God gave to Moses to make the holy tabernacle "according to the pattern" he was shown on Mt. Sinai.[5] The interrelationships among the Gospels, along with the other examples we have studied, demonstrate that spiritual realities realized in Christ were represented by prophetic patterns of God's making. The command to Moses proves to be an example of the very foreshadowing it suggests.

Proof and Doubt

Skeptics may sidestep the question of the Gospel pattern and typological coding by asking why we should have to go to such trouble to verify the Bible. If God is so important to our everlasting welfare, they ask, why are we not granted to see irrefutable miracles? The question assumes that God's primary interest ought to be proving to humans the bald fact of His existence, rather than in coaxing them out of moral corruption and leading them on a journey having Him as its goal and end. The challenge also ignores the barrier of sin that, according to the Bible, prevents direct communion between God and man.

Believers discern God working in their lives, sometimes even in ways

---

4   R. Joseph Hoffmann, *Jesus in History and Myth*, eds. R. Joseph Hoffmann and Gerald A. Larue (Buffalo: Prometheus, 1986), 143.

5   Heb 8:5; cf. Exod 25:40.

that can be called miraculous, but we do not see today great miracles like those performed by Jesus and the apostles, nor could such events function now as they did in the first century. God does continue to offer as evidence the lives of faithful Christians and a book to be examined and debated.

Often enough, those who examine the book conclude that it is no more than the work of men. However, in judging the Bible, as in judging much else, how we look has to do with what we see. The genius behind the Mona Lisa is apparent not from peering at the canvas through a microscope but from viewing the complete image with an appreciation born of insight. It is when we are willing to stand back and look at the Bible in faith, even if faith only in the possibility of its special character, that we can hope to glimpse the organic whole enlivened by God's Spirit.

The Deep Patterns of the Universe

The means by which we assemble a rational unity from the fragments of experience is referred to in New Testament Greek as *sunesis*, "understanding" or "comprehension." This capacity, which recommends the Scriptures' internal claim of divine authorship as the best explanation of typological coding, is also responsible for the breathtaking expansion of human knowledge through the sciences.

Science, like typological analysis, is a system of inferences from patterns. For example, observations of the way objects fall to earth and the way planets move in their orbits form a pattern that underwrites our concept of gravity and allows us to predict, among other things, that a satellite launched at a certain speed on a certain trajectory will begin orbiting the earth.

Patterns may be generated either by chance or by design. If the same number—say the number four—were to come up on three successive rolls of a die, we might assume that pure chance was responsible. But if chance generated the pattern of repeating fours, it would offer us no insight as to what we might expect on yet another roll of the same die. On the other hand, if the die were intentionally "loaded" to bias the result, then we could assume a high probability of getting a four when we rolled the die again.

What is true of die rolls is true of everything that we observe in the physical world. If the universe just happens to be the way it is without further explanation, then every event in the universe just happens to occur the way it does, and it is by pure chance that events seem to have an intelligible quality. Every event that occurs in an accidental universe is itself accidental, and the apparently predictable quality of physical events is a mirage. It hardly needs saying that such an idea is irreconcilable with science.

Science assumes a universe governed by rules in the form of physical laws.[6] Rules, however, owe their power to minds. For example, the rules of chess generate a predictable pattern in the movements of chess pieces because of the power those rules acquire from the minds of players. Similarly, the rules that generate order in nature must exist in a mind or minds capable of promulgating those rules across all of space-time.[7] And that, of course, is just what the Bible tells us.

God "leads forth the constellations," says the book of Job, by means of the "ordinances of the heavens," that is, through the laws governing astrophysics.[8] He makes the sun shine and the rain fall and gives "seed to the sower and bread to the eater," not (in most cases, at least) by miraculously setting aside physical laws, but by maintaining them.[9]

In the book of Job, God rhetorically asks the title character if he knows who causes the sun to rise each morning. Who sends forth the lightning, makes channels for the rain, generates snow and ice, and sets the courses of the stars?, he asks, before inquiring as to who gives various kinds of animals their unique characteristics.[10] God thereby

---

6 Physical laws are universe-governing principles for which scientific laws are the closest approximations available. Scientific laws include the field equations of Einsteinian astrophysics, the probabilistic wave functions of quantum mechanics and perhaps the arcane formulations of String Theory that relate large- and small-scale phenomena to one another.

7 For two excellent treatments of this argument, see John Foster, *The Divine Lawmaker: Lectures on Induction, Laws of Nature and the Existence of God* (Oxford: Oxford University Press, 2004) and Hugo A. Meynell, *The Intelligible Universe: A Cosmological Argument* (Totowa, NJ: Barnes & Noble, 1982); see also Meynell, "Hume, Kant and Rational Theism," www.leaderu.com/truth/3truth08.html.

8 Job 38:31-33; Jer 31:35.

9 Matt 5:45; Isa 55:10.

10 Job 38-41.

refers the law-governed processes of nature directly to his own creative prerogatives.

Using the present tense, as in Job, Amos says that Yahweh "forms the mountains, creates the wind, and reveals his thoughts to man."[11] The Psalmist acknowledges to God that "all your works you have made in wisdom."[12] The apostle Paul, speaking to the Lycaonians, said that God had left them with a testimony to his existence by sending rain and fruitful harvests, meaning not that rain fell by miraculous fiat on the plains of Asia Minor but that the system of laws governing the hydrologic cycle is evidence of a purposeful and dependable God.[13]

If a good God superintends the universe, why is it that throughout natural history volcanoes, hurricanes and other natural disasters have laid waste to living things, and animals have consumed one another to survive? The answer has to do with our inability, except through divine revelation, to see every aspect of the world's history clearly. From inside a corrupted world, corruption is all that is visible to the natural eye in any direction of either space or time. Beauty is still present, but it is scarred beauty—the beauty of something destined to be other than what we see it to be.

Here we need to remember what we discussed in Chapter 9 about God's purpose for man to have all earthly creation "in subjection." Subjection has to do primarily not with the power to destroy but the with the power to glorify that which has been subjected.[14] At the time of man's appearance God's creative works were "very good" and "complete," not in that there was nothing more to be done with them, but in that they had been brought to the ideal stage for man to play his divinely appointed role regarding them.

We at best can dimly conceive of how unfallen man, equipped with powers no human except Jesus has ever wielded, was supposed to have beautified the natural order. Instead, because of Adam's sin nature was crippled at the moment of birth and left "groaning" in misery, awaiting glorious liberation under the coming kingdom of Christ, the "last Adam."[15]

---

11 Amos 4:13.
12 Ps 104:24.
13 Acts 14:17.
14 Phil 3:21; Heb 2:8.
15 Rom 8:19-22; 1 Cor 15:45.

"Wail, for the world's wrong," wrote Shelley in his "Dirge." Exactly how the world can be in any meaningful sense "wrong" is unclear if, as Shelley believed, God does not exist. Instead, our cosmic discomfort is evidence that a rupture has occurred between us and the Source of life. Each of us must decide whether to cooperate with God's ongoing project to repair this breach through Christ.

God intends for men to "reach out for him and find him," Paul tells the philosophers of Athens, "though he is not far from each one of us."[16] Besides confirming that evidence of God lies close at hand, the verse suggests that God wants to accomplish something in us that requires our straining toward him. The Biblical principle that "from everyone who has been given much, much will be demanded" means that the more intelligent we are the more difficult the struggle for faith is likely to be.[17] Inviting us to undertake that struggle is God's way of searching for us, since he desires no one's eternal destruction.[18] Yet the Scriptures warn us against delaying to avail ourselves of God's grace: "Seek the LORD while he may be found; call on him while he is near."[19]

Admittedly, questions remain. Until now we have touched only lightly on the historical accuracy of the Bible. And, speaking of history, what are we to make of the less-than-savory record of nominal Christianity as far as wars, inquisitions and injustices of all kinds? What about the thousands of sectarian divisions that make the church resemble a poorly-sewn quilt? These are not questions that can be thoroughly entertained let alone settled in a book such as this, but in the final chapter we will look for scriptural directions in which to seek the answers.

---

16 Acts 17:27.
17 Luke 12:48.
18 2 Pet 3:9.
19 Isa 55:6; cf. 2 Cor 6:2.

19

The Word Alive

The story of mankind as revealed by archaeology has a bold division between the prehistoric and historical eras. Even before this division human society was organized in familiar ways, as is evident from the remains of Neolithic settlements, but social groups were limited in size. Prehistoric hunting, fishing, herding and farming all took place on a small scale by means of simple if well-crafted tools. Then, between 4000 and 3000 BC, material culture flowered. Dense populations, organized for large-scale agriculture and manufacturing, appeared in the valleys of four of the world's great river systems: the Nile in Egypt, the Indus in India, the Yellow River in China and Tigris-Euphrates in what is now Iraq.

It is the last of these regions that a consensus of historians has designated the "cradle of civilization." In the Tigris-Euphrates delta urban commerce buttressed by written laws and contracts was crowned by the emergence of poetic-religious literature. The center of this activity was ancient Uruk in the region called Sumer-Akkad, stretching from the site of Babylon to the Persian Gulf—the very place where the Bible says the first great cities were built: "The first centers of his kingdom were Babylon, Erech [Uruk], Akkad and Calneh, in Shinar [Sumer]."[1]

---

1   Gen 10:10.

Archaeology further agrees with Genesis that the Assyrians who founded Nineveh had migrated north from lower Mesopotamia.[2] And it confirms Genesis' subsequent portrayal of Egypt, Sumer-Akkad's nearest rival, as the empire whose shadow fell most heavily across Canaan from the patriarchal age to the rise of Assyria.

Until now we have been studying alignments between coded narratives and fulfillments, but we can see a correspondence as well between what archaeology and historiography tell us about the way civilization took shape and what we read in the Scriptures. The alignment is not exact, as if the Bible were giving us textbook history, but neither are the two detached from one another as if we were looking at objective reportage on one hand and on the other at the ethnic propaganda of a relatively minor culture that arose west of the Jordan river near the end of the second millennium BC.

The Reliability of Revelation

Believers are free to dismiss archaeology altogether or else cling to the idea, based on obsolete and jaundiced sources, that its findings are consistent with a highly literal reading of every verse of the Bible. What we are not free to do is adopt that attitude and make a reasoned appeal to those who are familiar with the full range of evidence on (and in) the ground. It may be possible to retreat from external facts into the closed vessel of personal belief, but can we recommend a faith that functions more as an escape hatch than a battle shield?[3]

Escape may be equally tempting for someone who finds that much of the conventional history of the ancient Near East is supported by fact and logic even after allowance is made for the fallibilities of archaeological science. There are plenty of tutors waiting to indoctrinate such a person in the Bible-is-bunk boilerplate so popular in colleges and universities. But one class of evidence cannot be admitted at the expense of another. We cannot evade the indications of a Creator when we look the world around us or fail to sense our estrangement from him when we turn inward to examine our hearts. Nor can we deny a strong if occasionally indirect connection between what scientific methods tell

---

2   Gen 10:11.
3   Eph 6:16.

us about the past and what the Scriptures say. Where the Bible and archaeology seem to be at odds, therefore, we should resist the temptation to grasp at shallow answers and instead bear in mind not only archaeology's limitations but the stylized nature of some Biblical history.

"Stylized" history refers to the use of literary devices to simplify an otherwise confusingly complex series of events. For example, we know by comparing genealogies from Exodus, 1 Chronicles, Ezra, Matthew and Luke with each other and with chronological notes elsewhere in the Scriptures that lists of generations have in places been abridged. To cite one example among many, just three generational links between Salmon and David are made to span the years-long conquest of Canaan plus the three-hundred-year period of the Judges.[4] One of the prophecies of Daniel invokes King Nebuchadnezzar as representative of the entire line of kings that followed him down to the conquest of Babylon by Media-Persia.[5]

It is easy to find stylistic devices employed on a small scale even in the New Testament. A comparison of the end of Luke's Gospel and the beginning of Acts, both written by Luke, shows that the Gospel's last few verses telescope several appearances of Jesus over the course of more than a month into a single scene occurring shortly after his death. Similarly, when we compare the summary of Israel's history from the seventh chapter of Acts with the book of Genesis, we find that two or more purchases of land by Abraham and his grandson Jacob have been combined into a single purchase attributed to Abraham.[6]

Also in Acts, one individual, Joseph, is used to represent all twelve of Jacob's sons.[7] Elsewhere in the Bible, Mark in his Gospel quotes the words of three prophets but "conflates" or combines them and attributes the resulting passage to just one prophet, Isaiah.[8] These and other examples demonstrate that although Biblical history is not hopelessly fuzzy, neither is it uniformly precise.

Archaeology for its part provides us with a number of certainties, such as the fact that the pyramids were built long ago. It also offers

---

4   Ruth 4:21-22.
5   Dan 2:32, 37-39.
6   Acts 7:16; cf. Gen 23:17-18; 33:19.
7   Acts 7:16; cf. Exod 13:19; Josh 24:32.
8   Mark 1:2-3; cf. Exod 23:20; Isa 40:3; Mal 3:1.

strong probabilities, such as the conclusion that the pyramids were built over many years by ancient Egyptians rather than by a lost civilization using sophisticated machinery. Even the range of centuries within which certain pyramids were constructed, and by which pharaohs, entail probabilities so strong that anyone who informs himself about the subject will hesitate to dispute them. Finer details or areas where evidence is scanty involve progressively weaker probabilities. When it is pursued judiciously, archaeology at least can offer us clues about where and to what degree stylization is likely present in the Biblical record.

We saw earlier how the interaction of Biblical and scientific knowledge—all of which comes from God—can work. In Chapter 15 I noted that Genesis locates the sun, moon and stars in the "expanse" of the sky below the highest clouds. Thanks to astronomy we know that the stars are located far above earth's atmosphere, and that Genesis must be referring to the appearance rather than physical mechanics of heavenly bodies.

In a similar way, fair-minded overviews of the Bible in relation to archaeology, such as the scholarly *On the Reliability of the Old Testament* by Kenneth Kitchen or Jefferey Sheller's popular-level treatment *Is the Bible True?*, confirm that as we move forward along the Biblical time line the Scriptures merge with the historiographic and archaeological evidence.[9] Or, to state it the other way around, the farther back in time we turn in the pages of the Bible, the more likely it is that events have been abbreviated and simplified in order to focus the reader's attention on God's progressive activity.

There are historical difficulties here and there even when we come to the New Testament, but some discrepancies between circumstantial evidence and written sources and between different written accounts are inevitable, as are questions about how to assemble isolated facts into a coherent narrative of the past. The Bible invites a certain number of difficulties simply by providing so much information. Problems we encounter must be weighed against abundant confirmation of people, places and events that can be gleaned from physical artifacts and from extra-Biblical writings.

---

9   See Kenneth A. Kitchen, *On the Reliability of the Old Testament* (Grand Rapids: Eerdmans, 2003); Jefferey Sheller, *Is the Bible True?* (New York: Harper-Collins, 2000).

When we read Bible's history of the kings of Judah and Israel as they contend with each other and surrounding nations, or follow Jesus as he preaches in the synagogues of Galilee and Paul and his fellow missionaries as they tour Greece and Asia Minor, we are on known historical terrain with landmarks all around us. It became apparent long ago that instead of being tied loosely to history as are, for example, the Iliad and the legends of King Arthur, the Bible is bound to it by tough sinews running in every direction.

The Refiner of Hearts

We may still fall short of satisfying those who insist that unless the Bible is factual in every detail we cannot trust it, much less advocate it as inspired. That logic holds up better in the abstract than it does when we start reading. I may not take it as fact that the earth's entire population came to listen to Solomon's wisdom or that Solomon made silver as common as stones in the streets of Jerusalem, but I cannot pretend ignorance of what those inspired statements indicate about Solomon's reputation as a sage and about the relative prosperity of Judah during his reign, nor can I miss their implication about God's plan to beautify the universe under the coming kingdom of Christ.[10]

When Jesus said that he had food to eat that the disciples did not know about or that Jairus' daughter had not died, he was not being factual by everyday standards.[11] He chose to punctuate his teaching with such statements in order to provoke deeper understanding and to test his listeners' motives. Sometimes the import of Jesus' words was revealed quickly, as when he spoke to the woman at the well about "living water." In other cases, the sense of a saying was not soon apparent. By telling his audience that they would have to eat his flesh and drink his blood, he provided the haughty with an excuse to reject him. "How can this man give us his flesh to eat?," they asked, but the answer came only to those patient enough to wait.[12]

To cite another example, it may have been years or even decades before Jesus' assurance that some of the disciples would not die before

---

10 1 Kgs 10:24, 27.
11 John 4:32; Mark 5:39.
12 John 6:53; cf. Ps 18:26.

they saw the coming of the kingdom was understood to refer to the Transfiguration.[13] The correct interpretation of other difficult passages, whether historical or prophetic, may be equally elusive. Everything in the Scriptures serves God's purpose unerringly, but his purpose is not simply to convey information. The goal of revelation is to convict us of sin and, further, to challenge our impatient natures and show us our need for humility. Even if our understanding is imperfect (and we are better off admitting as much, according to 1 Corinthians 8:2), we can comprehend enough to appreciate our position before God, the plan of salvation through Christ and the call to the "obedience of faith."[14]

Our own lives are randomly peppered with improbable events, as were the lives of people and nations of the past. So it should surprise us little when we find improbabilities where God was manipulating history for a special purpose, as he did with the nation of Israel and its forebears. In yet another category are the ordinarily impossible happenings or "nature miracles," including Noah's Flood, the plagues on Egypt, the exodus, the fall of Jericho and the "long day" of Joshua, that become credible only by existing within a larger scheme in which God's hand can be discerned.

By occurring outside the natural order a miracle may be obscured from view looking both forward and backward in time. People living just prior to such an event could not have seen it as they peered at the horizon of the future except with great difficulty through the lens of faith. Without the same lens we by looking backward into the past cannot see how an event of that kind could have happened, whether it is the parting of the Red Sea or the resurrection of Jesus.

If natural phenomena are inadequate to explain the characteristics of the Bible itself, we shouldn't wonder that they fail to account for all the events it describes. The same God who maintains the expected course of nature has the power to alter it for his own ends. From a spiritual perspective, one of the reasons nature proceeds relentlessly so much of the time is so that God can use miracles when and where his purpose calls for them.

Seeing God's hand at work in the Scriptures may be easier than seeing it in the history of Christianity. If the best sermon is the life of an exem-

---

13 Mark 9:1-7; cf. 2 Pet 1:16-18.
14 Rom 1:5.

plary believer, the strongest rebuttal is the failure of so many Christians and Christian institutions to behave in a manner worthy of the gospel.[15] However, objections based on the flaws of institutional Christianity, though weighty, ultimately fail. Divisions, strife, and corruption of both doctrine and morals are emphatically foretold not only by Jesus but by Paul and other New Testament writers.[16] We are led to expect that during the Gospel Age the church will be not so much an oasis standing out pristinely on a desert landscape as stalks of wheat alongside weeds. In this area as in others God reserves the right to test us by leaving us to navigate the treacherous shoals of organized religion by the light of his Spirit.[17]

It is a hard truth that godly devotion will never be popular. In those times and places where something claiming to be Christianity exercised political dominion, lusts of all kinds, and especially lust for power, were simply lacquered over with diluted virtue. It could hardly be otherwise, given that the wide and spacious road leading toward the abyss is traveled by many while relatively few persevere on the rock-strewn path of faith. Jesus even predicted that the love of the greater number would cool off.[18]

Paul left no doubt that preference of some believers for permissive "feel-good" teachers would assert itself, as would the desire of others to enthrone domineering spiritual bosses.[19] Ignorance may be a defense when it comes to some of these deviations, especially those turning on difficult theological questions, but the core teachings of the gospel are directly and repeatedly stated in the Bible. Likewise, on the majority of common ethical questions the Bible sets forth unmistakable if often unheeded principles of self-sacrifice, peacefulness, charity even toward enemies, modesty, moderation, chastity, as well as missionary fervor and eagerness for the coming of Christ's kingdom.

Even on controversial subjects such as premarital sex, homosexuality and the sanctity of unborn human life, the problem for many is not that the Bible is vague, but that it is uncompromisingly clear.

---

15 Phil 1:27.
16 Matt 7:22; 13:24-26; Acts 20:29-31, etc.
17 Matt 7:17-20; 1 Thess 5:21; 2 Tim 3:5.
18 Matt 24:10-12; Rev 2:4.
19 2 Cor 11:20; 2 Tim 4:3-4.

God does not leave us guessing about whether he will in the end bring forth a purified church, despite the failings of Christians. Prophetic coding can help us to see church history as part of God's unfolding plan to restore both his people and the creation. We noted Chapter 16 that one of the issues arising from that history, the seeming delay in the return of Jesus, is reflected in Moses' delay in returning to the congregation of Israel after ascending into God's presence at Sinai. Analyzing coded prophecy concerning the Gospel Age is a fascinating exercise, though one we must leave for another volume as we have the related subjects of coding in New Testament narratives and further evidence of the four-sided pattern of the Gospels.

If this book has done its job, it has demonstrated that there is more to the Bible than most of us have been led to expect—so much more that at best we have merely sampled its richness. Perhaps in doing so it has drawn aside the curtain of everyday appearance to offer a glimpse of what lies beyond. The window of revelation through which we peer at what Paul calls the "mysteries of God" will give us light to walk by even if questions are left waiting to be answered.

It is only with effort, though, that we can keep the veil from dropping once again in front of our eyes. Like most illusions, the seeming ordinariness of our surroundings can be either threatening or comforting. If the doctor hands us test results confirming a bleak prognosis, it is immediate impressions that we take refuge in. "I feel fine," we say to ourselves. "How can this paper with a few squiggles on it be more real than the present feeling that I am healthy?" The impression may resist only briefly the onslaught of reality but there is no denying its power.

Pilots-in-training, to cite another example, have to learn to rely on their instruments when visibility is poor. The temptation can be strong to trust the sensation that they are flying level or even gaining altitude when, in reality, they are descending.

C. S. Lewis once wrote that what posed the greatest challenge to his faith was not rational arguments against Christianity, since he thought these were decisively outweighed by arguments in its favor, but rather an emotional feeling of the world's emptiness.[20] The same may be true for every believer. The remedy is prayer accompanied by reflection, not

---

20 C. S. Lewis, "Religion: Reality or Substitute" in *The Seeing Eye* (NY: Random House, 1992), 57.

on the transitory physical circumstances that threaten to tyrannize over our thoughts, but on enduring spiritual realities.[21]

From personal experience I can testify that as often as we return to the words of inspired revelation we will find them brimming over with God's enlivening Spirit. It remains for us to discover afresh that "all the treasures of wisdom and knowledge" are to be found in the teachings and works, in the sinless life and redemptive death, in the resurrection, exaltation and eternal kingdom of the living Word, who says, "I will open my mouth in parables, I will utter things hidden since the creation of the world."[22]

---

21 2 Cor 4:18.
22 Matt 13:35.

Appendix

The Prodigal Son and the History of Israel

The following are points of alignment between the Parable of the Prodigal Son and the history of Israel's division into two kingdoms:

1) *There was a man who had two sons* (Luke 15:11). Ancient Israel consisted mostly of the descendants of two brothers, Judah and Joseph (Josh 18:5).

2) *The younger [son] said to his father, "Father, give me my share of the estate"* (Luke 15:12a). The descendants of Judah's younger brother Joseph withdrew from the united Israelite kingdom (1 Kgs 12:16-20).

3) *So [the father] divided his property between them* (Luke 15:12b). God made known that the division of the kingdom was according to his will (1 Kgs 11:29-31; 12:21-24).

4) *Not long after that, the younger son got together all he had, set off for a distant country and there squandered his wealth in wild living* (Luke 15:13). *This son of yours . . . squandered your property with prostitutes* (Luke 15:30). The northern monarchy turned its back on the Jerusalem temple and set up idolatrous shrines (1 Kgs 12:25-30). Northern Israel is said to have "gone to Assyria" and "called to Egypt" by seeking security in political alliances and by adopting foreign religious practices (Hos 7:11, NASB). They also indulged in sexual immorality. "The men themselves consort with harlots and sacrifice with shrine prostitutes" (Hos 4:14; cf. 6:10). "For they have gone up to Assyria . . . Ephraim has hired lovers" (Hos 8:9, NASB).

5) *After he had spent everything, there was a severe famine in that whole country, and he began to be in need* (Luke 15:14). In the book of Amos, addressed primarily though not exclusively to the northern kingdom (3:9, 14; 4:4; 5:6, 15; 6:6; 7:9-13), God says, " 'I gave you empty stomachs in every city and lack of bread in every town yet you have not returned to me' " (Amos 4:6; cf. Hos 2:8-9).

6) *So [the younger son] went and hired himself out to a citizen of that country* (Luke 15:15a). Instead of repenting under God's chastening, "Ephraim feeds on the wind; he pursues the east wind all day . . . He makes a treaty with Assyria and sends olive oil to Egypt" (Hos 12:1; cf. 8:10).

7) *[The foreign citizen] sent him to his fields to feed pigs. He longed to fill his stomach with the pods that the pigs were eating, but no one gave him anything* (Luke 15:15b-16). The northern kingdom was overthrown by Assyria in 722 BC and thousands of its prominent citizens were exiled far to the east (2 Kgs 17). Ezekiel was commanded to eat meager rations of course grains baked over a fire made with dung chips as a sign of the poverty of the Samaritan exiles. "The LORD said, 'In this way the people of Israel will eat defiled food among the nations where I will drive them' " (Ezek 4:13; cf. Hos 9:3).

8) *When he came to his senses, he said, "How many of my father's hired men have food to spare, and here I am starving to death! I will set out and go back to my father and say to him: 'Father, I have sinned against heaven and against you. I am no* *longer worthy to be called your son; make me like one of your hired men* ' " (Luke 15:17-19). Jeremiah prophesied that Israel would one day feel shame and turn again to God. "I have surely heard Ephraim's moaning: 'You disciplined me like an unruly calf, and I have been disciplined. Restore me, and I will return, because you are the LORD my God . . . I was ashamed and humiliated because I bore the disgrace of my youth' " (Jer 31:18-19). "Then she [the northern kingdom] will say, 'I will go back to my husband as at first, for then I was better off than now' " (Hos 2:7). "Take words with you and return to the LORD. Say to him: 'Forgive all our sins and receive us graciously' " (Hos 14:2).

9) *So he got up and went to his father. But while he was still a long way off, his father saw him and was filled with compassion for him; he ran to his son, threw his arms around him and kissed him* (Luke 15:20). Jeremiah expresses God's compassionate feelings for the northern Israelites. " 'Is not Ephraim my dear son, the child in whom I delight? Though I often speak against him, I still remember him. Therefore my heart yearns for him; I have great compassion for him,' declares the LORD" (Jer 31:20). "How can I give you up, Ephraim? My heart is changed within me; all my compassion is aroused" (Hos 11:8).

10) *But the father said to his servants, "Quick! Bring the best robe and put it on him [the younger son]. Put a ring on his finger and sandals on his feet. Bring the fattened calf and kill it. Let's have a feast and celebrate. For this son of mine was dead and is alive again; he was lost and is found." So they began to celebrate. Meanwhile, the older son was in the field. When he came near the house, he heard music and dancing.* (Luke 15:22-25). Two of the Father's gifts to the Prodigal, new clothes and a ring, also accompanied the exaltation of Joseph, the ancestor of the northern Israelites. "Then Pharaoh took his signet ring from his finger and put it on Joseph's finger. He dressed him in robes of fine linen and put a gold chain around his neck" (Gen 41:42). God promises that he will forgive and restore the people of the northern kingdom as the Father does the Prodigal. "I will heal their waywardness and love them freely" (Hos 14:4). "O Ephraim, what more have I to do with idols? I will answer him and care for him" (Hos 14:8). "I will bring back my exiled people Israel; they will rebuild the ruined cities and live in them. They will plant vineyards and drink their wine; they will make gardens and eat their fruit" (Amos 9:14). "Then maidens will dance and be glad, young men and old as well. I will turn their mourning into gladness; I will give them comfort and joy instead of sorrow" (Jer 31:13).

11) *The older brother became angry and refused to go in. So his father went out and pleaded with him. But he answered his father, "Look! All these years I've been slaving for you and never disobeyed your orders. Yet you never gave me even a young goat so I could celebrate with my friends. But when this son of yours who has squandered your property with prostitutes comes home, you kill the fattened calf for him!"* (Luke 15:28-30). The older brother proclaims his unfailing obedience even though he stands in defiance of his father's will. The older brother's attitude recreates that of Abijah (Abijam), the first Judean king to ascend the throne after the division of the kingdom. "[Abijah] committed all the sins his father had done before him; his heart was not fully devoted to the LORD his God, as the heart of David his forefather had been" (1 Kgs 15:3). In the narrative of 2 Chronicles 13:4-12, Abijah loudly condemns the northern kingdom, saying that the kingship was given to the descendants of David forever. He claims that Jeroboam, the first northern king, only succeeded in his rebellion because Solomon's son Rehoboam was young and weak—a distortion of the truth at best (cf. 1 Kgs 11:27-38; 2 Chron 10). He indicts the calf shrines and illegitimate priests of the north while declaring himself and all Judah to be unwavering in their devotion to Yahweh. "We are observing the requirements of the LORD our God," he says, "But you have forsaken him" (1 Chron 13:11).

"My son," the father said, "you are always with me, and everything I have is yours. But we had to celebrate and be glad, because this brother of yours was dead and is alive again; he was lost and is found" (Luke 15:31-32). There was a sense in which northern Israel was put farther away from Yahweh than was Judah, which retained the priestly and prophetic traditions even during its exile. "Then he rejected the tents of Joseph, he did not choose the tribe of Ephraim; but he chose the tribe of Judah, Mount Zion, which he loved" (Ps 78:67-68). "Then the LORD said to Hosea, 'Call [your daughter] Lo-Ruhamah, for I will no longer show love to the house of Israel, that I should at all forgive them. Yet I will show love to the house of Judah; and I will save them' " (Hos 1:6-7).

The parable leaves open the question of the response of the older brother to the father's plea, which encourages a forgiving attitude not just to Samaritans but to all classes of Israelites once looked upon as unclean. With the conversion of Samaritans and their incorporation into the early church, prophecies about the reconciliation of the brothers were fulfilled.

> *Ephraim's jealousy will vanish,*
> *and Judah's enemies will be cut off;*
> *Ephraim will not be jealous of Judah,*
> *nor Judah hostile toward Ephraim.*
> *—Isaiah 11:13*

Scripture Index

Scripture Index
(continued)

Scripture Index
(continued)

Scripture Index
(continued)

Scripture Index
(continued)

Scripture Index
(continued)

Scripture Index
(continued)

Scripture Index
(continued)

Scripture Index
(continued)

Scripture Index
(continued)

Scripture Index
(continued)

Scripture Index
(continued)

Scripture Index
(continued)

Scripture Index
(continued)

Scripture Index
(continued)

Scripture Index
(continued)

Scripture Index
(continued)

Scripture Index
(continued)

Scripture Index
(continued)

Printed in the United States
151824LV00003B/2/P